Garrison Carrasco

STRIVE FOR A 5
Preparing for the AP® World History Exam

Based on the 2016 / 2017 AP® World History redesigned curriculum.

Authored by
Kit Wainer
Leon M. Goldstein High School, Brooklyn, New York

With prior contributions from
Barbara Brun-Ozuna *Paschal High School, Fort Worth, Texas*
Ryba L. Epstein *Rich East High School, Park Forest, Illinois*
James Sabathne *Hononegah High School, Rockton, Illinois*
Lisa Tran *California State University, Fullerton*
Patrick Whelan *Saint Stephen's Episcopal School, Bradenton, Florida*

This product was developed to accompany

Ways of the World for the AP® Course
Third Edition
Robert W. Strayer | Eric W. Nelson

Y0-CAY-925

bedford, freeman & worth
high school publishers

Manufactured in the United States of America.

1 2 3 4 5   20 19 18 17

For information, write:
Bedford/St. Martin's
75 Arlington Street
Boston, MA 02116
(617) 399-4000

Or email:
socialstudies@bfwpub.com

ISBN: 978-1-319-03524-2

Contents

UNIT 2: PREP GUIDE 179

Preparing for the AP® World History Exam

Preface for the Students

By the time you open this book to help prepare you for the AP® World History Exam, you are likely already immersed in the study of world history. Your AP® World History course can be a deep and rewarding experience, demanding a high level of understanding and analysis as you read your textbook and consider other materials included in your course. If you work hard, you will find that this experience will hold great value beyond the AP® course or the AP® exam; you will have the intellectual tools to wrestle with complex ideas, to see connections between the past and the present, to write thoughtfully, and to know how to justify your thoughts as you prepare for college and adult life.

This book is designed to ease your way into a high score on the AP® World History Exam. Many students feel overwhelmed by the amount of material that the exam covers – after all, ten thousand years of human history is nothing to scoff at! Do not be daunted – you can master this vast amount of knowledge and walk into the exam confident that you have the knowledge and skills not only to do well, but to strive for a 5!

What's in This Book?

While this study guide is designed to accompany Strayer and Nelson's *Ways of the World for the AP® Course*, Third Edition, it can be used with almost any world history text. The guide follows the organization of the Strayer text and is divided into the six time periods of world history as described in the AP® World History Course and Exam Description, Effective Fall 2016. It follows a thematic narrative, making it an easy addition to any test review regimen. Dividing the content of this guide into these six chronological periods helps structure the learning of the main themes of the course and puts the details of events and ideas into an overall context.

Each part provides an overview of the main developments of that period, followed by a succinct summary of each chapter of *Ways of the World*. Each chapter is summarized using the five themes of AP® World History:

- Interaction between humans and the environment

- Development and interaction of cultures

- State-building, expansion, and conflict

- Creation, expansion, and interaction of economic systems

- Development and transformation of social structures

Following the thematic summaries are a set of Guiding Reading Questions with page numbers. Answer these questions as you study the chapters to build your knowledge and understanding of world history.

After the summaries of the chapters is a section on preparing for the AP® exam and includes two complete practice exams in the redesigned AP® format and style – with multiple-choice questions, a Document Based Question (DBQ), four Short Answer Questions (SAQ), and a Long Essay Question (LEQ) section (in which you may choose one of the two questions provided). Each essay will address at least one of four themes: causation, comparison, change and continuity over time, and periodization.

Notice this guide does not include answers to the exam questions. This is because some teachers like to use these practice exams for credit. Your teacher has access to the practice exam answers (for essays: what good answers will include), and can provide them to you, depending on his or her plans for utilizing this book in class.

Preface for the Teachers

Strive for a 5: Preparing for the AP® World History Exam is a student prep guide, designed to provide your students with a thorough review of the course material while practicing AP® test-taking skills that will help them on the AP® World History Exam.

Designed to pair seamlessly with *Ways of the World for the AP® Course*, Third Edition, by Robert W. Strayer and Eric W. Nelson, *Strive for a 5* applies a strong AP®-specific framework to the text's narrative and offers extended attention to the exam format and test-taking strategies. Either assigned as a core component of your test preparation coursework or recommended to students as an independently navigable review and practice tool, *Strive for a 5* is designed to familiarize students with the exam format, thematically organize and review key concepts, and provide cumulative practice exams. For students who are striving for a 5, there is no better preparation guide.

Features of this Prep Guide

Unit 1: Study Guide follow the textbook's structure and group course material into six chronological periods; these six parts closely correspond with the historical periodization of the AP® World History Exam. Within each part, **thematic chapter reviews** organize and summarize the major developments of each era using the five themes in world history and the key concepts relevant to that time period. Using this format allows students to review information in the categories that are often used in AP® World History Exam questions, especially the essay questions.

Unit 2: Prep Guide serves as an introduction to the AP® World History Exam and includes an overview of the exam, strategies for success, and essay-writing instructions. **AP®-style practice exams** conclude the Prep Guide portion of this book. Each practice exam includes multiple-choice questions, short-answer questions, a document-based question, and long-essay questions–in the same "redesign" style* that students will encounter on the AP® exam. The practice exams can be assigned as assessment, or students can independently measure their progress and areas in need of further review.

Note: We offer model answers for practice exams to only you. They are available on the book companion site at highschool.bfwpub.com for teachers only. This allows you to decide how to use the practice exams in this text.

*Based on the 2016 / 2017 AP® World History Curriculum Framework.

About the Author

Kit Wainer is a veteran Social Studies teacher with 28 years of experience in the New York City public school system. Kit is an AP® World History Exam Reader and also serves as a College Board Workshop Consultant for AP® World History. He currently teaches at Leon M. Goldstein High School in Brooklyn, New York.

UNIT 1
A Review of AP® World History & Ways of the World for the AP® Course, Third Edition

AP® WORLD HISTORY PERIOD ONE
Technological and Environmental
Transformations, to c. 600 BCE

PART ONE
First Things First:
Beginnings in History, to 600 BCE

AP® World History Key Concepts
    1.1:   Big Geography and the Peopling of the Earth
    1.2:   The Neolithic Revolution and Early Agricultural Societies

The Big Picture:
Turning Points in Early World History

The first unit for both the AP® World History course and this textbook covers the largest span of time of the six units. Four major turning points in human history occurred during this period; the first three are covered in Chapter 1 and the last in Chapter 2.

- **The Emergence of Humankind:** According to scientists, about 5 to 6 million years ago, several species of bipedal primates emerged in eastern and southern Africa. Eventually, this line led to *Homo sapiens*–modern humans–with large brains, the ability to use language and communicate abstract ideas, and the ability to create tools.

- **The Globalization of Humankind:** Around 100,000 years ago during the Paleolithic era (Old Stone Age), humans began to migrate out of Africa, armed with stone tools, the ability to use fire, and the ability to use language to work together in small groups of hunter-gatherers. People adapted to a variety of environments, from bitter cold tundras to burning hot deserts to grasslands and forests. Gradually, changes took place in the "tool kits" of human groups, helping them adapt to changing environmental circumstances. In addition, they developed art, religion, rituals, and stories (see Map 1.1, p. 4 and pp.16–17).

- **The Revolution of Farming and Herding:** By about 11,000 years ago, in separate regions in the Middle East, Asia, Africa, and the Americas, humans developed farming and animal husbandry; this development is often called the First Agricultural Revolution. This development has been called the single most important event in human history and has led to the growth of civilization as we know it today. The increased reliability of food sources also led to a population growth. The type of agriculture–or whether farming developed or not–depended on the climate and available plants and animals in a region. Some regions, typically dry grasslands, were more conducive to herding or pastoralism, while others provided enough food resources so that people continued as hunters, fishers, or foragers. The types of crop varied from region to region, such as potatoes in the Andes, grains in Eurasia, or corn (maize) in Mesoamerica. The Americas had relatively few domesticable animals—and no draft animals—compared to Afro-Eurasia, where goats, sheep, pigs, cattle, and later horses and camels were available (see Mapping Part One, pp. 8–9). The first farming villages were small, with people growing their own food and living without elaborate political or religious systems. Pastoral groups also remained small.

■ **The Turning Point of Civilization:** As farming provided a more reliable source of food, populations grew, and some settlements developed into civilizations. The earliest civilizations developed in seven separate areas between 3500 B.C.E. and 500 B.C.E. These First Civilizations gave rise to empires, cultural and religious traditions, new technologies, more hierarchical social and gender roles, and large-scale warfare.

AP® Themes in Part One:

Environment	Cultures	State Building	Economies	Social Structures
Initial human Migrations - Paleolithic Environmental transformations - Global warming and the Agricultural Revolution - Environmental effects of agricultural societies - Environmental basis of pastoralism - Environmental effects of First Civilizations - Environment and culture in Egypt and Mesopotamia	Paleolithic Religions - Stories from the Australian Dreamtime - Connections between religion and politics in the First Civilizations - Outlooks on the afterlife in Egypt and Mesopotamia - Cultural diffusion in the ancient world; ex.: Egyptian influence in Nubia, Crete, and Greece - Art in the Indus Valley Civilizations - Writing in the earliest civilizations	Political life in pre-state societies - Emergence of Chiefdoms - State building in the First Civilizations - Comparing political life in ancient Egypt and Mesopotamia - Flowering of an Egyptian empire - Sumerian incorporation into Akkadian, Babylonian, and Assyrian empires - Hittite invasion of Egypt and Babylonia - Diplomatic relations of Egypt and Mesopotamia	Gathering/Hunting technologies and economies - Breakthroughs to agricultural economies - Comparing Agricultural Revolutions; ex.: in Mesopotamia and Mesoamerica - Globalization of agriculture and resistance to it - Agriculture and Technological innovations - Emergence of pastoral economies - Conflicts between pastoral and agricultural peoples - Agriculture: setting the stage for civilization - Long-distance trade among ancient Afro-Eurasian civilizations	Paleolithic egalitarianism; ex.: among the San and Aboriginal Australians - Sedentary life among gathering/hunting peoples - Agricultural village life: gender, age, and kin - Pastoral Societies - Emergence of urban life - Class structures of early civilizations - The evolution of patriarchy - Consent and coercion in maintaining highly unequal societies

CHAPTER ONE
First Peoples; First Farmers: Most of History in a Single Chapter, to 4000 BCE

AP® World History Key Concepts

1.1: Big Geography and the Peopling of the Earth

I. Archeological evidence indicates that during the Paleolithic era, hunting-foraging bands of humans gradually migrated from their origin in East Africa to Eurasia, Australia, and the Americas, adapting their technology and cultures to new climate regions.

Ironically, the longest span of time for human history is covered in the AP period that has the least weight on the test. It is important to realize that this huge period is seen through a "panoramic" lens—big picture and not much fine detail. Modern humans first evolved in Africa about 200,000 to 250,000 years ago. Using more refined tools, they gradually moved from collecting edibles and scavenging dead animals to hunting, fishing, and gathering a wider range of foods. The population slowly grew, leading to the first really big idea in human history: migration. Humans migrated from Africa to almost every part of the globe, adapting to a wide range of environments from frozen tundra to grasslands, from forests to desert regions. How did this happen? It happened because humans were able to create new technology and because they were able to communicate and cooperate between members of family groups. You'll need to know the routes and time periods of these migrations to different regions in Eurasia, Australia, the Americas, and the Pacific Islands, as well as some of the archeological evidence and controversies about who migrated where and when. See Map 1.1 on pp. 16–17 of *Ways of the World* for likely migration routes and dates. Finally, you should be aware of some of the ways that humans adapted to new environments in Eurasia, Australia, the Americas, and the Pacific Islands using new tools, such as bone needles to make layered clothing, spears and spear throwers, woven nets and baskets, and pottery, to name just a few.

1.2: The Neolithic Revolution and Early Agricultural Societies

I. Beginning about 10,000 years ago, the Neolithic Revolution led to the development of more complex economic and social systems.

II. Agriculture and pastoralism began to transform human societies.

During the Neolithic era, which began approximately 10,000–12,000 years ago, most people continued living as hunters or fishers and gatherers while populations rose, especially in areas with abundant resources. In some areas, humans began to settle down—at least for part of the year—in small villages based on horticulture while they also continued hunting or fishing. At various times in different regions, settled agriculture emerged based on the available domesticable plants and animals. This deliberate cultivation of particular plants and animals is termed the Neolithic Revolution or Agricultural Revolution. Other regions less suited to agriculture—such as savannas and steppes—encouraged the development of pastoralism, in which people relied on the milk, meat, and blood of domesticated animals that they raised. The earliest known sites for settled agriculture were in the Fertile Crescent (see Map 1.4, p. 33). See also Map 1.3, "The Global Spread of Agriculture and Pastoralism" (pp. 30–31), for the sites where different plants and animals were first domesticated. Humans were now changing the environment, not just adapting to it. These new ways of exploiting the environment led to the development of new cultural, social, economic, and to a lesser extent, political patterns in both village life and pastoral communities.

Theme 1:
Interaction Between Humans and the Environment

Paleolithic humans adapted to different environments, while Neolithic humans modified their environments to greater and greater extents. Early humans were food collectors and scavengers. They developed tools such as hand axes and the use of fire and began to hunt and fish as well as collect foods such as berries, nuts, insects, and grains. As humans migrated out of Africa to other regions, they encountered many new environments—harsh tundra, forests, deserts, or large bodies of water—that required the creation of new tools. This migration was helped by the Ice Age, which lowered sea levels and created land bridges or narrower straits connecting regions such as the Americas, Indonesia, or Australia with Afro-Eurasia. New technologies such as layered clothing sewn with bone needles, spear throwers or bows, flaked stone tools, nets, and weaving allowed humans to enter into Ice Age Eurasia. Other species of human, such as Neanderthals in Europe or *Homo floresiensis* in Indonesia, became extinct soon after modern humans arrived. We don't know whether these other species died from being marginalized by the more technologically advanced *Homo sapiens* or whether disease or conflict killed them.

By the time of the Neolithic Revolution, humans had become proficient roving hunters and gatherers in many different environments, with about 70 percent of their food coming from gathering (often performed by women) and 30 percent from hunting (often undertaken by men). Perhaps as a response to environmental changes at the end of the last Ice Age, people began new methods of exploiting the environment, leading to the domestication of plants and animals and the rise of settled village life and pastoralism. This Agricultural Revolution created fundamental changes in the role of humans on the planet: they had become the shapers of their environment.

As people moved to agricultural life, they worked longer and harder for a more limited diet than that of their hunter-gatherer ancestors. The needs of agriculture led to drastic environmental change as a few domesticated crops replaced the variety of plants that had existed before. Both plants and animals were selectively bred to create desired results. Other environmental impacts included deforestation to grow food crops, terracing hillsides, digging irrigation canals, and soil depletion from overuse. In addition, new diseases passed from domesticated animals to humans.

Theme 2:
Development and Interaction of Cultures

Our knowledge of Paleolithic and Neolithic human culture is based almost exclusively on physical objects studied by archeologists. Archeological sites for early humans are scattered and often discovered by chance. Even when we find artifacts, we do not know with certainty what they mean because the people who made them are not alive to tell us nor can anthropologists observe them actually using their artifacts. Scholars therefore study the few remaining stone-age cultures (in places like the Amazon basin or Australia and New Guinea) to try to draw analogies between the life and artifacts of people today and those of our ancient ancestors. Planned burials with grave objects such as beads, ochre pigments, and flowers imply a belief system. Female statuettes unearthed throughout Eurasia (sometimes called the stone-age Venus) may be connected to the diffusion of religious ideas centered on female fertility and certainly show communication networks operating over large areas. Diffusion of artifacts such as the Clovis points in the Americas also point to a widespread network of communication. Dramatic cave paintings often depicting animals that were hunted or herded have been found in both Eurasia (Lascaux in Western Europe and Bhimbetka in

India) and Africa (Sahara and San rock art). In contemporary Australian stone-age cultures, the persistence of rock paintings and ceremonies associated with the Dreamtime provide a unique glimpse into what earlier Neolithic cultures may have been like.

During the Neolithic era, we begin to see the first monumental architecture, such as the complex at Göbekli Tepe in modern Turkey. Megaliths such as Göbekli Tepe and the more famous Stonehenge in England have been interpreted as religious centers or calendars to mark the solstices and equinoxes. Some archeologists argue that the need to feed the large number of people building and using such sites may have been one of the factors that encouraged a permanent horticultural lifestyle. The people living in early settlements in the Fertile Crescent, such as Ain Ghazal, created enigmatic statues, which may have represented deities, heroes, or leaders. Late in the Neolithic era, temples (with priests and priestesses), tombs, and their associated art developed in cities.

Theme 3:
State-Building, Expansion, and Conflict

This theme is not well developed in this time period. Hunting and gathering bands tended to be small, relatively egalitarian, and mobile. Large-scale conflicts did not seem to arise: why fight and lose some of your precious kinsmen if there was other territory to move to? Leadership roles seem to have been fluid and related to a specific need. True state building did not begin before there were permanently settled agricultural villages competing for land and resources. By the end of this period, more powerful leaders emerged. In agricultural areas such as Mesopotamia, secular and religious power was inherited and reinforced through the personal charisma of leaders, their ritual roles, their ability to redistribute wealth through gift giving, and their roles as battle leaders. Pastoral societies also developed first as relatively egalitarian kinship groups and moved toward clan or tribal leaders with greater wealth or power.

Theme 4:
Creation, Expansion, and Interaction of Economic Systems

Early humans were generalists, with each person creating the tools needed for exploiting the local environment for survival needs. However, very early in human history, items were exchanged or traded outside their place of origin: stone, flint, or special woods for tool making, decorative items (shells, feathers, pigments), new tools such as bone needles or Clovis points, and cultural artifacts such as carved figurines (see Theme 2).

The Agricultural Revolution sparked a rapid increase in the quantity and types of tools and weapons. Agriculturalists developed new technologies such as sickles, plows, kilns and potter's wheels, looms, sun-dried mud bricks, chisels, boats (including sails by Mesopotamians), and tools related to domestication of animals. Pastoralists invented saddles, bridles, harnesses, and new types of bows. Trade and communication systems expanded between villages, and between villages and the hinterlands that possessed resources that were not available locally. Often, pastoral groups transmitted goods and innovations across large areas between early civilizations and across ecological zones between pastoral and settled peoples. In the growing cities, wealth accumulated in the hands of leaders and priests. Priests, in addition to their religious roles, often controlled the exchange and creation of goods, organized large projects such as irrigation canals and monumental architecture, allotted fields, and controlled agricultural and artisanal labor.

Theme 5:
Development and Transformation of Social Structures

While most hunter-gatherer bands seem to have had gender-specific tasks (women more often were the gatherers, men the hunters), there seems to have been relative equality between the sexes. Little difference in material wealth or social power is evident. All people contributed to the collection of food needed for survival and all shared the same skills set.

However, the development of agriculture and pastoralism gradually changed that egalitarian social structure. Wealth in the form of arable land or herds of animals became more unevenly distributed. Society therefore became more stratified, and labor became more specialized. Early horticultural villages seem to have remained relatively more balanced in gender and social roles. Men continued to hunt, while women continued to provide many of the major agricultural innovations and much of the labor, using digging sticks and hoes to work their fields, creating looms to weave fibers from plants or animals, creating pottery to store food, and so on. Evidence for the continued strong role of women is found in the dominance of female images in art, in matrilineal descent (tracing descent through the mother's family), and matrilocal marriage patterns (men left their birth families to live with their wives). As more animals were domesticated and the use of animal-drawn plows spread, men took over the heavier agricultural labor and began to dominate.

Village-based lineage societies tended to reduce the equalities of earlier societies: elders controlled the labor forces and sought to control women's reproductive lives to ensure growth of the (now often patrilineal) lineage or kinship group. The growth of warfare led to the collection of captives who were placed in forced labor roles. Intensification of agricultural production and increased conflict seem to have led to the development of larger cities and chiefdoms, intensifying social stratification and the dominance of men over women.

Pastoral societies tended to retain more of the relative gender equality of earlier Paleolithic cultures, as evidenced by the burial goods of some women who seem to have held high status as warriors or healers and shamans.

Guided Reading Questions for Chapter 1

Seeking the Main Point What arguments does this chapter make for paying serious attention to human history before the coming of "civilization"? (Page 12)

Change What was the sequence of human migration across the planet? (Page 14)

Comparison How did Austronesian migrations differ from other early patterns of human movement? (Page 20)

Change In what ways did a gathering and hunting economy shape other aspects of Paleolithic societies? (Page 21)

Change Why did some Paleolithic Peoples abandon earlier, more nomadic ways and begin to live a more settled life? (Page 24)

Practicing AP® Historical Thinking How do you understand the significance of the long Paleolithic era in the larger context of world history? (Page 25)

Change What accounts for the emergence of agriculture after countless millennia of human life without it? (Page 28)

Comparison In what different ways did the Agricultural Revolution take shape in various parts of the world? (Page 32)

Connection In what ways did agriculture spread? Where and why was it sometimes resisted? (Page 36)

Change What changes did the Agricultural Revolution bring in its wake? (Page 37)

Comparison What different kinds of Societies emerged out of the Agricultural Revolution? (Page 41)

Practicing AP® Historical Thinking What was revolutionary about the Agricultural Revolution? (Page 46)

NOTES:

CHAPTER TWO
First Civilizations: Cities, States, and Unequal Societies, 3500 BCE—600 BCE

AP® World History Key Concepts

1.3 The Development and Interactions of Early Agricultural, Pastoral, and Urban Societies

I. Core and foundational civilizations developed in a variety of geographical and environmental settings where agriculture flourished, , including Mesopotamia in the Tigris and Euphrates River Valleys, Egypt in the Nile River Valley, Mohenjo-daro and Harappa in the Indus River Valley, Shang in the Yellow River (or Huang He) Valley, Olmec in Mesopamerica, and Chavin in Andean South America.

II. The first states emerged within core civilizations in Mesopotamia and the Nile Valley.

III. Culture played a significant role in unifying states through laws, language, literature, religion, myths, and monumental art.

The First Civilizations arose independently in the several millennia after 3500 B.C.E. You must be able to identify the locations of these civilizations (see Map 2.1, "First Civilizations," pp. 62–63) and understand the characteristics they shared as well as their unique characteristics.

- Sumer in ancient Mesopotamia
- Egypt along the Nile River in northeastern Africa
- The civilization of Norte Chico (and later the Chavín) in the coastal region of the Andes in present-day Peru
- The Indus Valley civilization in present-day Pakistan
- The Shang dynasty located in northern China
- The Oxus in what is today northern Afghanistan and Southern Turkmenistan
- The Olmecs of modern-day southern Mexico

Theme 1: Interaction Between Humans and the Environment

The First Civilizations arose in areas that had previously developed village agriculture, which was discussed in Chapter 1. All of these First Civilizations saw population increases due to intensified agricultural techniques that were adapted to their specific environments, ranging from lowland rain forest for the Olmecs, to desert oases for the Oxus, to desert punctuated by rivers for the Norte Chico people, to the river valleys of the Nile, Huang He, Tigris and Euphrates, and Indus. All of the First Civilizations were based on water management. Some, such as the Xia dynasty in China (a precursor to the Shang), dug canals to control devastating flooding. Others employed terraced fields, irrigation, and swamp drainage in their farming. The Egyptians used the regular flooding of the Nile Valley, which yearly brought rich mud that replenished fields and provided agricultural bounty. Larger populations meant increased demand for food. Overuse of fields, especially where slash-and-burn agriculture was being practiced (Olmecs) led to soil depletion. Intensive irrigation could lead to the fields becoming too saline, as in the Indus Valley. Deforestation—whether to clear land for agriculture or to harvest wood for fuel or construction—led to erosion. Periods of drought brought further stress. Whatever the cause, environmental degradation often led to lower crop yields and sometimes even to the abandonment of cities.

Theme 2:
Development and Interaction of Cultures

First Civilizations shared common cultural characteristics: more elaborate belief systems often rooted in fertility deities and supporting social and gender inequalities, writing and record-keeping systems, monumental art and architecture, and the explosion of the arts and literature. Distinctive writing systems emerged in most, but not all, of the early civilizations; the Oxus and the Andean regions, for example, did not develop true literacy. Writing served a number of functions, from celebrating the accomplishments of a society's leaders to recording transactions and taxes. Writing also gave birth to written laws such as the Code of Hammurabi (see Source 2.1 in *Thinking Through Sources* Document Reader Volume 1) and to literature (see Snapshot: Writing in Ancient Civilizations, p. 78). Monumental architecture (such as ziggurats and pyramids, tombs, temples, and palaces) and art (Olmec heads, Egyptian statues, etc.) reinforced the glory and power of the rulers and the gods.

Theme 3:
State-Building, Expansion, and Conflict

Archaeologists and historians have long debated the origins of the state. It is clear that agriculture was a necessary precondition, but it was not the only factor in the rise of the state. One theory is that the growing density of population and the relative scarcity of fertile land for farming meant that highly organized states had an advantage in the competition for resources. This competition usually led to warfare. Most of these civilizations followed a similar pattern of state building: coercion tactics to force people to obey authority and military might to expand control into new areas. The system of kingship (often divine kingship) also bound people to their leaders and priests. The Xia began the enduring concept of the Mandate of Heaven, linking the ruler as "the Son of Heaven" to the gods. The Egyptian pharaoh also ruled as a descendant of the gods, as most likely did the Olmec rulers. Some civilizations, such as in the Indus Valley, seemed to have a high level of coordination and planning (streets were laid out on a grid, uniform measurements, sewers, and "zoning") without signs of a king or other central ruler, leading to speculation that they may have been governed by a council of some sort.

Theme 4:
Creation, Expansion, and Interaction of Economic Systems

The economy of the early civilizations was based on agriculture, and control of the land was the major source of wealth. However, many skilled artisans created artifacts, textiles, pottery, weapons, and tools both for use within their own civilizations and for trade by merchants or gift exchanges between rulers. A number of early civilizations engaged in long-distance trade to obtain goods or materials (usually luxury items) that were not available locally. Many Indus Valley traders lived in Mesopotamia to facilitate trade between the two civilizations. Mesopotamia also had trade routes connecting it to Egypt and Central Asia. The Egyptians had similarly extensive trade routes, including to Nubia and the interior of Africa, the Red and Mediterranean Seas, as well as to their near neighbors in Mesopotamia. Trade often moved through middlemen, such as pastoral peoples, or through a series of merchant-traders working in a particular region. The Oxus civilization served as a hub in a trans-Eurasian trading network by conducting trade with China, India, Mesopotamia, and pastoral nomads of the steppes. The First Civilizations in the Americas, like the Olmecs and the Norte Chico people, developed in isolation from each other but did engage in more localized trade within their cultural region. The only item exchanged (indirectly) between the two regions was maize, which originated in Mesoamerica.

Theme 5:
Development and Transformation of Social Structures

Many of the First Civilizations witnessed an "erosion of equality" as these societies developed hierarchies of class and gender. Upper-class people with greater wealth were able to avoid physical labor and occupied the highest political, military, and religious positions within their societies. The majority of people were free commoners, but most of the early civilizations also developed systems of slavery, which varied greatly from place to place. This kind of slavery differed greatly from the slavery that developed in the Americas after the seventeenth century. Slavery in the First Civilizations was not perpetual in that the children of slaves could become free and was also not associated with race. The cities of Norte Chico show less signs of economic specialization than the other First Civilizations, and the enigmatic ruins of the Indus Valley show little evidence of social hierarchy.

The most significant social division within human societies was based on gender. Patriarchy has been the most pervasive gender system in human history, in which men were regarded as superior to women, men had legal and property rights denied to women, and men were far more active in governing. Women's roles were increasingly confined to the home and defined by their relationship to a male (father, husband, or son). There is much speculation about why patriarchy developed with civilization. One approach suggests that the intensification of agriculture and the shift to plow-based agriculture, which required the greater strength more often found in men, led to a decline in the status of women. The increase of warfare and combat may have also contributed to patriarchy; increased warfare led to the glorification of the warrior as well as an increase in the number of women who were captured as slaves. Finally, the development of private property may have helped shape early patriarchy; men wanted to ensure that only their own children inherited their land or wealth, and to do so, they attempted to control women's reproductive freedom.

Guided Reading Questions for Chapter 2

Seeking the Main Point What distinguished "civilizations" from earlier Paleolithic and Neolithicsocieties? (Page 60)

Change When and where did the First Civilizations emerge? (Page 60)

Change What accounts for the initial breakthroughs to civilization? (Page 68)

Change What was the role of cities in the early civilizations? (Page 69)

Change In what ways was social inequality expressed in early civilizations? (Page 71)

Change In what ways have historians tried to explain the origins of patriarchy? (Page 73)

Comparison How did Mesopotamian and Egyptian patriarchy differ from each other? (Page 75)

Change What were the sources of state authority in the First Civilizations? (Page 76)

Practicing AP® Historical Thinking In what ways might the advent of "civilization" have marked a revolutionary change in the human condition? And in what ways did it carry on earlier patterns from the past? (Page 80)

Comparison In what ways did Mesopotamian and Egyptian civilizations differ from each other? Page 80)

Connection In what ways were Mesopotamian and Egyptian civilizations shaped by their interactions with near and distant neighbors? (Page 85)

UNIT 1
A Review of AP® World History & Ways of the World for the AP® Course,
Third Edition

AP® WORLD HISTORY PERIOD TWO
Organization and Reorganization of Human Societies, c. 600 BCE to c. 600 CE

PART TWO
Second-Wave Civilizations in World History, 600 BCE–600 CE

AP® World History Key Concepts
2.1: The Development and Codification of Religious and Cultural Traditions
2.2: The Development of States and Empires
2.3: Emergence of Transregional Networks of Communication and Exchange

The Big Picture: After the First Civilizations: What Changed and What Didn't?

World history functions differently from other methods of studying history, partly because of the huge spans of time covered in the course and partly because of its comparative nature. *Ways of the World* uses the analogy of a camera lens zooming out to a panorama to cover large spans of time and zooming in to a middle or close view to look at some periods in more detail. Chapter 1 required the panoramic view; Chapter 2, a more mid-range view. This ability to shift "lenses" is a fundamental world history skill.

In order to consider the focus question, "After the First Civilizations: What Changed and What Didn't?" zoom out to consider the period from 3500 B.C.E. to 1750 C.E. The dominant development in this period is the spread of agriculture and civilizations based on agriculture. First-wave civilizations began the process around the globe but largely in isolation from each other. Although First Civilizations developed large and complex societies, all these societies collapsed. Mesopotamian city-states were absorbed into empires (such as Babylon and Assyria). Civilizations faded in Central Asia, the Indus Valley, and Norte Chico. During the first millennium B.C.E., Egypt fell to foreign invaders, the Olmecs abandoned their cities, and the Zhou dynasty kingdom in China fragmented into warring states. However, these urban, state-based civilizations set patterns that continued to shape their regions, while new civilizations emerged in Ethiopia and West Africa, Japan, Indonesia, and Southeast Asia. Second-wave civilizations, such as the Roman Empire, Han China, and Mayan city-states, rose and eventually collapsed. Third-wave civilizations (500 to 1500 C.E.) appeared: some, such as China, re-envisioned older patterns; in other regions, such as Western Europe, Russia, Japan, and West Africa, newer civilizations emerged and borrowed from older civilizations. Civilizations continued to trade and communicate with each other and with neighboring pastoral peoples.

Identifying changes that take place between one period and another or within a period, and, at the same time, identifying enduring continuities are two of the most important historical thinking skills. Identifying continuity usually requires a panoramic lens, while observing change often requires a closer zooming in to study specific details.

Part Two focuses thematically and comparatively on second-wave era (600 B.C.E. to 600 C.E.) civilizations in Eurasia and North Africa. Chapter 3 examines political frameworks and empires; Chapter 4 analyzes and compares cultural and religious traditions; Chapter 5 compares social and gender organizations; and Chapter 6 analyzes the extent to which the development of civilizations in inner Africa and the Americas parallel those of Eurasia or offer alternative paths.

Continuities in Civilization

- States and empires rose, expanded, and collapsed.
  - Monarchs continued to rule most of them.
  - Social and gender inequalities persisted, as did slavery.

- No technological breakthroughs produced new ways of organizing social or economic life.
  - Land-owning elites saw little reason for innovation, while peasants also did not produce innovations that would profit the landowners or themselves.
  - Merchants were dominated by the states and were often looked down on by ruling elites.

Changes in Civilization

- Population grew more rapidly than in in the Paleolithic era, with interruptions for pandemic diseases.
- Second- and third-wave states were larger than those of the First Civilizations.
  - States were more diverse.

- Rising and collapsing empires had consequences for the people under their dominion.
- Second- and third-wave civilizations generated many innovations within their spheres.
  - Distinctive wisdom traditions developed, such as Confucianism and Daoism in China; Hinduism and Buddhism in South Asia; Judaism, Zoroastrianism, Christianity, and Islam in the Middle East; and the rational scientific philosophy of Greece.

- Technological changes allowed humans to manipulate the environment in more profound ways.
  - China led the way with piston bellows, the draw-loom, silk-handling machinery, the wheelbarrow, draft harnesses for animals, the crossbow, iron casting, iron-chain suspension bridges, gunpowder and firearms, the magnetic compass, printing, paper, and porcelain.
  - India produced techniques for manufacturing cotton textiles and crystallizing sugar.
  - Roman achievements included building roads, bridges, aqueducts, the keystone arch, fortifications, and glassblowing.

- Some social hierarchies were modified.
  - India's caste system became more complicated.
  - Roman slaves and Chinese peasants sometimes rose in rebellion.
  - Women were often less subject to restrictions at the beginnings of a civilization, but   patriarchy became more intense as civilizations developed.

- Some Buddhist and Christian women found some opportunities for leadership and learning in convents.
- After the first-wave civilizations, networks of trade and communication grew more intense and far-flung.

■ Long-distance trade routes became regional and transregional in caravan routes across northern Eurasia and the Sahara, maritime trade in the Indian Ocean, river-based commerce in the eastern woodlands of North American, and in Mesoamerica and the Andes.

- Trade routes carried goods as well as culture and religions.
- Diseases, such as the Black Death, also spread along the trade routes.

AP® Themes in Part Two:

Environment	Cultures	State Building	Economies	Social Structures
Greek geography and environmental effects of Greek civilization - Environmental effects of Roman and Chinese civilizations - African landscapes and environmental limitations of agriculture - Environmental diversity in Mesoamerica and the Andes - Maya Environmental engineering - Ecological degradation: its role in the collapse of Maya civilization and the Roman Empire - "Verticality" in Wari and Tiwanaku - Geography and Continental variation - Iron making and deforestation in Meroë - The environment of Pacific Oceania and human impact on it - Ecological collapse in Rapa Nui	Cross-cultural perceptions in the ancient world - Chinese cultural traditions: Legalist, Confucian, Daoist - Evolution of Indian religious thought - Birth and spread of Buddhism - Artistic Representations of the Buddha - The Greek intellectual tradition and the spread of Greek culture in the Hellenistic era - Greco-Roman cultural synthesis and the attractions of Roman culture - Art and architecture in Pompeii - Cultural interaction in the Kushan Empire - Monotheisms of the Middle East: Judaism and Zoroastrianism - The rise and spread of Christianity - Chavín religious Movement - Moche art - Spread of Bantu Culture - *Mana* and *tapu* in Oceania	Eurasian empires of the second-wave era: • Persian • Greek (Alexander) • Roman: from Republic to empire • Chinese empires (Qin and Han) • Indian empires (Mauryan and Gupta) - City-states: Greek, Niger Valley, Maya, Teotihuacán - Greco-Persian Wars - Peloponnesian Wars - Vietnamese resistance to China - Chinese Relationships with northern "barbarians" - Slave rebellion in the Roman Empire - Meroitic and Axumite empires Wari and Tiwanaku States - Chiefdoms in Bantu Africa, the Americas, and Oceania	Persian commercial networks and agricultural systems - Chinese agriculture, metallurgy, and land-owning patterns - Economic condition of Chinese peasants - Merchants and state authorities in China - Economic functions of caste in India - Indian commercial and cultural network in the Indian Ocean Region - Slave labor systems in the Roman world - Pastoralism in Afro-Eurasia and its absence in the Americas - Economic specialization in the Niger Valley - Axumite trade Relationships - Patterns of economic and cultural exchange in North America - Wari and Tiwanaku Agriculture compared - Ritualized economic exchange in Oceania	Empires and the definition of masculinity - Class in China - Caste in India - Class and citizenship in Athens - Slavery in the Roman world - Patriarchy: • Evolution in China and Roman world • Athens/Sparta comparison • Variations in Oceania - Cities without states in West Africa - Female rulers in Meroë - Urban life in Teotihuacán - Social variation among Bantu speaking peoples - Social differences in Oceania

Chapter Three
State and Empire in Eurasia/North Africa, 600 BCE–600 CE

AP® World History Key Concepts

2.1: The Development and Codification of Religious and Cultural Traditions

I. Codifications and further developments of existing religious traditions provided a bond among the people and an ethical code to live by.

II. New belief systems and cultural traditions emerged and spread, often asserting universal truths.

III. Belief systems generally reinforced existing social structures while also offering new roles and status to some men and women. For example, Confucianism emphasized filial piety, and some Buddhists and Christians practiced a monastic life.

IV. Other religious and cultural traditions, including shamanism, animism, and ancestor veneration, persisted.

Long-distance trade flourished along the Silk Routes in northern Eurasia, the Mediterranean basin, the trans-Saharan routes, and the Indian Ocean. These networks allowed the spread of goods, technological innovations, and cultural traditions such as the "wisdom traditions" (Hinduism, Buddhism, Judaism, Zoroastrianism, and Christianity) and the rational philosophies of the Greek and Hellenistic world. *See Chapter 4 for more depth on this Key Concept.*

2.2: The Development of States and Empires

I. The number and size of key states and empires grew dramatically as rulers imposed political unity on areas where previously there had been competing states.

II. Empires and states developed new techniques of imperial administration based, in part, on the success of earlier political forms.

III. Unique social and economic dimensions developed in imperial societies in Afro-Eurasia and the Americas.

IV. The Roman, Han, Persian, Mauryan, and Gupta empires encountered political, cultural, and administrative difficulties that they could not manage, which eventually led to their decline, collapse, and transformation into successor empires or states.

After the collapse of the first-wave civilizations, some new civilizations grew in the shadow of the original ones, borrowing from their earlier cultures and political systems, while new states also arose on the fringes of previous civilizations. This chapter focuses on the political development of empires in Eurasia and North Africa. You will need to know all of the following empires, as well as their locations:

- Qin and Han in China (See Map 3.5, p. 123)
- Mauryan and Gupta (See Map 3.6, p. 133)
- Greek city-states (See Map 3.2, p. 111)
- Persian (See Map 3.1, p. 109)
- Hellenistic (See Map 3.3, p. 115)
- Roman (See Map 3.4, p. 119)

The Chinese empires incorporated much of the traditions of the First Civilization in that region. Following the collapse of the original Indus Valley civilization and the migration of the Aryans to the Indian subcontinent, the Mauryan and Gupta empires arose in a politically and culturally fragmented South Asia. The Greek, Roman, and Persian cultures arose on the fringes of the old civilizations of the Fertile Crescent. All of these empires created strong militaries and administrative systems that would cope with the expanded size and multicultural nature of their conquered territories. Inevitably, these second-wave civilizations (also called classical civilizations) fell, often from a combination of invasions from peoples on the periphery of their control and internal problems they could not resolve. *See Chapter 5 for more depth on social issues in these empires and Chapter 6 for the empires outside Eurasia.*

2.3: Emergence of Transregional Networks of Communication and Exchange

I. Land and water routes became the basis for transregional trade, communication, and exchange networks in the Eastern Hemisphere.

II. New technologies facilitated long-distance communication and exchange.

III. Alongside the trade in goods, the exchange of people, technology, religious and cultural beliefs, food crops, domesticated animals, and disease pathogens developed across far-flung networks of communication and exchange.

You will need to know the long-distance trade routes: the Silk Routes in northern Eurasia, the Mediterranean basin routes, the trans-Saharan routes, and the Indian Ocean routes. Goods, technological innovations, cultural traditions, crops, and diseases spread along these new or intensified trade networks. The Roman, Chinese, and Indian empires had little direct contact but were linked loosely by trade networks. The Persians and Greeks were geographically close and engaged in direct conflict with each other. The Hellenistic empires, following the conquests by Alexander the Great, blended and spread the cultures of the old Greek territories through Egypt, the Middle East, and South Asia. The Romans later conquered much of the territory around the Mediterranean and incorporated many of the cultural traditions of Greek and blended Hellenistic cultures, which they spread in turn to Western Europe.

Theme 1: Interaction Between Humans and the Environment

Negative environmental impacts arose from the second-wave empires due to increasing populations and their exploitation of resources. More land and forests were cleared for cultivation, and the face of the land was changed by human activity. Greek cities deforested hillsides for wood to process metals, such as iron, creating erosion and thinning soil. On the other hand, the mountainous geography of the Peloponnesian peninsula meant that Greek city-states remained relatively small and diverse and did not combine to create an empire until conquered by Philip of Macedon. The Romans, Persians, and Chinese drained swamps, diverted rivers, built canals, and created aqueducts to help bring food and water to their growing cities. Mild Mediterranean climates allowed both Greeks and Romans to conduct public life outdoors in the agora or forum. Passes in the Hindu Kush mountains northwest of India allowed different groups to migrate, creating cultural and linguistic diversity and contributing to political fragmentation in the region. India enjoyed relatively brief periods of imperial rule under the Maurya and Gupta. Second-wave empires also built or expanded cities, especially as new bureaucratic and cultural centers or trade hubs, but these empires also might destroy the urban centers of conquered people (such as Carthage). The concentration of people and domesticated animals led to epidemic diseases, which also spread along the trade routes, like the plague that hit Athens during the war with Sparta. Even though population grew during this period because of more intensive agriculture, the rate of increase was slow due to disease and warfare. The fall of second-wave empires, especially in Europe, led to a decline in urban populations.

Theme 2:
Development and Interaction of Cultures

The second-wave empires had a huge impact on culture. Linguistically, in some cases (like China and Rome) empires created unifying national languages. The Hellenistic empires spread Greek language and culture to the edges of India and created cultural centers such as Alexandria in Egypt. Classical Greek philosophy, literature, drama, and art influenced Rome, and through it, Western Europe. Despite many minorities and different spoken languages and dialects, China developed a common written language that enabled the government to extend its rule and laws. Rome also spread the use of Latin throughout its territories and made it the language of law and government.

Empires created monumental architecture, including palaces, temples, tombs, walls and fortifications, and public buildings, to reinforce the power and majesty of the empire. Greco-Roman temples, gymnasia, theaters, and racetracks sprang up in far-flung corners of the Hellenistic and Roman empires. China's Great Wall, which was built to keep out nomadic tribes who periodically invaded the northern part of the country, projected the power of the Qin and Han emperors, as did the construction of elaborate palaces and royal tombs. The Persians encouraged artistic, religious, and cultural expressions from their conquered peoples and, like the Hellenistic empires, created a fusion of architectural and artistic styles. Gupta rulers presided over a golden age, building temples and encouraging the study of literature, science, medicine, and mathematics (especially the number system using nine numerals and zero). *Chapter 4 will discuss the religions and wisdom traditions of classical Eurasia in more detail.*

Theme 3:
State-Building, Expansion, and Conflict

This chapter focuses primarily on the techniques that second-wave empires used to conquer and consolidate territory, administer these large territories to maintain order, and extract economic gain and the internal failures that led to their collapse. The needs of empire produced some commonalities in state building, yet the different cultures and locations of the empires created some important differences. One of these differences concerned the amount of participation individuals had in their government. Greek city-states had the most direct participation of adult male citizens, followed by the Roman Republic. In contrast, Asian monarchies, such as the Persian Empire or the Qin dynasty, placed almost absolute power in the hands of the king. Romans held out the possibility of citizenship and the protection of the Roman legal system and military to encourage loyalty among conquered people. The Chinese accepted minorities who adopted Chinese language and culture. The Persian, Hellenistic, and Indian empires ruled diverse peoples with varying degrees of cultural, if not political, tolerance.

Second-wave empires created bureaucracies to administer their territories, common legal systems, and systems of taxation. Examples of bureaucratic systems included the satraps and "eyes and ears of the King" in Persia, the Han professional bureaucracy trained in royal academies, and Mauryan rule according to the *Arthashastra*, a manual for pragmatic and moral rule. Romans used a military basis for governing their empire, despite maintaining the ideals of "the Senate and people of Rome" from the days of the Republic. All empires relied on strong militaries, both to create and expand their empires and to maintain control over conquered peoples. All used architecture and art to reinforce imperial prestige. All used the support of religion to justify imperial rule: the Han Mandate of Heaven; the Roman deification of the emperor; the Persian absolute monarchy incorporating Zoroastrian imagery; and Alexander the Great allowing himself to be made a god by the Egyptians.

The second-wave civilizations in Western Europe, India, and China overextended themselves geographically for their level of technological development and became unable to effectively administer their empires. In addition, social conflict, political divisions, and financial problems also weakened second-wave civilizations. Ironically, the Huns (steppe nomads called the Huna in India and Xiongnu in China) invaded all three weakened empires. While the Gupta and Han dynasties fell, India and China changed little culturally. The Chinese culturally assimilated the nomads and relied on Confucian models to rebuild a centralized state after a period of collapse. In Western Europe, however, the advance of the Huns forced warlike Germanic tribes into the heartland of the empire. Once inside the weakened empire, these groups established small Germanic kingdoms, each with its own culture and identity, which at first controlled the Roman emperors and then eventually displaced them. Over time, the Germanic tribes adopted Christianity, and the Church played a unifying role in the hybrid civilizations that followed. However, Western Europe did not recover as a unified state.

Theme 4:
Creation, Expansion, and Interaction of Economic Systems

The unification of large territories into empires promoted trade by creating roads and canals, providing uniform legal and tax codes, and creating common languages and currencies. Some empires, such as the Persian, Roman, and Chinese, fostered communication networks by creating thousands of miles of roads or canals, while also standardizing weights and measures, coinage, and tax systems. Expanded transregional trade routes, such as the Silk Routes, trans-Saharan routes, and Indian Ocean basin routes, allowed the diffusion of inventions, ideas, and goods. Some inventions, such as new saddles or harnesses, directly helped trade, as did stone bridges built by the Romans or suspension bridges built by the Chinese. The domestication of the camel created new options for crossing the Sahara or Taklamakan deserts. China was the center of much of this technological invention, including such items as the magnetic compass, gunpowder, new techniques for iron smelting, silk-handling machinery, new harnesses for draft animals, wheelbarrows, porcelain, paper, and printing. Roman innovation was largely in the area of construction and engineering, with the use of the keystone arch in bridges and aqueducts, cement, and durable roadbeds; Romans also excelled in glassblowing. India, the focus of the Indian Ocean trading system, led in the production of textiles, such as cotton, and the technology used to crystalize cane syrup into sugar crystals. With the collapse of the second-wave civilizations, long-distance trade declined.

Theme 5:
Development and Transformation of Social Structures

Second-wave empires accelerated social stratification and the dominance of patriarchal gender systems. Wealth concentrated in the hands of a few, while conquered people often became slaves, driving out the small landholder. Sparta, for example, maintained a large population of helots, conquered people who lived in slave-like conditions. In some cases, the ideals of a warrior society led to increased domination of women. For example, in Rome, the masculinity of upper-class male citizens was defined in part by a man's role as a soldier; this meant that in private he exercised absolute control over his wife, children, and slaves. *Chapter 5 discusses the social consequences of classical empires in more detail.*

Guided Reading Questions for Chapter 3

Seeking the Main Point How might you assess—both positively and negatively—the role of empires in the history of the second-wave era? (Page 107)

Comparison How did Persian and Greek civilizations differ in their political organization and values? (Page 108)

Change How did semi-democratic governments emerge in some of the Greek city-states? (Page 111)

Connection What were the consequences for both sides of the encounter between the Persians and the Greeks? (Page 113)

Connection What changes did Alexander's conquests bring in their wake? (Page 114)

Change How did Rome grow from a single city to the center of a huge empire? (Page 118)

Comparison Why was the Chinese empire able to take shape so quickly, while that of the Romans took centuries? (Page 122)

Explanation Why were the Roman and Chinese empires able to enjoy long periods of relative stability and prosperity? (Page 123)

Change What internal and external factors contributed to the collapse of the Roman and Chinese empires? (Page 129)

Practicing AP® Historical Thinking In comparing the Roman and Chinese empires, which do you find more striking–their similarities or their differences? (Page 131)

Comparison Why were centralized empires so much less prominent in India than in China? (Page 132)

Chapter Four
Culture and Religion in Eurasia/North Africa, 600 BCE–600 CE

AP® World History Key Concepts

2.1: The Development and Codification of Religious and Cultural Traditions

I. Codifications and further developments of existing religious traditions provided a bond among the people and an ethical code to live by.

II. New belief systems and cultural traditions emerged and spread, often asserting universal truths.

III. Belief systems generally reinforced existing social structures while also offering new roles and status to some men and women. For example, Confucianism emphasized filial piety, and some Buddhists and Christians practiced a monastic life.

IV. Other religious and cultural traditions, including shamanism, animism, and ancestor veneration, persisted.

2.3: Emergence of Transregional Networks of Communication and Exchange

III. Alongside the trade in goods, the exchange of people, technology, religious and cultural beliefs, food crops, domesticated animals, and disease pathogens developed across far-flung networks of communication and exchange.

Chapter Four zooms in on cultural developments in the second-wave or classical civilizations. Some religious traditions such as animism and polytheism, which often included female deities, persisted from earlier eras —especially in areas outside of the cities. Second-wave civilizations often modified existing traditions: Vedic traditions in India were the basis of Hinduism; the beliefs of the ancient Hebrews in the Middle East were the foundation of Judaism and Christianity (and, later, Islam); and the Mandate of Heaven and veneration of ancestors endured for centuries in China.

The period around the sixth century B.C.E. saw the seemingly unrelated development of new religious beliefs in many parts of Eurasia/North Africa, creating traditions that still influence the world today. New or reforming religious leaders include Siddhartha Gautama (the Buddha), Zarathustra, and the Hebrew prophets. Philosophical or "wisdom traditions" developed in Greece (especially Athens) and China (Confucianism, Daoism, and Legalism). These wisdom traditions tended to focus on secular concerns rather than on the divine. Buddhism, especially the historical Buddha, also focused on the enlightenment of the individual through right action and meditation instead of on the divine. Hinduism, Judaism, and Zoroastrianism all moved toward monotheism and remained associated with particular groups of people. They did not proselytize (seek converts) outside the original group. However, all three did spread by migration or through merchants to regions outside of their places of origin. Buddhism and, later, Christianity became proselytizing universal religions, spreading far beyond their origins in India and Judea respectively (see Map 4.1, p. 175). The Chinese wisdom traditions spread within China's sphere of influence in East Asia to places such as Korea, Vietnam, and Japan. The rational, logical philosophies of the Greeks spread throughout Alexander's Hellenistic Empire and were taken up by the Romans— and, later, the Arabs—with profound influences on scientific, philosophical, and political thought in the

Western world and beyond. Use the Snapshot on page 151 to review the thinkers and philosophies of the second-wave era. You may also wish to add the names of the sacred literature or major works associated with each of these traditions.

Theme 1:
Interaction Between Humans and the Environment

Refer to Chapter 3 for a more in-depth discussion of this theme.

Theme 2:
Development and Interaction of Cultures

In Greece, an explosion of artistic and literary forms emerged in the early part of this period. In addition, Greeks assumed that through rational thought and scientific questioning humans could discover the explanation for natural phenomena instead of attributing them to the actions of divine beings. In Athens, philosophical questioning was also applied to social and political issues. The questioning and writings of Greek philosophers like Socrates, Plato, and Aristotle impacted Western thought long after Athens ceased to be independent.

The Warring States era in China led to different approaches to restoring order and tranquility. When the Qin reconstituted the empire following the Warring States era, the concept of the heavens favoring the ruler (known as the Mandate of Heaven) was already a tradition. Qin Shihuangdi, the first emperor, also adopted Han Fei's doctrine of Legalism to subdue all opposition. Legalism was based on a very negative view of humanity, featuring clear, strict laws with harsh punishments for anyone who broke the law or offended the emperor. Partly because of this harsh system, the Qin dynasty was very short-lived. The next dynasty, the Han, moved away from Legalism and adopted the philosophy of Confucius. Confucianism sought to restore the harmony of a past golden age through the governance of educated gentlemen who led through moral example and concern for their followers' well-being; the superior man demonstrated virtue and care for the inferior in the relationship, while the inferior person owed respect and obedience. Education was highly valued in China, partly because Confucius believed that humans were able to improve their moral lives through education. Later, the civil service would require rigorous examinations based on Confucian learning. The third solution to the turmoil of the Warring States period was Daoism. Its founder, Laozi, rejected the Confucian emphasis on education and service to the government. Instead, one would withdraw from the world and study the *dao*, the way of nature that governed all natural phenomena. Daoism became popular with the people, but instead of competing with each other, Daoism and Confucianism tended to be complementary.

Hinduism did not have a single founder. Like Judaism and Zoroastrianism, it was specific to a certain people and territory. The basis of religion in India was the Vedas, a collection of prayers, hymns, and rituals passed down in Brahmin families by oral tradition and later written down in Sanskrit. Brahmins were responsible for proper ritual observances, which they controlled through their knowledge of the Vedas, but dissatisfaction grew because of their exclusive control and the high fees they charged. The central philosophical concepts of Hinduism were outlined in the Upanishads. Brahman, the World Soul, was the unifying force that underlay all creation. The individual soul (*atman*) was a part of Brahman and could be reunited with the Brahman, according to the laws of *karma*, after many cycles of rebirth (reincarnation) if the individual followed pure action appropriate to his or her social station or caste. Hinduism became the underpinning of the caste system and gender inequality, as codified by the *The Laws of Manu*.

Siddhartha Gautama was the founder of Buddhism. He challenged the Brahmins' control of ritual and the caste system's control of individuals' attempts to achieve enlightenment. The core of Buddhist beliefs are found in the Four Noble Truths—essentially that suffering is inevitable, but that by ending attachment to material things and by meditation, one can achieve *nirvana* (enlightenment) in this lifetime. Buddhism became a universal religion and spread outward from India. In India itself, Buddhism gradually disappeared as it was reabsorbed into Hindu beliefs.

Around the sixth or seventh century B.C.E., Zarathustra (Zoroaster) created a monotheistic religion out of Persian polytheism. While Zoroastrianism did not become a universal religion, it had great influence on Judaism and, through it, Christianity. Zarathustra spoke of a benevolent deity, Ahura Mazda, who was in a cosmic struggle with the forces of evil. A savior would appear and, after a final judgment day, those who had aligned themselves with the forces of light would be rewarded with resurrection of the body and eternal life in paradise, while those who had aligned themselves with the evil forces of darkness would be condemned to eternal punishment.

The Hebrews worshipped one god (Yahweh) who had formed a covenant with their ancestor Abraham and had guided them out of Egypt to the Promised Land, Canaan. Yahweh was seen as the creator of the natural world, working through history and speaking directly to humans. Prophets like Isaiah and Amos helped transform rituals that were temple-based and controlled by priests into concern for social justice and moral action. Like Hinduism, the Jewish sacred text (the Torah) had first been passed down in oral tradition and was only written down after the Jews had returned to Jerusalem from captivity in Babylon. Like Hinduism and Zoroastrianism, Judaism did not become a proselytizing religion.

The founder of Christianity was Jesus, who came from a Jewish family in Roman-controlled Judea. He inherited the Jewish tradition of intense personal devotion to a single deity and its emphasis on moral action and social justice. After Jesus' death, his followers professed belief in his divinity. Paul, an early convert to Christianity, transformed Christianity from a local sect into a universal religion by his missionary activity in the eastern portion of the Roman Empire. Paul emphasized that all people, not just Jews, could follow Jesus' teachings. For the first 600 years, Christianity was predominantly found in the Asian and African portions of the Roman Empire—especially the area that is now Turkey and northern Africa. Later, the Germanic tribes in Western Europe that had defeated the western Roman Empire accepted Christianity, making it the dominant religion in Europe.

Theme 3:
State-Building, Expansion, and Conflict

There are some ways in which religions and the wisdom traditions directly interacted with the state. In China, the Qin dynasty used Legalism as a way to secure rule and eliminate opposition. Confucian philosophy became the official belief of the Han dynasty and became the foundation for the civil service system that continued into the twentieth century. The Mandate of Heaven justified dynastic rule: the "heavens" approved of the ruler who behaved in the manner of a Confucian gentleman, seeing to the welfare of his people and conducting himself as a moral example. Zoroastrianism became the dominant religion of Persian kings of the Achaemenid dynasty. Judaism and, later, Christianity were persecuted by the polytheistic Roman Empire, which relied on the cult of divine caesars to legitimize Roman rule. Christianity later became the official religion of the Roman Empire, and in other areas, such as Armenia and Axum (Ethiopia). The desire to maintain a stable rule led some Roman emperors to encourage Christians to decide on one official or orthodox version among the many that arose in the first three centuries following the life of Jesus. The Eastern Empire, centered on Constantinople, rejected the supremacy of the Roman pope and developed into the Eastern Orthodox Church, which, in turn, supported the Byzantine Empire for the next 1,000 years. Pluralism and tolerance for different beliefs generally characterized India, although Emperor Ashoka converted to Buddhism and raised stupas (mound-like structures containing Buddhist relics) throughout his realm in an attempt to encourage people to follow his example. *Refer to Chapter 3 for a more in-depth discussion of this theme.*

Theme 4:
Creation, Expansion, and Interaction of Economic Systems

Religions often spread along trade routes. Hinduism spread into Southeast Asia along land and sea routes. Buddhism followed later and also expanded along the Silk Road into China and East Asia. Buddhism also spurred trade in Buddhist religious artifacts and scriptures. Jewish merchants traveled along the trade routes to Asia, Europe, and Africa, especially after the destruction of Jerusalem and the Diaspora. Buddhism and Christianity, as universal religions seeking converts, profited especially from the ability to move along trade routes that were made relatively safe by the second-wave empires. *Refer to Chapter 3 for a more in-depth discussion of this theme.*

Theme 5:
Development and Transformation of Social Structures

The tendency of monotheistic religions to envision God as male contributed to continued patriarchal dominance of women. The early Christian church reflected Jesus' acceptance of women in leading roles, but later conformed to prevailing patriarchal beliefs as articulated by Paul and later church fathers. Christianity and Buddhism both allowed women some autonomy in separate monastic communities, but not in secular life or religion outside the cloistered walls. In Confucian China, families were male dominated, with children (even adult children) owing filial piety toward their parents. Women were completely subservient to their fathers, husbands, and—when widowed—their sons. This view of women as subservient to male family members was shared by most of the religions of this period but was especially stringent in China and India. Even the Greek philosophers generally believed women to be inferior to men.

Religion and wisdom traditions also affected class identity. In China, the Qin favored warriors and farmers as essential to the state. The Han, shaped more by Confucian ideas, placed great emphasis on the scholar-gentry at the top of the class structure, followed by farmers who were essential to supporting the large population. Hinduism codified existing social groups into a more stringent caste system, with the Brahmins as the highest class, followed by warriors, merchants, and laborers. In contrast to the caste system in India, upward mobility was possible in China: even a peasant could, through diligent scholarship, rise to become part of the scholar-gentry class. Both Buddhism and Christianity opposed traditional class structures, so both drew significant numbers of early converts from the lower classes. Daoism was also popular among the people of China, and its philosophy underlay the Yellow Turban peasants' revolt. *Refer to Chapter 5 for a more in-depth discussion of this theme.*

Guided Reading Questions for Chapter 4

Seeking the Main Point   Fundamentally, religions are basically alike. Does the material of this chapter support or challenge this idea? (Page 149)

Comparison   What different answers to the problem of disorder arose in classical China? (Page 150)

Description Why has Confucianism been defined as a "humanistic philosophy" rather than a supernatural religion? (Page 152)

Comparison How did the Daoist outlook differ from that of Confucianism? (Page 155)

Change In what ways did the religious traditions of South Asia change over the centuries? (Page 158)

Comparison In what ways did Buddhism reflect Hindu traditions, and in what ways did it challenge them? (Page 160)

Comparison What is the difference between the Theravada and Mahayana expressions of Buddhism? (Page 161)

Change What new emphases characterized Hinduism as it responded to the challenge of Buddhism? (Page 164)

Practicing AP® Historical **Thinking** How did the evolution of cultural traditions in India and China differ during the era of second-wave civilizations? (Page 164)

Connection What aspects of Zoroastrianism and Judaism subsequently found a place in Christianity and Islam? (Page 165)

Description What was distinctive about the Jewish religious tradition? (Page 166)

Description What are the distinctive features of the Greek intellectual tradition? (Page 168)

Comparison How would you compare the lives and teachings of Jesus and the Buddha? In what different ways did the two religions evolve after the deaths of their founders? (Page 172)

Change In what ways was Christianity transformed in the five centuries following the death of Jesus? (Page 173)

Practicing AP® Historical Thinking How might you understand the appeal of Buddhism and Christianity as opposed to the more rationalist approaches of Greek and Confucian philosophy? (Page 180)

CHAPTER FIVE
Society and Inequality in Eurasia/North Africa, 600 BCE–600 CE

AP® World History Key Concepts

2.1: The Development and Codification of Religious and Cultural Traditions

I. Codifications and further developments of existing religious traditions provided a bond among the people and an ethical code to live by.

II. New belief systems and cultural traditions emerged and spread, often asserting universal truths.

III. Belief systems generally reinforced existing social structures while also offering new roles and status to some men and women. For example, Confucianism emphasized filial piety, and some Buddhists and Christians practiced a monastic life.

IV. Other religious and cultural traditions, including shamanism, animism, and ancestor veneration, persisted.

2.2: The Development of States and Empires

I. The number and size of key states and empires grew dramatically as rulers imposed political unity on areas where previously there had been competing states.

II. Empires and states developed new techniques of imperial administration based, in part, on the success of earlier political forms.

IV. The Roman, Han, Persian, Mauryan, and Gupta empires encountered political, cultural, and administrative difficulties that they could not manage, which eventually led to their decline, collapse, and transformation into successor empires or states.

Second-wave (or classical) civilizations continued the social hierarchies and gender inequalities that arose in the First Civilizations. This chapter focuses on the different ways that empires in China, Rome, and India expressed these inequalities. The landowning classes achieved wealth by exploiting the labor of the mass population, a pattern that continued until the Industrial Revolution. Roman state religion moved from a polytheistic cult of the emperor to Christianity. Late Roman emperors ended persecutions against Christians and saw them as a group who were therefore loyal to the emperor. They chose Christians for administrative roles, even when Christians were still a minority in the empire. Two of the Eurasia civilizations suffered from rebellions of the lower classes against state control: Chinese peasants rose in the Yellow Turban Rebellion, while slaves like Spartacus rebelled against their masters in Rome. Perhaps because of strong deference to the *varnas* (four broad social groups set forth in *The Laws of Manu* and supported by Hindu beliefs), class rebellion—as opposed to regional attempts to throw off the control of the empire—was less likely in India. In addition, belief systems both supported and, in some cases, undercut the hierarchies of class and gender. For example, Confucian hierarchies and the Mandate of Heaven upheld the Han Empire, and Hinduism provided common beliefs throughout culturally diverse India, while upholding the social structure. Buddhism and Christianity cut across class and caste, holding all (males) to be equal within their beliefs. Patriarchy continued to be dominant in all three empires, with some lessening of restrictions on women in times of political crisis.

Concerning gender roles, women, such as Boudica in Britain or the Trung sisters in Vietnam, sometimes led resistance movements to both Roman and Han expansion. One woman, Empress Wu, became the ruler of China in the Tang dynasty, although her rule was such an affront to Chinese ideas about the proper role of women that no other woman was allowed to reign for centuries. Elite women were usually closely confined to the home and forbidden from assuming public roles. Again, belief systems tended to reinforce patriarchy, with women finding some small escape in Christian and Buddhist convents.

Theme 1:
Interaction Between Humans and the Environment

Refer to Chapter 3 for a more in-depth discussion of this theme.

Theme 2:
Development and Interaction of Cultures

Chinese scholar-gentry were often the creators of elite Chinese culture. They were highly educated and wrote books or painted nature scenes in addition to fulfilling the official duties of their positions. In Rome, slaves often held positions of teachers, artists, or scribes. Throughout second-wave civilizations, women rarely received an equal education to that of men in similar social classes. Greek city-states varied in their attitudes toward women. Sparta, for example, allowed women more freedom than Athens, but both retained patriarchy. A few exceptional women demonstrated learning and culture, such as Aspasia in Periclean Athens, but most were kept firmly inside the doors of their homes and not taught to read. Buddhism and Christianity both ignored class structure in seeking converts—a person from any class could achieve salvation or reach nirvana. All belief systems reflected strong gender biases. Women who became Christian or Buddhist nuns could, at least partially, escape from patriarchal control. *See Chapter 4 for more discussion of this theme.*

Theme 3:
State-Building, Expansion, and Conflict

Slaves in all three empires most often were captured in warfare as the empire expanded. Of the three empires, only the Roman Empire based much of its economy on slave labor, leaving Rome open to frequent slave rebellions such as the Spartacus revolt. In India and China, peasants performed agricultural and other low-level labor. The Chinese state was often faced with peasant rebellions, such as the Yellow Turban Rebellion, which weakened the Han Empire. In India and Rome, warriors had relatively high prestige, but in China, scholar-gentry were favored and warriors were disdained because they did not contribute to the creation of food or goods. Occasionally, on the fringes of imperial expansion, women took leadership roles in defending their homes from Roman or Chinese conquest; but in general, women were not involved in the military or in governing. In China, state officials were chosen and promoted in rank by passing exams based on Confucian principles. Administrators in Rome came from the military and elite, but educated slaves held many lower offices. Empress Wu ruled China during the Tang dynasty, but all other rulers of these empires were male. *See Chapter 3 for more on this theme.*

Theme 4:
Creation, Expansion, and Interaction of Economic Systems

Although merchants and trade were important to Qin and Han China, they were widely viewed as unproductive, greedy, and materialistic. In addition, merchants were often forced to loan large amounts of money to the state and were actively discriminated against. Neither India's nor China's economy benefitted much from slavery, unlike the Roman Empire, whose economy was based on slave labor. Slaves provided between 30 and 40 percent of the labor force, especially on the large estates (*latifundia*) and in the mines. In second-wave empires, the elites often found ways to avoid taxation, pushing the burden onto lower classes, leading to economic problems that helped destabilize the empires. Female slaves often served as domestic servants, actresses and entertainers, or simply as prostitutes. Male slaves filled a variety of roles including agricultural labor, skilled craftsmen, gladiators—even accountants, scribes, and teachers. *See Chapter 3 for more on this theme.*

Theme 5:
Development and Transformation of Social Structures

All second-wave civilizations were sharply divided along class lines. Each civilization had slight differences, however. As in the First Civilizations, wealth meant access to and ownership of land. Classical China was able to offer some means of social mobility through the famous exam system. Although this system certainly favored the rich and well-connected, it was possible for intelligent young men from very limited means to rise to the level of a scholar and thus into the bureaucracy that administered the empire. Most often, the scholar-gentry class reflected the twin influences of education and wealth. The majority of people in China were peasants—some lucky enough to own their land, while others worked as tenants on large estates. Although peasants were exploited, they were lauded in official Chinese documents. Merchants, however, were often seen as unproductive and materialistic. Although there were relatively few slaves in Han China, they did exist, especially as status symbols for the wealthy.

In Mauryan and Gupta India, the caste system—the rigid, inherited hierarchy—developed over centuries. The four main groups, or varna, had religious justification and consisted of the Brahmins, priests and teachers; the Kshatriya, warriors and rulers; Vaisya, the cultivators, merchants, or craftsmen; and the Sudras, who were laborers. Outside the caste system were the Untouchables, who performed tasks considered to be ritually polluting, such as slaughtering animals or burying the dead. These castes were divided into multiple sub-castes, known as *jatis*, which were based on occupation. There were also a small number of slaves, often criminals, debtors, or prisoners of war. Slaves did have some legal protection. Because the caste system was tied into religious beliefs about reincarnation, there was relatively little upward mobility or upheaval—in contrast to the peasant and slave revolts occurring in the other two empires. However, new migrants were incorporated into a *jati*, and entire *jati* could be upgraded into a higher caste, creating some mobility within the caste system.

In the Mediterranean region, however, slavery was common. The Greek city-states relied on slave labor, and some estimates state that 30 to 40 percent of the Roman Empire's population was slaves, mostly captured as prisoners of war. This large slave population worked the fields of the *latifundia* and competed with free laborers and craftsmen, ultimately undermining the economy and state. Romans sometimes manumitted (freed) their slaves, and slaves could save money and buy their freedom. Freed slaves could become full citizens. Members of Rome's upper class were known as patricians; they were landowners who controlled the Senate in the days of the Republic. Toward the end of the Republic, wealthy commoners could also join the elite. The widespread use of slaves severely limited the viability of artisans or other "middle" classes.

Patriarchy permeated the second-wave empires—although restrictions tended to be more pronounced in urban areas for elite women than for lower-class or rural women. In general, women were expected to be obedient to their fathers, then their husbands, and finally (as widows) to their sons. Women's subservience to men was justified by Confucian texts, Hindu religious writings (such as *The Laws of Manu*), or long-held ideals of the Greco-Roman matron. In China, women's roles fluctuated. When pastoral peoples invaded, society was in collapse, or order was threatened, women were able to expand their roles. Some, like the Empress Wu, were able to take over and rule. Within the Greek city-states, Spartan women were allowed more freedom relative to their sisters in other states, such as Athens. They married men who were closer to their own age, were expected to engage in athletics so they would have strong children, were respected for giving birth (a woman who died in labor was considered a warrior who had died in battle), and were not secluded.

Guided Reading Questions for Chapter 5

Seeking the Main Point To what extent were the massive inequalities of second-wave civilizations generally accepted, and in what ways were they resisted or challenged? (Page 192)

Description How would you characterize the social hierarchy of China during the second-wave era? (Page 193)

Change What class conflicts disrupted Chinese society? (Page 196)

Description What set of ideas underlies India's caste-based society? (Page 199)

Comparison What is the difference between varna and jati as expressions of caste? (Page 200)

Practicing AP® Historical Thinking How did India's caste system differ from China's class system? (Page 203)

Comparison How did the inequalities of slavery differ from those of caste? (Page 204)

Comparison How did Greco-Roman slavery differ from that of other classical civilizations? (Page 205)

Change In what ways did the expression of Chinese patriarchy change over time, and why did it change? (Page 210)

Comparison How did the patriarchies of Athens and Sparta differ from each other? (Page 213)

NOTES:

CHAPTER SIX
Commonalities and Variations:
Africa, the Americas, and Pacific Oceania, 600 BCE-1200 CE

AP® World History Key Concepts

2.1: The Development and Codification of Religious and Cultural Traditions

III. Belief systems generally reinforced existing social structures while also offering new roles and status to some men and women. For example, Confucianism emphasized filial piety, and some Buddhists and Christians practiced a monastic life.

IV. Other religious and cultural traditions, including shamanism, animism, and ancestor veneration, persisted.

2.2: The Development of States and Empires

III. Unique social and economic dimensions developed in imperial societies in Afro-Eurasia and the Americas.

3.1: Expansion and Intensification of Communication and Exchange Networks

I. Improved transportation technologies and commercial practices led to an increased volume of trade, and expanded the geographical range of existing and newly active trade networks.

II. The movement of peoples caused environmental and linguistic effects.

3.2: Continuity and Innovation of State Forms and Their Interactions

I. Empires collapsed and were reconstituted; in some regions new state forms emerged.

3.3: Increased Economic Productive Capacity and Its Consequences

I. Innovations stimulated agricultural and industrial production in many regions.

Partly because the Agricultural Revolution (and its effect on population growth) began in Eurasia, the First Civilizations and their second-wave successors contained most of the population of the earth. This chapter explores both agricultural civilizations and smaller cultures that developed outside of Eurasia. Africa had significant contact with Eurasia through the Indian Ocean and Mediterranean trade routes, but the Americas developed without contact from the Afro-Eurasian world. The groups that developed urban sedentary civilizations—the Maya and Teotihuacán in Mesoamerica (see Map 6.2, p. 242), the Chavín, Moche, Wari, and Tiwanaku in the Andes (see Map 6.3, p. 247), Meroë and Axum in northeastern Africa (See Map 6.1, p. 235)—displayed many of the characteristics developed in First Civilizations: intensive agriculture, more complex political and religious life, monumental architecture and art, trade links with distant regions, stratified societies reflecting different specializations, and an explosion in technology. However, settled agriculture that was productive enough to support an urban population without being supplemented by hunting and foraging developed more slowly in the Americas and sub-Saharan Africa because they lacked the available grains and domesticable draft animals found in Eurasia. Some of these cultures did not share the stark social or gender hierarchies characteristic of Eurasian empires and developed their own ways of organizing agricultural villages and towns. The Bantu-speaking peoples spread their methods of agriculture, religious beliefs, and language throughout much of sub-Saharan Africa (see Map 6.1, p. 235). The Niger Valley was also the site of agricultural communities that did not turn into imperial states. In North America, the Pueblo peoples in the southwest and the mound builders in the southeast also developed agriculture and urban centers without an empire (see Map 6.4, p. 256).

Theme 1:
Interaction Between Humans and the Environment

Eurasia was estimated to possess 80 percent of the population of second-wave civilizations, while Africa made up 11 percent and the Americas between 5 and 7 percent. In addition, with the exception of llamas and alpacas, draft animals were not available in either the Americas or (except by importation) in sub-Saharan Africa. This accounts for the continued use of hoes and digging sticks instead of plows in most regions (Meroë was a major exception). Metallurgy (especially iron) was also much less developed in these two areas, with Meroë and, later, West Africa being the main sites for iron technology. Ironworking caused environmental degradation as trees were cut down to provide fuel for smelters. While Meroë was blessed with sufficient rainfall to make it less dependent on irrigation agriculture, water control continued to be important in all these regions. In the Niger River delta, a group known collectively as the Bantu-speaking peoples slowly spread new agricultural techniques, domesticated animals such as cattle, and their tool-making technology southward and eastward from their ancestral home.

In Mesoamerica, civilizations such as the Maya and Teotihuacán in the Valley of Mexico relied on farming corn, chilies, beans, and squash in a variety of ecological regions from rain-forested lowlands to cold, high mountainous regions. The land was terraced, swamps were drained, mountain ridges were flattened, and water management systems developed—all in order to transform the land for intensive agriculture. Andean cultures also adapted to a wide variety of ecological regions, including high plateaus and mountains where potatoes and llamas were raised; mid-level valleys where crops such as cotton and food crops like maize, chilies, and cacao grew; and coastal regions that relied on fishing and bird guano (excrement) as fertilizer for crops. Farmers developed a raised-field system to drain water away from crops in swampy areas and dug canals that controlled rain water or snow melt from the mountains. In contrast to the urban civilizations of Mesoamerica and the Andes, most North American cultures were semi-sedentary. The mound builders (Hopewell culture) in eastern North America developed agriculture independently and relied on crops such as sunflower seeds, sumpweed, goosefoot, gourds, and squash for part of their staple food, augmented by hunting and gathering. Around 900 C.E., maize-based agriculture arrived from Mexico and allowed for larger settlements, such as Cahokia. Maize agriculture, supplemented by squash and beans, also reached the Pueblo people where it allowed for a very sudden rise in permanent villages in the deserts of the Southwest. Agricultural civilizations in the Americas and the Nile Valley struggled to cope with changes in climate (such as prolonged drought), deforestation, and soil exhaustion from over-farming, which hastened their demise.

Theme 2:
Development and Interaction of Cultures

Many capital cities of these civilizations continued the pattern of monumental architecture and royal tomb art, which exemplified the power of the rulers. Meroë, in contact with Egyptian civilization up the Nile River, created monumental architecture like tombs, pyramids, and sculptures and was ruled by sacred monarchs. The kingdom of Axum created huge obelisks and adopted Coptic Christianity in the 400s. Their successor state, Ethiopia, continued to be a predominantly Christian country, even though Islam was sweeping the region. Bantu-speaking people spread their language, ancestor veneration, dancing, drum music, and respect for women as agricultural workers throughout much of sub-Saharan Africa. The people of Jenne-jeno produced elaborate masks and statues representing ancestral spirits.

In both Mesoamerica and Andean America, temple architecture, accurate solar calendars, complex mathematics, and ritual sacrifices performed by priests and sacred kings were important. The Hopewell culture was characterized by large earth mounds; some of them appear to be burial mounds, while others might have astronomical purposes. In the southwest, sunken houses and kivas (sunken religious spaces) were surrounded by multi-storied, interconnected, aboveground structures known as pueblos. While the Mesoamericans developed writing (the Maya used both glyphs and syllabic symbols), none of the other peoples in the Americas did. In the Andean region, the Chavín created a pan-Andean religious movement that became the basis for later civilizations. Moche warrior-priests performed shamanistic rituals and ruled a region along the northern coast of modern Peru. Tombs of the warrior-elite contained great riches and beautiful artifacts. Wari and Tiwanaku shared a cult of an Andean Staff God.

Theme 3:
State-Building, Expansion, and Conflict

Civilizations in Sub-Saharan Africa and the Americas were not as large as those in Afro-Eurasia, but they nevertheless controlled quite a bit of territory. Teotihuacán, for example, controlled an area of around 10,000 square miles and over 100,000 people. In the Andean regions, several successive civilizations arose, such as the Chavín and Moche along the coast, and the Wari and Tiwanaku in the Andes. Later civilizations, such as the Inca, built on the administrative and military techniques their predecessors established. Meroë and Axum, linked in trade with the Eurasian empires, developed their own strong states in northeastern Africa. Meroë was ruled by sacred kings (and queens) similar to the pharaohs of Egypt. Axum, on the Horn of Africa, was built on controlling trade with Rome and the Indian Ocean trade routes. Monumental architecture, such as obelisks, reinforced the grandeur of these kings. In contrast, some civilizations, such as the Maya, existed as separate city-states that fought each other for prisoners to sacrifice in religious rituals. Archeology at Jenne-jeno in the Niger River region reveals central towns surrounded by smaller villages dedicated to specific crafts (such as iron smelting), which also did not unite into larger empires.

Theme 4:
Creation, Expansion, and Interaction of
Economic Systems

Each of these civilizations relied on agriculture and trade for economic success. The kingdom of Axum relied on very efficient plow-based agriculture, unlike the majority of sub-Saharan Africa that relied on hoes and digging sticks. Axum controlled the trade between the Indian Ocean ports along the African coast and the African interior by controlling Adulis, the largest port on the east African coast. Smaller civilizations such as the city-states along the Niger River valley flourished in small clusters of villages devoted to special economic activities such as ironsmiths, cotton weavers, leather workers, and potters. All three non-traditional second-wave civilizations—the mound builders, the pueblo, and the Bantu—seem to have traded over a large region for luxury items such as feathers, precious stones, animal hides, and ivory. The Bantu appear to have incorporated sugarcane and bananas from Indonesia and ironworking from the north (likely Meroë/Axum). The domestication of the camel allowed greater movement of trade goods across the Sahara. Mesoamericans had guilds of merchant traders who carried luxury goods from the hinterland and between cities by canoe and foot. Burial mounds in the Hopewell culture show evidence of trade goods coming from as far away as Yellowstone, the Gulf of Mexico, and the Great Lakes. Pueblo people traded with Mexico along the turquoise road. In the Andes, the Wari and Tiwanaku created roads where llama caravans allowed goods to be traded between regions.

Theme 5:
Development and Transformation of Social Structures

Urban civilizations in these more remote areas continued the pattern of Eurasian empires, with stratified social classes consisting of ruling elites (often ruling as shamanistic mediators between humans and the gods), merchants, skilled artisans, servants, agricultural laborers, and slaves. However, Jenne-jeno in West Africa and the Bantu-speaking peoples did not seem to have major differences in wealth (and, we assume, social classes). Sub-Saharan Africa also seems to have been less sharply patriarchal than Eurasia. Meroë had at least ten women who ruled in their own right and, unlike Egypt, were portrayed as women and not as men (as Hatshepsut had been). Bantu-speaking people believed in separate spheres for men and women, but valued both; women continued to be respected as the primary agricultural workers, while men continued as hunters and warriors. The elite of Mesoamerica and Andean America were thought to be divine, similar to beliefs in Meroë.

Guided Reading Questions for Chapter 6

Seeking the Main Point To what extent did the histories of Africa and the Americas parallel those of Eurasia? In what ways did they forge new or different paths? (Page 230)

Comparison What similarities and differences are noticeable among the three major continents of the world? (Page 230)

Connection How did the history of Meroë and Axum reflect interaction with neighboring civilizations? (Page 234)

Description How does the experience of the Niger Valley challenge conventional notions of "civilization"? (Page 239)

Comparison With what Eurasian civilizations might the Maya be compared? (Page 243)

Connection In what ways did Teotihuacán shape the history of Mesoamerica? (Page 244)

Connection What kind of influence did Chavín exert in the Andes region? (Page 247)

Description What features of Moche life characterize it as a civilization? (Page 248)

Description What was the significance of Wari and Tiwanaku in the history of Andean civilization? (Page 249)

Practicing AP® Historical Thinking What features common to all civilizations can you identify in the civilizations of Africa and the Americas? What distinguishing features give each of them a distinctive identity? (Page 251)

Connection In what ways did the process of Bantu expansion stimulate cross-cultural interaction? (Page 253)

Comparison In what ways were the histories of the Ancestral Pueblo and the Mound Builders similar to each other, and how did they differ? (Page 255)

NOTES:

UNIT 1
A Review of AP® World History & Ways of the World for the AP® Course,
Third Edition

AP® WORLD HISTORY PERIOD THREE
Regional and Transregional Interactions, c. 600 CE to c. 1450 CE

PART THREE
An Age of Accelerating Connections, 600 CE –1450

AP® World History Key Concepts

3.1: Expansion and Intensification of Communication and Exchange Networks

3.2: Continuity and Innovation of State Forms and Their Interactions

3.3: Increased Economic Productive Capacity and Its Consequences

The Big Picture: Defining a Millennium

How do scholars decide what defines the ending of one stage of history and the beginning of another? This question corresponds to the AP® historical thinking skill of periodization – the ability to categorize historical events into meaningful epochs and to determine transitional phases in the historical narrative. For this textbook, the period chosen is roughly a millennium: 600 c.e. (the fall of the second-wave civilizations) to 1450 c.e. (the voyages of Columbus). Scholars do not have a very accurate way of describing this period; "postclassical" or "medieval" are terms that are often used, but apply most specifically to Europe. *Ways of the World* has chosen to call this era before the beginning of the modern world the era of third-wave civilizations.

Third-Wave Civilizations: Something New, Something Old, Something Blended

One of the reasons why scholars do not have a very accurate way of describing this period is because of the "rather different trajectories of various regions of the world during this millennium." This means that it is difficult to find ways to characterize this period without violating the reality for regions outside Eurasia. However, there are some regional patterns that emerge.

First, the globalization of civilizations that were unique yet still drew on that of their predecessors continued. Common features included states and cities, specialized economies, social stratification, and gender inequality.

- New, smaller civilizations arose along the East African coast (like the Swahili city-states) and engaged in the Indian Ocean trade.

- In West Africa, the kingdoms of Ghana, Mali, and Songhay controlled the trans-Saharan trade.

- Kievan Russia borrowed culture from the Mediterranean region and controlled trade between the Baltic and the Black Sea.

- In East Asia, Japan, Korea, and Vietnam borrowed from China.

- Srivijaya and the Angkor kingdom borrowed from the Hindu and Buddhist traditions of South Asia.

Next, a new civilization arose: Islam, a civilization defined by its religion, began in the seventh century in Arabia and expanded rapidly (see Map 9.2, p. 372) to control much of North Africa and the Middle East.

- Another pattern was the persistence or reconstitution of second-wave civilizations into the third-wave era.

- The Byzantine Empire continued the pattern of Roman Christian civilization until 1453.

- After a period of fragmentation, the Sui, Tang, and Song Chinese dynasties restored political unity and Confucian traditions.

- Indian civilization continued patterns of cultural diversity, caste, and Hinduism.

- In Mesoamerica, the collapse of the Maya and Teotihuacán led to the success of the Mexica (Aztec) empire.

- In the Andes, the Incas incorporated previous centers of civilization into a large empire.

A final pattern followed the collapse of the Roman Empire in Western Europe: the decentralized rule of smaller successor states, which created a civilization that blended Greco-Roman and Germanic elements where kings and church leaders attempted to maintain links with the religion and culture of the classical Mediterranean world. Western Europe, a backwater in the first part of this millennium, began to emerge after 1000 as a group of competitive, expansive states.

The Ties That Bind: Transregional Interaction in the Third-Wave Era

The variety of regional developments makes it difficult to identify truly transregional patterns, but clearly there was an increased rate and degree of exchange between cultures, whether through trade, migration, or conquest. In some areas, "local cosmopolitan regions" emerged: island Southeast Asia, the Swahili states, Central Asian cities, the Islamic Middle East, parts of Western Europe, and the Inca Empire. Accelerating trade had several consequences.

- **Long-distance trade** routes such as the Silk Roads in Eurasia, the Indian Ocean basin, the trans-Saharan routes, and along the Mississippi and other rivers grew considerably during this period. Trade passed along not only goods, but people, religious ideas, technology, and even pathogens. New products became known through the trade routes, and in some regions, people began to produce goods for that trade instead of for a local market. People who controlled trade often became quite wealthy.

- **Larger empires** were another characteristic of the third-wave civilizations. The empires often provided stability and security and encouraged trade, such as the West African savanna empires or the Tang dynasty. Large empires also meant more diversity, as different groups of people came under the sway of one state, such as the Inca or the Islamic empire. The largest empires were created by pastoralists or nomadic peoples: Arabs, Berbers, Turks, Mongols, or Aztecs.

■ **Religions spread** along the trade routes protected by large empires. Hinduism, Buddhism, Christianity, and Islam all expanded outside their original location to become world religions.

■ **Technologies spread** to different regions. Technology such as silk manufacturing, the sugar crystallization process, cotton textile manufacturing, the Hindu-Arabic number system, the concept of zero, and corn (maize) production diffused to regions far beyond their original creation.

■ **Diseases spread** to become transregional pandemics, such as the Black Death.

■ **Travelers along the trade routes become a major focus of historical interest,** whether merchants, missionaries, migrants, soldiers, or bureaucratic administrators. This focus on travel raises the following questions:

- What happens when strangers from different cultures meet?

- How did external stimuli cause change within societies?

- How did societies or individuals choose what to accept and what to reject from other cultures, and what modifications did they make to the foreign ideas or technologies?

A masculine, warrior culture meant that much of the "work" of building empires and administering them, establishing trade routes, spreading religions, and so on was predominantly the realm of men, and most of our historical sources from this time come from men. Third-wave civilizations mostly provide "men's history"; however, women often had a stronger local role, and their labor contributed to making goods that entered long-distance trade. Gender roles varied over time and between regions and groups of people.

AP® Themes in Part Three:

Environment	Cultures	State Building	Economies	Social Structures
Long-distance commerce and environmental variations - China and northern barbarians: interaction across an ecological frontier - Ecological patterns in Arabia - Islam's "Green Revolution" - Ecology, agriculture, and technology in Europe - Environmental effects of European economic growth in the Middle Ages - Pastoralism as an Environmental adaptation - Environmental effects of Mongol conquests - Disease as a historical actor: the Black Death - Australian Environmental adaptations	Spread of Buddhism in Asia - Indian cultural influence in Southeast Asia - Cross-cultural and perceptions of "others" - Assimilation and resistance: Buddhism in China - The rise of Islam - Cultural encounters: Islam in India, Anatolia, West Africa, and Spain - Christianity: • Contraction in Asia and Africa • Expansion in Europe and Russia • Conflicts between Roman Catholic and Eastern Orthodox - Faith and reason in European Christianity - Cultural exchange in the Mongol Empire - Varying perceptions of the Mongols - Islam and the European Renaissance	The development of Southeast Asian states - The development of Swahili city-states - The development of West African empires - State structure in Song and Tang China - In the shadow of China: state building in Korea, Vietnam, and Japan - Rise and fragmentation of an Arab Empire - The Byzantine state - A new Russian state - Rise of a state system in Europe - The Crusades - Pastoral empires - The Mongol conquests: comparing China, Persia, and Russia - Comparing 15th-century states: Chinese, European, Islamic world - Comparing European and Chinese maritime Voyages - Aztec and Inca empires	Silk Road trading Networks - Indian Ocean trading networks - Trans-Saharan trading networks - Commercial networks in the Americas - China's economic Revolution - Chinese Technological innovations - Islam and the making of a hemispheric exchange network - European Technological borrowing and innovation - Comparing European and Chinese economic Patterns - Mongol Empire as a Eurasian economic Network - Networks of connection in the 15th century	Slavery in West African civilizations - Women in Song dynasty China - Comparing women's lives in Korea, Vietnam, and Japan - Chinese elites at Leisure - Women in Mongolruled China - Men and women in early Islam - Women and work in the emerging European Civilization - European feudalism as a social system - Urban societies in medieval Europe - Commonality and variation in pastoral societies - Women in pastoral Societies - Social variations and gender roles in 15th-century societies - Gender parallelism in the Aztec and Inca empires - Gender roles among the Iroquois

CHAPTER SEVEN
Commerce and Culture, 600-1450

AP® World History Key Concepts

3.1: Expansion and Intensification of Communication and Exchange Networks

I. Improved transportation technologies and commercial practices led to an increased volume of trade, and expanded the geographical range of existing and newly active trade networks.

II. The movement of peoples caused environmental and linguistic effects.

III. Cross-cultural exchanges were fostered by the intensification of existing, or the creation of new, networks of trade and communication.

The primary focus of this chapter is the development and intensification of transregional trade networks: the Silk Roads across Central Asia (see Map 7.1, p. 285), the Indian Ocean Basin (see Map 7.2, p. 292), the trans-Saharan routes (see Map 7.4, p. 304), and the less dense trade routes in the Americas (see Map 7.5, p. 308). Also, make sure to review the Snapshot charts of goods traded in the different regions, such as the goods traded on the Silk Roads on page 286 and across the Indian Ocean basin on page 294. Trade routes most often connected different environmental regions – the goods or agricultural products produced in one area might not be able to be found in another area with a different geography. All of these routes generated wealth and led to the development or expansion of urban centers like the Swahili city-states or Cahokia. This expanded trade relied on new technology like the sternpost rudder, magnetic compass, astrolabe, lateen sail, and the domestication of camels. Expanded trade also facilitated the exchange of more than just trade goods; religions, culture, languages, agricultural products, human populations (whether merchants, travelers, or slaves), and disease were all transported along the trade routes. Much of the trade was conducted by independent merchants, who often lived in diaspora communities along the trade routes, but in some cases, as with the Incas, trade was strictly controlled by the state. Languages spread with the merchants, such as Sanskrit into Southeast Asia or Arabic into East Africa. New languages also developed, such as Swahili – based on the Bantu language group, but written in Arabic and using Arabic loan words. Environmental effects include the dissemination of new crops, such as bananas, maize, yams, or sugar to new locations; the exploitation of forests for rare woods, animals and birds, or ivory; or the spread of diseases such as the Black Death.

3.2: Continuity and Innovation of State Forms and Their Interactions

I. Empires collapsed and were reconstituted; in some regions new state forms emerged.

II. Interregional contacts and conflicts between states and empires encouraged significant technological and cultural transfers, including transfers between Tang China and the Abbasids, transfers across the Mongol empires, transfers during the Crusades, and transfers during Chines maritime activity led by Ming Admiral Zheng He.

The expansion of trade encouraged urban growth along important junctures in trade routes, such as the Swahili city-states in East Africa or Gao and Timbuktu in West Africa, as well as creating opportunities for new kinds of states like Srivijaya (see Map 7.3, p. 296), built on the Strait of Malacca, a choke point in the sea trade routes between the South China Sea and the Indian Ocean. Culture, including technology, traveled along the trade routes. Some technological transfers aided exploration, such as the sternpost rudder and lateen sail or the spread of camel domestication from Asia to northern Africa. Others included transferring the special products of one region to another, sometimes by "industrial espionage." For example, silk production technology was a closely guarded secret in China, but was transferred to other regions such as Korea or the Byzantine Empire, dispersing silk manufacturing. Sometimes agricultural products were transferred, such as sugarcane to India; maize to the Ancestral Pueblo people, the Mound Builders, or the Andean region; or bananas to Madagascar and Eastern Africa.

Religion also spread through the travels of merchants. Judaism, Christianity, Hinduism, Buddhism, and Islam were all carried to distant lands by merchants. Buddhism traveled the eastern ends of the Silk Roads between India and China and followed Hinduism into Southeast Asia. Conversion to Buddhism was voluntary and demonstrated the symbiotic relationship between the trade and religion; wealthy Buddhists spent quite a bit of money promoting Buddhist traditions and acquiring Buddhist artifacts, while Buddhist travelers, whether monks or merchants, helped fuel long-distance trade. Similarly, the cultures of peripheral regions in East and Southeast Asia were influenced by dominant trading partners. For example, Vietnam, Japan, and Korea became part of China's sphere of influence. Other areas in Southeast Asia were influenced by Indian culture because of the trading relationship between those areas and the Hindu kingdoms of South Asia. The temple of Angkor Wat is a prime example of Hindu and, later, Buddhist cultural influence in Southeast Asia. Islam spread throughout the Indian Ocean basin and in Western Africa in much the same way as Buddhism did along the Silk Roads; conversion was voluntary and offered advantages to local rulers in terms of trade and culture, including a written language. Islam also cemented societal hierarchies and inherited kingship lines.

3.3: Increased Economic Productive Capacity and Its Consequences

I. Innovations stimulated agricultural and industrial production in many regions.

II. The fate of cities varied greatly, with periods of significant decline and periods of increased urbanization buoyed by rising productivity and expanding trade networks.

III. Despite significant continuities in social structures and in methods of production, there were also some important changes in labor management and in the effect of religious conversion on gender relations and family life.

Cities contracted or became extinct in the face of over-extended agriculture (Chaco Canyon), shifting of trade routes due to combat or invasion (inner Asian cities after the breakup of the Han and invasion of pastoral peoples), or exposure to trade-borne diseases (such as the Black Death, which devastated many cities in Eurasia and northern Africa). Trade also contributed to the creation of cities or their expansion, such as Dunhuang along the Silk Road, Venice in the Mediterranean trade, or the Swahili city-states in East Africa. Long-distance trade also permitted the transportation of slaves from one region to another. Women were most often used as domestic servants or concubines, while men were often agricultural laborers, miners, porters, or even government officials. Some African slaves even ended up in the Abbasid caliphate.

Theme 1: Interaction Between Humans and the Environment

Since Eurasia is on an east–west axis, much of the agricultural products or domesticated animals available in one region could be grown or raised in another along the same lines of latitude. In the Americas and Africa, all continents on a north–south axis, much modification was needed to transport animals or crops into totally different zones; rain forest, deserts, high mountains – all served to limit trade and the transfer of crops or animals. This explains the more rapid expansion of crops across Eurasia and the relatively long time it took for maize to spread beyond its origins in Mesoamerica to the Andes or northeastern woodlands. One of the most important environmental issues in the increased trade was when Malay sailors learned to use the monsoons (seasonal winds in the Indian Ocean region) to travel over open sea instead of hugging the coastline (see Map 7.2, p. 292). Along with new navigation technology and shipbuilding techniques, the Indian Ocean became a "common highway" for traders from China to the Swahili cities.

Theme 2:
Development and Interaction of Cultures

Cultures interacted in unprecedented ways as the intensity of economic exchanges increased. The most obvious example is the spread of religions. Specifically, Buddhism, Islam, Hinduism, and even Christianity came to new areas via trade routes, and linked far-flung people with a common belief system. Great monumental structures, such as the Hindu temples of Angkor Wat, Buddhist temples such as Borobudur in Indonesia, or the mosques and Islamic universities of Timbuktu, speak to cultural diffusion along trade routes. Similarly, intellectual knowledge such as mathematics, medical innovations, and hydrologic technology spread. Foodstuffs, such as rice, noodles, sugar, and citrus, spread across Eurasia, while Malay sailors spread bananas, coconuts, and cocoyams to Madagascar. Kings in East African city-states converted to Islam, wore silk and used porcelain dishes from China, and used a language composed of Bantu words written in Arabic script. Lastly, travelers recorded their journeys and gave new insight into the cultures they encountered, such as Ibn Battuta and Marco Polo.

Theme 3:
State-Building, Expansion, and Conflict

State expansion was often linked to controlling needed trade routes. States garnered wealth from trading and taxing those who traded. West African states such as Ghana and Mali became extremely wealthy because they controlled the gold–salt trade across the Sahara. Their gold monopoly allowed them to create armies to take over more territory and to protect the trade routes. Srivijaya controlled the strategic straits of Malacca and also became incredibly wealthy by charging ships that passed through the narrow strait. Pastoralists (such as the Mongols or Berbers) controlled trade through steppes and desert regions. The Mongols (see Chapter 11) created a huge land empire stretching from China to Eastern Europe, and a rejuvenated Silk Road trade flourished under their protection.

Theme 4:
Creation, Expansion, and Interaction of Economic Systems

Along with the much-coveted silks, commodities such as cotton textiles from India, hides and furs from Russia, lapis lazuli from the Middle East, and olive oil and wine from the Mediterranean region traveled across the land routes collectively known as the Silk Roads. These trails stretched in various directions from Luoyang in the east to Tyre in the west. They circumvented the Taklamakan desert to the north and to the south, linked with routes going northward for Baltic amber and furs and timber from Siberia, and stretched southward into Barygaza in India as well as into the Persian Gulf.

The goods traded within the Indian Ocean basin (the Sea Roads) included many of the same goods that were transmitted overland along the Silk Roads; however, because ships could carry more than camels or donkeys, nonluxury goods such as rice, pepper, sugar, wheat, and timber traveled via the Indian Ocean trade network. As new technology was employed, the volume of trade across land and sea increased. In addition, traders engaged in economic warfare and espionage by smuggling trade secrets from one area to another. For example, knowledge of how to raise silk worms was smuggled out of China and helped the Byzantines, Persians, Japanese, and Koreans learn how to produce the much-coveted silk cloth, thus expanding the silk industry. Malay sailors learned how to use the seasonal monsoon winds to navigate the Indian Ocean, therefore connecting the east coast of Africa with Asia.

The trans-Saharan trade routes across Africa (or Sand Roads) originated as trade routes between the various cities in Sudanic Africa and were transformed by the importation of the camel. Once the camel came to West Africa, regional trade expanded into a large network of trade routes that exchanged salt, gold, ivory, and slaves within West Africa and to the cities around the Mediterranean Sea.

In the Americas, long-distance trade routes became increasingly important. These American trade routes were not as direct or well-established as those in the Afro-Eurasian area, but luxury goods such as obsidian and turquoise traveled their way southward from North America into Mesoamerica, while the knowledge of the cultivation of maize traveled northward to the Ancestral Pueblo people and the Mississippi Valley, and indirectly travelled south to the Andes. The pochteca (independent merchant guild) controlled trade in the Aztec Empire. In the Andean region, however, the Inca state created thousands of miles roads and exerted absolute control over trade.

Theme 5: Development and Transformation of Social Structures

Interregional trade affected social structures. One of the most obvious is that although men often undertook the trade, women often created the items that were traded. This was especially true in silk. Women were responsible for raising silk worms and creating silk cloth. Trade also increased the social complexity in areas that had previously not been a central part of the trade network. Also, because of expanded long-distance trade, slaves could be taken long distances from their homes – even to different continents. For example, slaves from non-Islamic stateless societies in Africa were used as agricultural laborers by the Abbasid in the modern region of southern Iraq. Finally, access to coveted luxury goods from distant lands cemented the differences between the ruling elite and the commoners. Rulers were almost always male, and traditional matrilineal descent patterns changed in favor of patriarchal forms of political, economic, and social powers.

In the Aztec Empire, the pochteca (independent merchants' guild) lived separately from the permanent residents of cities, married only among themselves, and sometimes served as spies for rulers. In the Inca Empire of South America, the state controlled the storage and dispersion of food and other goods, requiring a system of recordkeeping by a highly trained class of accountants.

Guided Reading Questions for Chapter 7

Seeking the Main Point In what ways did long-distance commerce act as a motor of change in pre-modern world history? (Page 283)

Change What lay behind the emergence of Silk Road commerce, and what kept it going for so many centuries? (Page 284)

Significance What made silk such a highly desired commodity across Eurasia? (Page 286)

Connection What were the major economic, social, and cultural consequences of Silk Road commerce? (Page 287)

Change What accounted for the spread of Buddhism along the Silk Roads? (Page 288)

Connection What was the impact of disease along the Silk Roads? (Page 290)

Change What lay behind the flourishing of Indian Ocean commerce in the post-classical millennium? (Page 294)

Connection In what ways did Indian influence register in Southeast Asia? (Page 295)

Connection What was the role of Swahili civilization in the world of Indian Ocean commerce? (Page 299)

Practicing AP® Historical Thinking To what extent did the Silk Roads and the Sea Roads operate in a similar fashion? How did they differ? (Page 300)

Connection What changes did trans-Saharan trade bring to West Africa? (Page 302)

Comparison In what ways did networks of interaction in the West-ern Hemisphere differ from those in the Eastern Hemisphere? (Page 306)

NOTES:

CHAPTER EIGHT
China and the World: East Asian Connections, 600–1300

AP® World History Key Concepts

3.1: Expansion and Intensification of Communication and Exchange Networks

I. Improved transportation technologies and commercial practices led to an increased volume of trade, and expanded the geographical range of existing and newly active trade networks.

II. The movement of peoples caused environmental and linguistic effects.

III. Cross-cultural exchanges were fostered by the intensification of existing, or the creation of new, networks of trade and communication.

The fall of the Han dynasty led to several hundred years of political fragmentation. Large numbers of Han Chinese migrated southward during these unsettled years, which were marked by frequent incursion from steppes pastoralists such as the Xiongnu and Jurchen, who intermarried with the northern Chinese. Buddhism grew rapidly in China as Confucianism lost favor. Large populations in the south were possible because of improved agricultural techniques and water management, as well as the importation of new strains of rice. Old-growth forests were felled and hillsides were terraced, all in an effort to grow enough to feed the ever-increasing population.

During the Tang and Song dynasties, China led the world in technology and was once again the center of transregional trade. China took control of the Silk Roads and also opened or expanded many interior trade systems along canals and rivers. Using advanced shipbuilding and navigational techniques, Chinese merchants ranged throughout Southeast Asia and the Indian Ocean. Uniform taxes and tariffs and the use of paper money and bank drafts, as well as China's openness to foreign merchants, led to significant improvements in trade. China learned to deal with people they considered to be barbarians through a system of tribute exchanges or through military conflict when all else failed. China remained the "superpower" of the region and affected the political, social, cultural, and economic systems of nearby Korea, Vietnam, and Japan.

3.2: Continuity and Innovation of State Forms and Their Interactions

I. Empires collapsed and were reconstituted; in some regions new state forms emerged.

II. Interregional contacts and conflicts between states and empires encouraged significant technological and cultural transfers.

The Sui dynasty rebuilt a centralized state in China, followed closely by the Tang and Song dynasties. Confucian and Daoist ideals were reinvigorated and absorbed many aspects of Buddhism, which came to be seen as a foreign religion and associated with conquest. The Confucian examination system was reestablished, and the political system endured (with a brief Mongol interruption) until the twentieth century. China's technological advances — such as printing, porcelain making, steel making, the magnetic compass, shipbuilding techniques, medical advances, and gunpowder — found their way across Afro-Eurasia along the trade routes, often disseminated by Muslim merchants.

3.3: Increased Economic Productive Capacity and Its Consequences

I. Innovations stimulated agricultural and industrial production in many regions.

II. The fate of cities varied greatly, with periods of significant decline, and with periods of increased urbanization buoyed by rising productivity and expanding trade networks.

III. Despite significant continuities in social structures and in methods of production, there were also some important changes in labor management and in the effect of religious conversion on gender relations and family life.

As Song Chinese moved south to escape the invasions of steppes nomads, they greatly modified the land around the Yangzi River valley through intensive agriculture to accommodate the higher population level; they brought in new, high-yield rice strains from Vietnam (Champa rice), improved water control over river flooding and irrigation, cut down trees, terraced hillsides, and dug canals. China could support the highest population in the world and at the time was the most urbanized country. Large cities rose further south, away from invaders, while the northern population dropped. Cities included large administrative capitals and growth was also fueled by increased industrialization and foreign trade. Social structures reflected the traditional values established under the Han; the scholar-gentry class continued to be in charge, but merchants could become exceedingly wealthy because of the reestablished trade networks. While Chinese agriculture continued to be based on the labor of free peasants and tenant farmers, some changes did occur. For example, requiring cash payments of rents instead of payment in kind meant that peasant households had to produce something to sell, often goods that could be traded to the growing internal urban markets or on long-distance trade networks. Gender roles in the Song dynasty also returned to what was perceived as proper Confucian submission of women, especially women of the upper class. It was at this time that the practice of foot binding began. While aspects of Chinese culture and its political and economic structure influenced Korea, Japan, and Vietnam, these nations on China's periphery often retained much of their own traditions on social and gender roles.

Theme 1: Interaction Between Humans and the Environment

China saw both population increases and decreases during this period. Invasions from steppes nomads and warfare caused populations to decline or move south to escape warfare; raging epidemic diseases such as the Black Death also took their toll. Overall, more intensive agriculture was made possible by improved techniques, such as terracing, using fertilizer (night soil or human feces), canal and flood control, and the importation of new crops, such as Champa rice, led to rapidly rising population numbers as well as increased population density and urbanization. This intensive agriculture, in addition to clear-cutting forests to provide power for kilns and metalworking, tended to destroy the original ecology of a region. Some farmers switched to cash crops instead of growing food, which they now purchased from expanded internal markets.

Theme 2:
Development and Interaction of Cultures

China had a complicated relationship with cultures on its periphery. When China was strong, its expansion and control strongly impacted surrounding peoples such as the nomadic and seminomadic steppes people to the north, non-Han southern peoples, and surrounding states such as Vietnam, Korea, and Japan. China, as the middle kingdom, believed that their emperor ruled "all under heaven." Non-Chinese people could become accepted as civilized if they adopted Chinese language and writing, dress, customs, and cultural beliefs. Peripheral states often took part in a tribute system where they acknowledged both the cultural and military superiority of the Chinese and offered elaborate gifts or tribute to the emperor, who would reciprocate with token gifts. When China was weak, however, as in the period following the collapse of the Han dynasty and during the Tang dynasty, it paid vast amounts of tribute to its northern neighbors to prevent invasion, even offering Chinese princesses to barbarian leaders as wives to try to maintain peaceful borders.

China's cultural impact on its neighbors led to the adoption of Confucian values and education in Vietnam, Korea, and Japan. These regions also learned Buddhism from Chinese monks, adopted Chinese ideograms for their local languages, modeled their governments, economic systems, and, in the case of Japan, their cities, on Chinese models. However, this cultural borrowing was piecemeal; for example, Japanese and Korean landowners and nobility retained control of their governments without adopting a merit-based system, women often retained slightly more independence (for example, Japanese samurai women were expected to learn martial arts; Vietnamese women like the Trung sisters led rebellions against Chinese rule; and none adopted foot binding), and Chinese ideograms were adapted to local language phonetics.

Chinese philosophy within China changed. Confucianism was devalued following the fall of the Han and ensuing political fragmentation, and Buddhism became an alternative that promised solace. However, when central rule was restored under the Sui, Tang, and Song, a new form of Confucianism was restored as the center of government. This new form, called Neo-Confucianism, incorporated elements of Buddhism and stressed even stronger submission for women and adherence to Confucian hierarchies. The examination system was expanded with the help of printing, which made more texts available.

Theme 3:
State-Building, Expansion, and Conflict

China regained its central governmental unity under the Sui dynasty. It rebuilt and extended canals (see Map 8.1, p. 326 for the location of the Grand Canal) and attempted to expand its borders to include Korea. This military venture was unsuccessful and exhausted the dynasty's finances, leading to its collapse. The Tang dynasty continued traditional Chinese models: strong central control by an emperor supported by a theoretically merit-based bureaucracy trained through a strenuous Confucian academic tradition and civil service examinations (though in actuality, the landed gentry still had a significant role in governing). Six ministries were established (personnel, rites, finance, army, justice, and public works), and a Censorate oversaw the operations of the other branches. This basic system remained intact until the twentieth century, despite changes in dynasties. Tang China was considered the best-run state in the world and expanded its control along the Silk Roads. The Tang suppressed Buddhism in China, partly because it conflicted with Confucian hierarchical support for dynastic rule and partly because it was seen as a foreign religion at a time when China was recovering the core of Chinese culture expressed through Neo-Confucianism. Toward the end of Tang rule, Vietnam managed to win its independence from direct Chinese rule. As northern nomadic tribes such as the Khitan and Jurchen took over regions along the northern border, the next dynasty, the Song, moved southward. By the end of the thirteenth century, another group of steppes nomads, the Mongols, seized control of the entire empire and ruled until the mid-fourteenth century. Japan copied many aspects of China's culture and governance but remained more feudal than the centralized middle kingdom.

Theme 4:
Creation, Expansion, and Interaction of Economic Systems

After the restoration of centralized government with the Sui dynasty, and continuing with the Tang and Song dynasties, China regained its dominance in world trade and industry. Constructing the Grand Canal and other internal waterways allowed more direct trade within the country. Low-cost transportation allowed bulk materials, not just luxury goods, to be shipped and permitted farmers to specialize in production of items for trade because they could buy food in the local market instead of having to grow it themselves. Silk cloth and other handicrafts were produced for internal and interregional trade. The production of iron for armor, arrowheads and other weapons, monastery bells, and agricultural tools soared not only in large-scale, state-run smelters but also in small backyard furnaces. Production of paper and printing presses increased the volume of information and scholarly texts. Gunpowder, new navigational techniques, and improved designs for shipbuilding all added to China's growth and strength. China was the most commercialized country in the world under the Tang and Song. In addition, the Tang took control of the eastern half of the Silk Roads into Central Asia through the Tarim basin (see Map 8.1, p. 326). Large amounts of trade goods, such as Chinese silks and porcelain, traveled westward; tribute arrangements also increased the amount of Chinese goods flowing west and north to the pastoral people of the steppes, as well as other goods being imported into China from the west and Central Asia. This trade greatly influenced cultures on China's periphery.

Theme 5:
Development and Transformation of Social Structures

The influence of pastoral nomads – during the period after the fall of the Han, the rise of Turkic empires during the Tang, and the collapse of the Song under the Mongols – led to some loosening of traditional Confucian hierarchies, especially the subordination and confinement of women. However, the traditional Chinese values expressed in Neo-Confucianism meant that during most of this period women were forced into submission, and the social hierarchy established under the Han remained relatively constant.

The Song practice of foot binding was a new factor that demonstrated the renewed subordination of women and was thought to create beautiful, tiny feet that distinguished upper-class Chinese women from the barbarians. Women also lost control of silk weaving, but they continued to be the major producers of silk worms and thread. Women did have increased opportunities running restaurants, selling fish and vegetables, or working as domestic servants, dressmakers, concubines, or performers. In contrast, women's property rights expanded, as did their education (at least for elite women).

In Korea, Chinese influence saw a regression of women's freedom as the Confucian system became more popular. Also, the landowning gentry in Korea maintained far more control than did their counterparts in China; the meritocracy was less effective in providing social mobility in Korea. Vietnam, in contrast, more heartily adopted the civil service examination system and thus maintained greater social mobility than Korea.

While Japan copied Chinese bureaucratic principles, the Japanese did not adopt China's social structure or views on the role of women. Unlike Song China, Japanese women escaped foot binding and had considerably more freedom. Also, the warrior virtues of the samurai were at the core of Japanese feudal society, whereas warriors were not highly regarded in China's social structure.

Guided Reading Questions for Chapter 8

Seeking the Main Point Chinese history has often been viewed in the West as impressive per-haps, but largely static or changeless and self-contained or isolated. In what ways might the material in this chapter counteract such impressions? (Page 324)

Change Why are the centuries of the Tang and Song dynas-ties in China sometimes referred to as a "golden age"? (Page 325)

Change In what ways did women's lives change during the Tang and Song dynasties? (Page 331)

Connection How did the Chinese and their nomadic neighbors to the north view each other? (Page 333)

Connection What assumptions underlay the tribute system? (Page 334)

Connection In what ways did China and the nomads influence each other? (Page 336)

Connection In what ways did China have an influence in Korea, Vietnam, and Japan? In what ways was that influence resisted? (Page 337)

Comparison In what different ways did Japanese and Korean women experience the pressures of Confucian orthodoxy? (Page 343)

Practicing AP® Historical Thinking In what different ways did Korea, Vietnam, Japan, and northern nomads experience and respond to Chinese influence? (Page 345)

Connection In what ways did China participate in the world of Eurasian commerce and exchange, and with what outcomes? (Page 346)

Change What facilitated the rooting of Buddhism within China? (Page 349)

Change What were the major sources of opposition to Buddhism within China? (Page 352)

CHAPTER NINE
The Worlds of Islam: Afro-Eurasian Connections, 600–1450

AP® World History Key Concepts

3.1: Expansion and Intensification of Communication and Exchange Networks

I. Improved transportation technologies and commercial practices led to an increased volume of trade, and expanded the geographical range of existing and newly active trade networks.

II. The movement of peoples caused environmental and linguistic effects.

III. Cross-cultural exchanges were fostered by the intensification of existing, or the creation of new, networks of trade and communication.

The expansion of Islamic empires created the first hemisphere-wide trading and communication network involving Africa, Asia, South Asia, and Europe (see Map 9.3, p. 383). Distant regions such as Central Asia and sub-Saharan Africa became more closely linked to the major trading systems (Indian Ocean, Mediterranean, Silk Roads, and Saharan routes) through the spread of Islamic empires. Muslim merchants continued advances in shipbuilding and navigation, such as improving the astrolabe by adding azimuths for determining location at sea. Islam was friendly to merchants and trade if conducted fairly, unlike the more hostile attitude toward merchants in other cultures (such as China and Christian Europe). The economic system of the *Dar al-Islam* (land under Islamic rule) often borrowed from the Persians and employed many commercial techniques that facilitated trade, in addition to enjoying the advantages of a common language (Arabic), system of taxation, and laws. The spread of Islam, whether by armies, merchants, or Sufi mystics, was accompanied by the spread of Arabic, the language used in the sacred texts of the Quran and *hadiths* (sayings of the prophet Mohammed). Arabic became a common trade language, and many previously unwritten languages, such as Swahili, came to be written in Arabic script. The creation of a hemisphere-wide trade network also contributed to the spread of different crops, agricultural and water management techniques, and agricultural implements. In some areas, such as Muslim Spain, Central Asia, or sub-Saharan Africa, syncretism or cultural blending occurred alongside the diffusion of Islam and Arabic culture.

3.2: Continuity and Innovation of State Forms and Their Interactions

I. Empires collapsed and were reconstituted; in some regions new state forms emerged.

II. Interregional contacts and conflicts between states and empires encouraged significant technological and cultural transfers.

The rapid expansion of Islam (see Map 9.2, p. 372 and Map 9.3, p. 383), first through conquest by Arab armies and later through conversion, brought the core of Afro-Eurasia under the control of one group. State rule evolved from military conquest to the creation of new forms of governance. The military forces sweeping out of Arabia led to the ultimate downfall of the Byzantine Empire, Christian kingdoms in Spain, and the Sassanid Empire (Persia) before moving to take control of the trade routes and confronting China at the Battle of Talas River in Central Asia in 751. This rapid expansion led to an empire that was united by a common faith, with no separation of religion and governance.

The first four Rightly Guided Caliphs had all been companions of the prophet Mohammed. After their deaths, a split emerged in Islam between the Sunni and the Shia. The Sunnis believed that the caliphs should be chosen by the Islamic community; the Shia held that leadership should derive from the blood relatives of Muhammad. While Persia became Shia and maintained Farsi as their language, much of the rest of northern Africa, Spain, and the Middle East were Sunni Arabs and used Arabic as the language of government. The Umayyad caliphate following the Rightly Guided Caliphs was replaced by the Abbasids, who were strongly influenced by Persian traditions. Persian culture, architecture, administrative techniques, and court ritual had a huge impact on Muslim rule in Iran, India, Central Asia, and the Ottoman Empire. The Abbasids soon lost all but nominal control over outlying regions and were ultimately conquered by the Mongols, who destroyed their capital of Baghdad.

3.3: Increased Economic Productive Capacity and Its Consequences

I. Innovations stimulated agricultural and industrial production in many regions.

II. The fate of cities varied greatly, with periods of significant decline, and with periods of increased urbanization buoyed by rising productivity and expanding trade networks.

III. Despite significant continuities in social structures and in methods of production, there were also some important changes in labor management and in the effect of religious conversion on gender relations and family life.

Persian water management techniques helped increase agricultural production throughout the Dar al-Islam. Crops, including sugar, cotton, and citrus, were widely diffused. Urban areas grew as administrative, religious, or trade centers. Mecca, for example, saw millions of pilgrims each year during the hajj. Baghdad was built as the capital of the Abbasid caliphate. Gao became a religious and educational center in West Africa, and the Swahili city-states grew in East Africa as a result of trade in the Indian Ocean basin.

Islam also brought changes to social and gender roles. All believers were equal in the eyes of Allah, so there was no distinction in prayer and no rigid caste system. This encouraged conversion of lower-caste people in South Asia, for example, and encouraged slaves to adopt Islam as a means to end their servitude. Women were also considered to be equal religiously and gained more property rights under the Quran. However, women were still clearly subordinate to their husbands. Some regional traditions of veiling and sequestration of women became more common and widespread and were later identified as Muslim customs.

Theme 1: Interaction Between Humans and the Environment

Because of the arid environment in the Arabian Peninsula, Arab culture originated with nomadic tribes who searched for pastures and oases with water and shade for their animals (usually sheep, goats, and camels). Some oases developed into agricultural villages and trading centers that later developed into cities. Islamic empires united Afro-Eurasia in trade networks, leading to great environmental change. New agricultural products and practices became widespread; rice, sugarcane, sorghum, "hard" wheat, citrus, bananas, and other tropical fruits found their way westward. In addition, water management systems (such as the qanat system – drilling into a mountainside to create a tunnel to bring water for irrigation and drinking to distant places) and plantation systems with slave labor created an "Islamic Green Revolution" that increased the food supply and caused an increase in population density and urbanization. New technology that entered the Islamic world from the east (like gunpowder, water drilling, cotton and silk textile manufacturing, and papermaking) was passed through to other regions under Islamic control.

Theme 2:
Development and Interaction of Cultures

The founder of Islam, Muhammad Ibn Abdullah, was originally a trader along the routes that connected Arabia with the Levant and Mesopotamia, where Judaism, Christianity, and Zoroastrianism were all practiced. Consequently, he was familiar with several spiritual concepts that were later found in Islam, such as an all-powerful male Creator God, spiritual warfare between good and evil, an eternal heaven for the faithful as well as hell for nonbelievers. As Islam developed from a tribal religion into a universal religion, Islamic culture and the Arabic language spread as well. The Islamic world tolerated other monotheistic religious followers, particularly Christians and Jews as *dhimmis*, or "people of the book," which was unusual for this period. However, because of its tolerance, Islam looked quite different in the various regions it conquered.

Not long after Muhammad's death, a split developed in the *umma* (community of believers). Some followers, later known as Sunnis, believed the caliph should be selected by the entire Islamic community; those who believed that leadership should come from the line of Ali and Husayn, who were related to the prophet Mohammad, became known as the Shia. The division has never been reconciled. Other subgroups also developed, including the mystical Sufis (who served as missionaries and traders) and, much later, the Sikhs, who blended Islam with Hinduism.

Islam created the first truly international, hemispheric empire in history; its network reached from Spain to India, from the Mediterranean across the Sahara into West Africa and along the East African trading coastline. Its principles of faith, sometimes condensed into the Pillars of Islam (belief in one all-powerful God, obligations for prayer, charity, fasting during Ramadan, and completing a hajj [pilgrimage] to Mecca), wove a web of interconnectedness; yet, local traditions also shaped Islamic civilization outside of the Arab-controlled areas of the Middle East and North Africa.

Islam reached India via Turkic warriors invading from the Asia steppes. Although Islam proved attractive to disillusioned Buddhists and the lower castes of Hinduism and provided some tax relief, Muslims remained a minority population. In the early sixteenth century, Sikhism, a new religious movement developed; it incorporated elements of Islam (monotheism) with Hindu concepts (reincarnation and karma). Hinduism, however, remained dominant in South Asia.

The Byzantine Empire was defeated by Muslim Ottoman Turks with the fall of Constantinople in 1453. The Turkish conquerors offered many benefits to the conquered population, and Islam was not as foreign to monotheistic Christians, Jews, and Zoroastrians as it had been to Hindus and Buddhists. Sufis facilitated conversion as they established schools, hospitals, and other public works. Perhaps because a much larger proportion of the population was Turkish, as opposed to the smaller Turkic population in India, the Ottoman Empire emerged with a distinctive Turkish culture; the language was Turkish, and elements of Turkish shamanism found their way into the cultural fabric.

A different pattern of expansion and conversion occurred in West Africa where traders instead of warriors carried the message across the Sahara into Ghana, Mali, Songhay, and Kanem-Bornu. The earliest converts to Islam were the ruling elites of these kingdoms because Islam provided a source of literate officials to assist with administration and bureaucracy. Islam also offered African merchants important trade ties. In West Africa, cities became centers of government administration and trade as well as centers of Islamic religious and intellectual life. Islam did not spread quickly to rural areas, which clung to the ancient African religions and traditions.

Islam penetrated the Iberian Peninsula from North Africa early in the eighth century. To a great degree, Muslims, Christians, and Jews lived in better harmony here than elsewhere. The fine arts and sciences flourished, including medicine, astronomy, architecture, literature, and art. By 1000, Spain was perhaps 75 percent Islamic, and many of its cultural practices had spread to others, whether they converted or not. By the late tenth century, toleration began to fade. Christians began to invade from the north in an effort to reclaim Spain, and Crusaders' armies attempted to retake Jerusalem in the East. A more strict and fundamental form of Islam entered Spain from North Africa, and relationships among the three religions changed as Muslims avoided contact with Christians and imposed several limitations on them.

The Reconquista (the reconquest of Muslim Spain by the Christian monarchs Ferdinand and Isabella) was completed in 1492. Possibly the most important impact of Muslim Spain was its intellectual activity, making an abundance of Islamic and classical Greek learning available to backward Europe.

Theme 3:
State-Building, Expansion, and Conflict

The creation and rapid spread of the Islamic Empire was remarkable; by 750, Islam encompassed all of the Arabian Peninsula, stretched across North Africa and into the Iberian Peninsula, across Persia into South Asia, and northward into the Central Asian steppes. The defeat of the Chinese at the Battle of the Talas River halted Chinese westward expansion. Muslim military might began as a defense against other Arabs hostile to the new religion and gradually grew into an imperial army. New lands, rich agricultural areas, and profitable trading networks were brought under Muslim rule.

As the Arab Empire grew, its caliphs were transformed from tribal leaders into absolute rulers, often patterning themselves after the political administration of the Byzantine or Sassanid (Persian) emperors they had recently fought. Included in this transformation was the acquisition of a bureaucracy, standing armies, taxes, and currency, as well as dynastic rivalries and succession disputes. The Umayyad (630–750) and the Abbasid (750–1258) dynasties followed the first caliphs. The empire did not distinguish between secular and religious rule; the caliph was the leader of both the religion and the government. Sharia (Islamic law) was developed to create a way to govern justly, behave properly, and create a good society following the teachings of the Quran and *hadith*. The unity of the *umma* did not last long; different regions broke away as local rulers became strong enough to assert individual control over their particular territory, while maintaining nominal allegiance to the caliph in Baghdad. By the tenth century, little political unification remained, even as the religion and culture it created continued to spread to different parts of the Eastern Hemisphere. The Abbasids were conquered by the Mongols, who swept down from the steppes and destroyed Baghdad. *See Chapter 11 for more detailed discussion of the Mongols.*

Theme 4:
Creation, Expansion, and Interaction of Economic Systems

As Islam spread throughout Arabia, across the North African coast, and northeast into Southwest Asia and beyond, it created an immense network of economic and cultural exchanges. Commercial activity was respected in the Islamic world (Muhammad had himself been a trader) as opposed to Christendom, China, and South Asia. The pilgrimage to Mecca also encouraged travel and exchange among the faithful, and the desire of urban elites for luxury goods stimulated craftsmanship and trade. Baghdad, the Abbasid capital, became a cosmopolitan city with goods and services from across the hemisphere. Arab and Persian merchants became the dominant players in such exchanges across the third-wave civilizations and were active in the Mediterranean, across the Silk Roads and Saharan routes, and in the Indian Ocean basin. Agricultural production in Spain was the highest in Europe during the early centuries of Islamic rule, and Córdoba was one of the most splendid and cosmopolitan in the world at this time. Many new economic tools, often of Persian origin, helped expand trade, such as forms of banking, letters of credit, business partnerships, and contracts.

Theme 5:
Development and Transformation of Social Structures

Socially, Islam assumed the equality of all believers before Allah. This religious egalitarianism encouraged conversion among some groups, such as lower-caste people in India. Although the Quran offered women specific protections – such as property and inheritance rights and the prohibition of female infanticide or marriage by capture – less freedom was allowed in other areas – such as ending polyandry (the practice of taking multiple husbands) or freedom of movement in public. Early Arab Muslim practices were also more liberal toward women than those of the Abbasid Empire, where elite women were confined not only in public but also in private areas of the home called harems.

Strict seclusion was not possible for women of lower economic status, whose economic activity was needed outside the home. Some Sufi groups, however, allowed women as equal members or had separate groups for women similar to the nuns of Buddhism and Christianity. A few educated women were poets or became teachers of the faith; these teachers were also called *mullahs*, the same term that was applied to male teachers of the faith. However, most women were limited to a narrow sphere that centered on their family obligations.

At first, there was little attempt to convert conquered peoples to Islam, only to bring them under Islamic rule. People from monotheistic religions were promised freedom of worship, if not political equality. The *dhimmis* were granted protected status and incurred a special tax. In some areas, such as the Iberian Peninsula and the Ottoman Empire, Christians and Jews could rise to prominent positions in government and society.

Guided Reading Questions for Chapter 9

Seeking the Main Point In what ways did the civilization of Islam draw on other civilizations in the Afro-Eurasian world? And in what respects did it shape or trans-form those civilizations? (Page 364)

Description In what ways did the early history of Islam reflect its Arabian origins? (Page 366)

Description What did the Quran expect from those who followed its teachings? (Page 367)

Change How was Arabia trans-formed by the rise of Islam? (Page 369)

Change Why were Arabs able to construct such a huge empire so quickly? (Page 372)

Explanation What accounts for the widespread conversion to Islam? (Page 374)

Comparison What is the difference between Sunni and Shia Islam? (Page 375)

Comparison In what ways were Sufi Muslims critical of main-stream Islam? (Page 377)

Change How did the rise of Islam change the lives of women? (Page 380)

Comparison What similarities and differences can you identify in the spread of Islam to India, Anatolia, West Africa, and Spain? (Page 384)

Change In what ways was Anatolia changed by its incorporation into the Islamic world? (Page 385)

Practicing AP® Historical Thinking "Islam had a revolutionary impact on every society that it touched." What evidence might support this statement, and what might challenge it? (Page 390)

Description What makes it possible to speak of the Islamic world as a distinct and coherent civilization? (Page 392)

Connection In what ways was the world of Islam a "cosmopolitan civilization"? (Page 393)

CHAPTER TEN
The Worlds of Christendom: Contraction, Expansion, and Division, 600–1300

AP® World History Key Concepts

3.1: Expansion and Intensification of Communication and Exchange Networks

I. Improved transportation technologies and commercial practices led to an increased volume of trade, and expanded the geographical range of existing and newly active trade networks.

II. The movement of peoples caused environmental and linguistic effects.

III. Cross-cultural exchanges were fostered by the intensification of existing, or the creation of new, networks of trade and communication.

After the collapse of the Roman Empire in the West, long-distance trade plummeted as Roman roads fell into disrepair and social order disintegrated leaving small chiefdoms competing for control. Additionally, there was a series of invasions from groups such as the Muslims, Magyar/Huns, and Vikings (see Map 10.3, p. 429). Recovery began after 1000 when the invasions ended, partly stimulated by the Crusades (see Map 10.4, p. 435), which reintroduced a taste for Eastern luxury goods. Contact with Muslims in Spain and elsewhere led to improvements in shipbuilding and knowledge of gunpowder. In the eastern Mediterranean, the Byzantine Empire (see Map 10.1, p. 417) maintained trade ties with Asia and, along with the Italian city-states (such as Genoa, Florence, and Venice), was responsible for most of Asian or African goods entering Europe. Another trading network stretching from the Atlantic, to the Baltic, into Russia, and south to Constantinople was created by the Vikings. An indigenous trade network slowly grew in Western Europe; the Hanseatic cities in the north and the trade fairs centered in France helped begin the rebuilding process.

3.2: Continuity and Innovation of State Forms and Their Interactions

I. Empires collapsed and were reconstituted; in some regions new state forms emerged.

II. Interregional contacts and conflicts between states and empires encouraged significant technological and cultural transfers.

The Byzantine Empire continued the existence of Greco-Roman culture and ruled for a thousand years after the fall of the western Roman Empire until it was conquered by the Ottoman Turks in 1453. The Byzantines continued the Roman struggle against the Persian Empire, which weakened both and contributed to their losses to Muslim armies.

In Western Europe, the collapse of Rome created a power vacuum in which competing Germanic chiefs attempted to carve out kingdoms. Ultimately, the need to fend off outside invaders, such as the Arabs, Magyars, and Vikings, led to improved military techniques and the adoption of feudalism, a decentralized form of governance where individual fighters swear allegiance to a lord, promising to provide warriors at the lord's need in exchange for protection, land, and justice. Except for a brief attempt to reconstitute the Roman Empire in the West under Charlemagne (see Map 10.2, p. 426), decentralized government remained the norm until the High Middle Ages (1000–1300) when new centralized states like England, France, and Spain began to emerge. Unlike China, European states remained separate and competed against each other (see Map 10.3, p. 429). Some areas saw the rise of new, hybrid states; for example, Kiev was created by Vikings (Rus) and Slavic people but adopted Byzantine ideas of absolute power in the hands of an emperor, the Cyrillic writing system based on Greek, and Eastern Orthodox Christianity. New trade goods entering Europe, funneled through the Byzantine Empire and Muslim sources, also brought new ideas and technology (see Snapshot: European Borrowing, p. 439), which fueled the European economy and intellectual thought.

3.3: Increased Economic Productive Capacity and Its Consequences

I. Innovations stimulated agricultural and industrial production in many regions.

II. The fate of cities varied greatly, with periods of significant decline, and with periods of increased urbanization buoyed by rising productivity and expanding trade networks.

III. Despite significant continuities in social structures and in methods of production, there were also some important changes in labor management and in the effect of religious conversion on gender relations and family life.

The economy and agricultural practices declined during the years following the fall of the Roman Empire in the West. Long-distance trade virtually disappeared in the regions conquered by Germanic tribes and agricultural land turned into wasteland. Population dropped, and most of the remaining population was rural, tied to the land in an effort to grow enough to survive. Contact with Muslim Spain, the Crusades, and the rise of Italian trading city-states (as well as trade through Constantinople) led to significant borrowing in technology; new plows, horse collars, wheelbarrows, and spinning wheels increased rural productivity.

A generally warming trend in weather, the use of crop rotation, and new agricultural implements led to a gradual population increase. Some cities also began to increase in size for the first time since the fall of Rome. Kiev, as capital of the empire created by the Rus, was also a trade link between the Baltic and Constantinople. Italian city-states continued to prosper based on trade with the Byzantines and the Muslim world, and cities such as Córdoba and Granada rose in Muslim occupied Spain. Paris, Bologna, and other cities became university centers.

Both the social and gender structure changed after the fall of Rome as Germanic and Greco-Roman influences blended into a new entity. Women remained under patriarchal control but were able to participate in many craft guilds; however, by the fifteenth century, they were pushed out of most guilds.

Theme 1:
Interaction between Humans and the Environment

The fall of Rome led to vast areas of land falling into disuse. Disease, warfare, and invasion led to a 25 percent drop in population in urban centers outside of the Italian peninsula. The monastery movement stimulated the reclamation of wasteland and intensification of agriculture. Gradually, as order was restored, peasant and serf-based agriculture began to revive.

By the High Middle Ages, a more efficient feudal labor system, relative freedom from invasion, a warming climate, and technological innovations (such as the heavy wheeled plow, improved horse collar and iron horseshoes, wheelbarrow, and the three-field system of crop rotation) provided sufficient food to cause a population rebound. Towns along old Roman trade routes began to grow, as did centers for secular and church administration (including universities and cathedral towns). Italian cities continued to grow to service the Mediterranean trade.

Theme 2:
Development and Interaction of Cultures

Much of northern Africa was Christian when Muslim armies swept out of Arabia. Gradually, much of the population converted to Islam, recognizing similar beliefs in one God and an afterlife of reward or punishment, as well as similar rituals of purification. Some groups, such as the Coptic-speaking Christians in Egypt, remained as minority *dhimmis* under Muslim rule. Others, such as the Ethiopian Church in Axum, maintained their allegiance to Christianity, even though Muslim-ruled territories cut them off from much exchange with other Christians.

The Mediterranean world was a cultural crossroads where Germanic invaders, Muslim Arabs, Byzantine Greeks, and the remainder of Rome in the West as personified by the Catholic Church mixed and merged. Missionaries continued to spread Christianity into the northern parts of Europe and to convert Germanic and Nordic rulers. Christian practices were melded with local traditions, and traditional pagan sacred sites often became the location for new churches.

Both the Byzantine Empire and Muslim Spain were areas of cultural contact, but in different ways. The Byzantine Empire continued the practice of ancient Greek learning and transmitted this cultural heritage to the Islamic world and the Christian West. Byzantine religion spread north and east into the Balkans and Russia. Muslim Arab conquerors of Spain tolerated Christians and Jews as *dhimmis*, some of whom rose quite high in the court. Cultural interchange in the Muslim world produced advances in medicine, science, and mathematics, as well as an attempt to rationalize Aristotelian science and religious belief. European intellectuals travelled to places such as Córdoba to learn.

In Western Europe, a new culture was being created, combining remnants of Greco-Roman culture, the culture of Germanic tribes, and influences from the Roman Catholic Church. Latin continued as the language of the Church and of all literate people in Western Europe. Members of the Church also provided expertise for the new Germanic rulers to draw on to create their governments, legal systems, and taxation systems. Medieval scholars, such as Thomas Aquinas, also attempted to reconcile the natural philosophy of the classical world with Christian beliefs. Europeans also demonstrated a passion for new technology borrowed from the East and often improved upon these advancements. Key figures such as Roger Bacon stimulated empirical scientific thought, leading ultimately to the Scientific Revolution and the Enlightenment.

Theme 3:
State-Building, Expansion, and Conflict

The eastern half of the Roman Empire, later known as the Byzantine Empire, continued to preserve Greco-Roman culture and governance for a thousand years after the fall of Rome. Their Eastern Orthodox version of Christianity was closely linked to the emperor, combining leadership of both church and state in a relationship known as caesaropapism. The Byzantine court was filled with elaborate rituals, separating the emperor from the people and even from other nobles. The capital, Constantinople, was a lynchpin in the trade between Asia and the Mediterranean, and that trade provided revenue for the empire.

While the more densely populated and more strategically situated Byzantine Empire was not taken over by the Germanic tribes or the Huns, they did mount a centuries' long rear-guard action against the forces of Islam. First the Byzantines lost North Africa and the Middle East, then Muslim armies gradually chipped away at Anatolia, the Byzantine heartland, and southeastern Europe until only the city of Constantinople remained. The Byzantines were helped by strong fortifications around their capital and the use of weapons such as Greek fire and artillery. Their war with Persia and later the destruction left by the Crusaders, who destroyed part of Constantinople's fortifications and attacked its people whom they considered to be heretics, further weakened the empire until the Ottoman Turks finally took the city in 1453, using superior cannon and siege technology to destroy the remaining walls.

Western Europe suffered a series of invasions that drastically altered the culture and forced the urbanized people of the Roman Empire into decline. First, the Germanic tribes overthrew the last Roman emperor, dividing the territory among the tribes such as the Franks, Lombards, Visigoths, and Vandals (see Map 10.1, p. 417). Gradually, these tribal chiefdoms incorporated elements of Roman rule, preserved by the Church. Charlemagne and his Carolingian dynasty attempted to restore unified rule under one king and one God in the Roman model; the unification did not outlast Charlemagne. As a new hybrid system of governance was developing, more invasions from Muslims, Magyars, and Vikings occurred until approximately 1000 (see Map 10.3, p. 429). The need to repel frequent invasions led to decentralized rule based on mutual obligations between landed nobles and their rulers; this system is known as feudalism. By the eleventh century, new national states had begun to emerge like France, England, the Scandinavian states, and Spain as it reconquered the Iberian Peninsula. The Holy Roman Empire remained a more traditional and decentralized collection of local feudal nobles owing allegiance to a common monarch.

Christian Europeans were also invaders; the Crusades and the Reconquista (see Map 10.4, p. 435) were attempts to retake lands in the hands of Muslims. While the Reconquista was ultimately successful in driving Muslims and Jews from Spain, the Crusades had little effect on the Middle East. However, the taste for Eastern luxuries, such as spices and silks, stimulated European interest in long-distance trade. New states, like Kiev in southern Russia, also arose on the periphery of the old Roman Empire. Kievan Russia shared more than religion with the Byzantine Empire; it also adopted Byzantine attitudes toward absolute rule uniting state and religion as well as elaborate court rituals. When the Byzantine Empire fell to the Ottoman Turks (1453), Russia considered itself the "third Rome," the direct inheritors of the Roman Empire.

Theme 4:
Creation, Expansion, and Interaction of Economic Systems

The fall of Rome to Germanic tribes and the emergence of Arab Muslims sundered the unified Mediterranean trading system, plunging much of Europe into a "dark age" where virtually all long-distance trade ceased. A trickle of goods still made its way through Constantinople and to the Italian city-states such as Venice and Genoa where some goods were traded across the Alps. In Western Europe, the feudal political structure was paralleled by manorialism, characterized by local agricultural estates that were virtually self-sufficient and worked by serfs. Gradually, order was restored, and a taste for Asian luxuries stimulated by the Crusades helped the European economy rebuild. New trade routes were created by the Vikings, linking the Baltic and Russia with Constantinople. Powerful craft guilds controlled production of commodities such as textiles and metalworking. Chartered towns, independent from local feudal lords, grew as trade and economic centers. Free-trade towns, such as the Hanseatic cities, flourished in northern Europe. Technology spread from Asia, often through Muslim merchants, which Europeans used and adapted to stimulate economic growth in the High Middle Ages. After the fall of Constantinople, all trade with Asia and Africa had to pass through Muslim-controlled lands, where Christian merchants were subject to extra taxes. Merchants and princes began to look to the Atlantic instead of the Mediterranean for possible long-distance trade.

Theme 5:
Development and Transformation of Social Structures

A new society, blended from Germanic, Greco-Roman, and Christian traditions, was created in Western Europe after the fall of Rome. Unlike China, a much-glorified military elite emerged at the top of the social classes. The need to support armed men and horses for heavy cavalry (knights) without much cash or trade revenues led to the creation of the feudal system, where lords gave land (to be worked by peasants or serfs) to their retainers in exchange for mutual obligations of defense and loyalty. A small middle class of university-educated men, like doctors, lawyers, and church theologians, grew, while guildsmen and merchants populated the towns.

The basis of the society was agricultural labor bound to the land as serfs. Unlike slaves, serfs could not be sold but were passed along with the land as chattel. The Church had its own hierarchy, also based on land worked either by monks or by serfs, from the Pope, through cardinals and bishops, to abbots, monks, and priests.

Women had more freedom in the earlier part of the period, both in convents and in craft guilds, such as spinning, weaving, brewing, and baking. They had obligations to their feudal lord to be paid by labor or in kind. By the High Middle Ages, women were pushed out of most of the crafts, except for spinning and midwifery (and prostitution), and lost much of the independence that they had previously enjoyed in convents.

Guided Reading Questions for Chapter 10

Seeking the Main Point In what different ways did the history of Christianity unfold in various parts of the Afro-Eurasian world during the third-wave era? (Page 410)

Comparison What variations in the experience of African and Asian Chris tian communities can you identify? (Page 412)

Continuity and Change In what respects did Byzantium continue the patterns of the classical Roman Empire? In what ways did it diverge from those patterns? (Page 416)

Comparison How did Eastern Orthodox Christianity differ from Roman Catholicism? (Page 418)

Connection In what ways was the Byzantine Empire linked to a wider world? (Page 421)

Connection How did links to Byzantium transform the new civilization of Kievan Rus? (Page 423)

Change What replaced the Roman order in Western Europe? (Page 425)

Change In what ways was European civilization changing after 1000? (Page 429)

Change What was the impact of the Crusades in world history? (Page 434)

Practicing AP® Historical Thinking How did the historical development of the European West differ from that of Byzantium in the third-wave era? (Page 437)

Change In what ways did borrowing from abroad shape European civilization after 1000? (Page 438)

Comparison Why was Europe unable to achieve the kind of political unity that China experienced? What impact did this have on the subsequent history of Europe? (Page 441)

Comparison In what different ways did classical Greek philosophy and science have an impact in the West, in Byzantium, and in the Islamic world? (Page 443)

CHAPTER ELEVEN
Pastoral Peoples on the Global Stage: The Mongol Movement, 1200–1450

AP® World History Key Concepts

3.1: Expansion and Intensification of Communication and Exchange Networks

I. Improved transportation technologies and commercial practices led to an increased volume of trade, and expanded the geographical range of existing and newly active trade networks.

II. The movement of peoples caused environmental and linguistic effects.

III. Cross-cultural exchanges were fostered by the intensification of existing, or the creation of new, networks of trade and communication.

The major new empires in Eurasia during this period did not come from the core or foundational First Civilizations, but from pastoral nomads who lived in dry grasslands or steppes, areas unsuitable for agriculture. For centuries, pastoralists had facilitated trade with and between settled peoples, had provided innovations in transportation and weaponry (such as the stirrup, camel saddle, and compound recurve bow), and had originated religions such as Judaism and Islam.

In West Africa, the Almoravids took control of the gold trade and then crossed the Mediterranean to take control southern Spain. Turkic tribes spread westward from Central Asia, becoming a major force in the spread of Islam. The Ottoman Turks took Anatolia from the Byzantines and replaced much of the local culture; the Turkish language replaced Greek, and Islam replaced Christianity.

The most impressive pastoral empire was that of the Mongols, who created the largest land empire ever seen in Eurasia. The Mongols, however, had little long-term impact on culture or language in most of the regions they conquered; instead, they often adapted to the civilizations of the settled peoples they defeated. The Mongols did have a huge impact on Eurasian trade, however. They protected and taxed merchants across their realms and contributed to the rebirth of the Silk Routes, allowing crops, technology, religions, and knowledge to flow across Eurasia at a greater rate than ever before.

Environmentally, the Mongols destroyed agricultural resources and irrigation systems when conquering a region, and new crops were dispersed to different regions following the *pax Mongolica* (Mongol peace). The most significant environmental impact was the spread of the Black Death from Central Asia across the Mongol trade routes, creating a pandemic reaching much of Eurasia and northern Africa.

3.2: Continuity and Innovation of State Forms and Their Interactions

I. Empires collapsed and were reconstituted; in some regions new state forms emerged.

II. Interregional contacts and conflicts between states and empires encouraged significant technological and cultural transfers.

The collapse of the second-wave empires had huge consequences; in particular, they created opportunity for peoples on the periphery of empires to assert themselves on a larger stage. Often, these groups were pastoralists (see Snapshot: Varieties of Pastoral Societies, p. 460). Pastoralists, like the Xiongnu, Turkic peoples, or Mongols, often raided and harassed settled states, such as China. When the Chinese state was strong, the pastoral incursions were a nuisance, not a threat. When the Chinese state was weak, it was forced to pay tribute to the tribes in order to prevent invasion. During the Tang dynasty, the northern part of China was ruled by pastoralists, and the greatest pastoral empire of all – the Mongols – captured Song China and ruled as the Yuan dynasty. For the most part, the Mongols in China remained culturally distinct and had little lasting effect on China. Other pastoral empires included the Seljuk Turks, who took military control of the Persian Empire and adopted the title of sultan (the Abbasids remained in nominal control); they were defeated by the Mongols to form the Il-Khanate of Persia.

The Mongol conquest was devastating to the heavily populated agricultural region and cities such as Baghdad. The Mongols themselves were changed by this conquest; they adopted Islam, drew heavily on Persian administrative techniques, and some became farmers and intermarried with local people.

In Russia, the Mongols of the Golden Horde destroyed the Kievan Rus. However, because the rich steppes to the southeast provided ample pasture for Mongol horses and livestock, they continued a pastoral life, requiring tribute from Russian princes instead of governing them directly. This indirect rule allowed the princes of Moscow to become powerful and eventually throw off Mongol control. There was little cultural transfer between the Christian Russians and the Mongols, who assimilated with the Kipchaks and adopted Islam. Mongol control of the major trade routes in Eurasia promoted cultural transfer. The Mongol capital, Karakorum, became a multicultural center open to craftsmen and merchants of many far-flung regions. Chinese technology, art, and medicine moved westward, Muslim astronomy and crops moved east to influence the Chinese, and the comparatively backward Western Europe benefitted from new crops, technology, and knowledge without having to undergo Mongol conquest. *See Chapters 8, 9, and 10 for discussion of this Key Concept for East Asia, the Arab empires, and Europe.*

3.3: Increased Economic Productive Capacity and Its Consequences

I. Innovations stimulated agricultural and industrial production in many regions.

II. The fate of cities varied greatly, with periods of significant decline, and with periods of increased urbanization buoyed by rising productivity and expanding trade networks.

III. Despite significant continuities in social structures and in methods of production, there were also some important changes in labor management and in the effect of religious conversion on gender relations and family life.

In some regions, such as the Middle East, Mongol invasion meant great destruction to both urban centers and the agricultural system that supported them. The overall effect of the interchange along Mongol-protected trade routes stimulated trade and technology. One of the most significant transfers, however, was disease; the Black Death (bubonic plague) swept along the trade routes, killing between 25 percent and 50 percent of the populations of Eurasia and northern Africa. The social consequences were huge in some regions. For example, much of Western Europe experienced a significant drop in population among the serfs and laborers, leading to changes in the social system; laborers demanded higher wages and freedom from serfdom. Another, shorter-term impact of the pastoral invasions was a lessening of patriarchy. Mongols and other steppes people allowed women much more active social and economic roles and even participation in political and military power.

Theme 1:
Interaction Between Humans and the Environment

The most important role of nomads to the global historical record was their ability to adapt to environments unsuitable for agriculture. The domestication of the horse and the development of skilled horseback riding were pivotal for the success of pastoralists in Eurasian grasslands. Camels provided the same advantages in arid environments such as Arabia and the Sahara. Ranges and herd sizes (usually goats, sheep, horses, or camels) increased, as did the ability to transport shelters and goods. Pastoral skills such as hunting and riding, along with improved technology (such as horse and camel saddles, stirrups, smaller compound or laminated bows that could be fired while on horseback or camelback) provided military advantages over sedentary civilizations. Mongol trade routes fostered the spread of religions, agricultural products (such as carrots and lemons to China from the Middle East), and technology (such as the stirrup and gunpowder).

At the same time, Mongol attacks devastated local populations who resisted. Khwarizm, Kievan Russia, and the Abbasid Empire were crushed by the Mongols, their people were killed or enslaved, and their cities were destroyed. The Mongols had different priorities than those of settled civilizations and often converted agricultural land into pasture. As a result, Persian and Iraqi irrigation systems were neglected and destroyed, causing immense damage to these agricultural societies. On the other hand, new cities were built, such as the Mongol capitals of Karakorum in Mongolia and Khanbalik in China, or existing cities grew in response to renewed trade across the Silk Roads. Another environmental impact of the vast Mongol trading system was the ease with which epidemic disease could be spread. The Black Death began in Central Asia and spread outward to affect most of the hemisphere except Sub-Saharan Africa or the tundra regions of northern Eurasia (see Map 11.2, p. 482).

Theme 2:
Development and Interaction of Cultures

Nomads are often seen as the world's first connectors between various cultures as they migrated from one pastureland to another. They carried exotic commodities, unique plants and seeds, technology, and religions from place to place; as a result, they spurred innovation and creativity among sedentary civilizations. With the development of horseback and camel riding, nomads were able to travel farther than before and expand their realm of influence. The Xiongnu (see Map, p. 463) in the third and second centuries B.C.E., provoked by Chinese incursions into their territory, created a military confederacy that was instrumental in the demise of both the Roman and Han empires. Later nomadic groups performed similar functions (Huns, Turks, Germans, Arab Bedouins, Magyars, Vikings, Almoravids). A major turning point in history was the conversion of Turks to Islam, which gave these nomadic Central Asian tribal peoples cultural cohesion that afforded them the ability to create one of the major third-wave Islamic civilizations and become a major source of spreading Islam and Turkic languages as they penetrated Afro-Eurasia.

The most expansive pastoralist people, the Mongols, had a small cultural impact, leaving behind no new universal faith, language, or organizational skills. To control conquered populations, the Mongols distributed population clusters of one culture among those of another culture or sent them to other areas of the empire where their services as skilled craftsmen, bureaucrats, or military experts were required. In China, some Mongols sampled Daoism or Buddhism, though most remained true to their ancient animistic beliefs. While they adopted many Chinese luxuries, such as wearing silk, the Yuan dynasty did not attempt to assimilate into Chinese society. The Mongolian occupation, however, impacted the succeeding Ming dynasty, which attempted to return to a pure Chinese culture and reestablish Confucian values.

In Persia, members of the Mongolian court assimilated much of the Persian culture, and a number of Mongols actually became farmers, married local people, and converted to Islam. When the Mongolian dynasty in Persia collapsed in 1330, the Mongols were not driven out (as they were in China and Russia) because they had become so assimilated into Persian culture that divisions among the cultures no longer existed.

After the Mongols destroyed Kiev, they collected tribute from but did not occupy Russia. The nearby grasslands allowed the Mongols to continue their nomadic culture, near the Kipchak people from whom they adopted Islam. The center of Russian culture, however, shifted from Kiev to Moscow. In addition, the tolerant Mongolian attitude toward religion allowed the Eastern Orthodox Church to flourish as it received exemption from many taxes.

Theme 3:
State-Building, Expansion, and Conflict

The traditional pastoral unit was the clan or tribe, and different clans or tribes were often at war with each other. Sometimes a charismatic leader would be able to unite the tribes to create new empires, but because steppes tribes were organized around family and kinship relationships, maintaining unification was a challenge. The Xiongnu north of China established perhaps the earliest such nomadic empire. The largest nomadic empire was that of the Mongols, who united the steppes tribes and attacked established civilizations such as Song China and Abbasid Persia (see Map 11.1, p. 466).

The charismatic leader Chinggis Khan created the most powerful military in the world at the time, defeating neighboring tribes and harnessing their skills as cavalry to create a Mongol Empire. Continued expansion kept his warriors unified and provided loyalty through the distribution of wealth and other rewards. Although he and his descendants created the largest Eurasian land empire, they were not successful in every military venture; they withdrew from Eastern Europe, were defeated by the Mamluks at Ain Jalut in 1260, failed twice to invade Japan due to typhoons, and failed to penetrate the tropical jungles of Southeast Asia. Chinggis organized his army in groups of hundreds, thousands, and ten thousands (similar to the Roman legions), dispersed warriors from defeated steppes tribes among Mongolian warriors, and borrowed military techniques developed by other cultures, such as gunpowder, battering rams, and catapults from the Chinese. Chinggis's terrifying reputation preceded him; many cities surrendered rather than fight and be annihilated. As his territory expanded, Chinggis created Karakorum, a capital city in the Mongolian homeland. A centralized bureaucracy evolved, staffed with scholars from all reaches of the growing empire, as did a type of "Pony Express" system to relay messages, information, and decrees that also helped facilitate unification and trade. Mongol rulers often continued or drew on the governmental administration already in place at the time of conquest.

In China, the southern Song dynasty was not conquered until Chinggis's grandson, Khubilai, became the Great Khan. The Mongols initiated practices that irritated the Chinese, such as using foreigners (particularly Muslims) as administrators, bypassing Confucian scholars at the highest levels of government (positions which were reserved for Mongols), eliminating the civil service examinations, and allowing women to sit in councils. In addition, Mongols favored merchants and artisans over scholar-bureaucrats. As a result of social resentment, rising taxes, floods and famine (which created peasant rebellions), endemic outbreaks of plague and disease, and increasing factionalism among the Mongols themselves, the Chinese were able to combine forces and push the Mongols back north to the steppes.

The weakened Abbasid Empire collapsed in 1258 with the conquest and slaughter of Baghdad, the capital. The Mongols made use of institutions already in place, including the bureaucratic system, leaving much of the political administration in Persian hands. The demise of the Mongols in Persia was the result of cultural assimilation rather than military or political conquest. Kievan Rus was also in a state of decline at the time, with regional princes unable or unwilling to unite against a common enemy. Mongol weaponry and siege tactics had become increasingly more sophisticated after coming into contact with the Chinese. Mongolian control of Russia was basically indirect; taxes were extensive and frequent. The degree of control and exploitation was unequal, however, allowing some areas of Russia to prosper while devastating others. Moscow became the new governmental and military center, with the Muscovite princes eventually throwing off Mongol rule.

Theme 4:
Creation, Expansion, and Interaction of Economic Systems

Mongols loved the products of artisans from settled areas; one of the motivating factors for expansion was the desire to take these products from the cultures that produced them. They consistently promoted commerce and the exchange of goods in various ways, like standardizing weights and measures, providing financial assistance for caravans, and offering tax breaks for merchants. In addition, the Mongol peace (*pax Mongolica*) brought the two ends of Eurasia in closer contact than ever before and created a vibrant new phase of trade along the various Silk Roads. It created sub-networks in the process and overland trade networks that linked with maritime systems through the South China Sea and the Indian Ocean. When the vast land empire of the Mongols collapsed and land-based trade became dangerous again, trade and travel shifted to a maritime system, utilizing connections already established during Mongolian control.

Theme 5:
Development and Transformation of Social Structures

Social relationships in nomadic societies differed from those in sedentary civilizations; populations were smaller and were composed of kinship-based groups. In times of crisis, these kinship-based groups or clans would sometimes come together into larger tribes. The mobility required for nomadic life prevented rigid social or political stratification, but the leader was usually the most talented in whatever skills were considered the most important to the clan. One of Chinggis Khan's greatest challenges was figuring out how to override the tribalism that would have torn his newly unified Mongolian state apart. He accomplished this by scattering members of different tribes among members of other tribes. Loyalty was inspired by Mongol commanders sharing experiences, food, clothing, sleeping quarters, hardships, and victories with their warriors. Mongol military commanders were at the front of the battle, leading and inspiring their men, and merit and valor were quickly rewarded. The flow of wealth from conquered peoples benefitted all involved, although not all equally, and the standard of living rose for almost all participants.

Status in Mongolian society rested upon talents, abilities, or skills. Consequently, those of lesser status in settled cultures suddenly found themselves valuable under Mongol rule, particularly if they were unusually skilled in language, trade, scholarship, or craftsmanship. However, a skilled individual could be relocated hundreds of miles away from home and family to serve the Mongols. The Mongols usually kept a distinct division between them and their conquered peoples, though Mongol assimilation in Persia serves as an obvious exception. The Kievan Rus had little to offer the Mongols, and the Mongols maintained their cultural identity by living outside that civilization and maintaining their pastoral way of life. Mongols also went to great efforts to remain culturally and socially detached from the Chinese, forbidding intermarriage and prohibiting Chinese scholars from learning Mongolian script.

Mongolian women always had more independence and freedom of movement than women in agriculturally based societies. As much as possible, they continued their lifestyle of the steppes, freely associating with men, riding their own horses, participating in hunting excursions with their husbands, sitting in council, or becoming warriors. Foot binding and seclusion, characteristic of Chinese women, were not adopted by the Yuan dynasty.

Guided Reading Questions for Chapter 11

Seeking the Main Point What has been the role in world his-tory of pastoral peoples in general and the Mongols in particular? (Page 458)

Comparison In what ways did pastoral societies differ from their agricultural counterparts? (Page 459)

Connection In what ways did pastoral societies interact with their agricultural neighbors? (Page 461)

Significance In what ways did the Xiongnu, Arabs, Turks, and Berbers make an impact on world his-tory? (Page 463)

Description Identify the major steps in the rise of the Mongol Empire. (Page 467)

Practicing AP® Historical Thinking What accounts for the political and military success of the Mongols? (Page 472)

Change How did Mongol rule change China? In what ways were the Mongols changed by China? (Page 473)

Comparison How was Mongol rule in Persia different from that in China? (Page 476)

Comparison What was distinctive about the Russian experience of Mongol rule? (Page 478)

Connection What kinds of cross-cultural interactions did the Mongol Empire generate? (Page 481)

Change Disease changes societies. How might this argument apply to the plague? (Page 484)

NOTES:

Chapter Twelve
The Worlds of the Fifteenth Century

AP® World History Key Concepts

3.1: Expansion and Intensification of Communication and Exchange Networks

I. Improved transportation technologies and commercial practices led to an increased volume of trade, and expanded the geographical range of existing and newly active trade networks.

II. The movement of peoples caused environmental and linguistic effects.

III. Cross-cultural exchanges were fostered by the intensification of existing, or the creation of new, networks of trade and communication.

Chapter 12 provides an overview of the world in the fifteenth century – just as the hemispheres were about to be permanently linked. Much of the world was not governed by empires; people in Australia, Siberia, the Arctic coastal regions, and parts of Africa (see Map 12.3, p. 514) and the Americas (see Map 12.5, p. 523) continued to use stone-age technology. Some people, particularly in Australia and along the northwest coast of North America, lived in hunter-forager bands or villages, while other people, such as the Igbo in West Africa and the Iroquois in eastern North America, lived in agricultural villages. Still others were nomadic pastoralists, such as the Turkic tribes in Central Asia and the Fulbe of West Africa. However, the dominant story of this period resides with civilizations in both hemispheres.

Both hemispheres witnessed an intensification of trade networks, such as the *pochteca* of the Aztecs, Andean trade controlled by the Incas, Indian Ocean trade under Islamic control, trans-Saharan trade under the Songhay, and trade between the Safavid, Mughal, and Ottoman Islamic empires. The expansion or destruction of empires, however, damaged trade; the collapse of Mongol empires hurt trade on trans-Eurasia land routes, while the fall of Constantinople to the Ottoman Turks damaged Christian European trade with Asia. In other regions, migrations led to new connections, such as the Fulbe in Africa and the continued Polynesian migrations in Oceania. Some trade existed between North and South America by ocean-going canoe, but trade routes were mostly limited to regional trade. Environmental effects of trade included not only the diffusion of food crops but also of diseases. Technological improvements in shipbuilding and navigation, exemplified by the Chinese and Portuguese, rendered ships more capable of open-ocean voyaging and prepared the way for global connections in the sixteenth century. Cultural changes included the continued expansion of Islam in Africa, following merchants and Sufis in West Africa and the migration of the Fulbe in Central Africa, and the adoption of Quechua and the cult of the Incas throughout the Andean empire.

3.2: Continuity and Innovation of State Forms and Their Interactions

I. Empires collapsed and were reconstituted; in some regions new state forms emerged.

II. Interregional contacts and conflicts between states and empires encouraged significant technological and cultural transfers.

In the Americas, new state forms emerged. The Mexica (Aztecs) took control of much of Mesoamerica, imposing tributary relationships with existing city-states (such as the Maya and Toltec) for luxury goods, textiles, clothing, weapons, and slaves for sacrificing to the Aztec gods. In the Andes, the Incas also asserted control over preexisting cultures such as the Chavín, Moche, Wari, and Tiwanaku, but asserted more direct, bureaucratic rule under an emperor believed to be divine. In contrast, in North America the Iroquois League created limited government. In Africa, the Igbo created a stateless society. *See Chapters 7 through 11 for discussion of this Key Concept for Afro-Eurasia.*

3.3: Increased Economic Productive Capacity and Its Consequences

I. Innovations stimulated agricultural and industrial production in many regions.

II. The fate of cities varied greatly, with periods of significant decline, and with periods of increased urbanization buoyed by rising productivity and expanding trade networks.

III. Despite significant continuities in social structures and in methods of production, there were also some important changes in labor management and in the effect of religious conversion on gender relations and family life.

The Americas experienced many economic improvements during the fifteenth century. In Mesoamerica, the Aztecs/Mexica transformed the lake and swampy area around their capital, Tenochtitlán, with canals, causeways, and floating islands (*chinampas*) where food and flowers were grown. The Incas continued the Quechua practiced of raised-bed agriculture (called *waru-waru*) with channels between the beds to control rainwater. Aztec trade was managed by the *pochteca*, an independent guild, while the Incas directly controlled trade in the Andes. Social roles for men and women were clearly defined, but patriarchy was less entrenched than it was in Eurasia. For example, women could be local rulers among the Aztecs, and descent was reckoned from both father and mother. In the Inca culture, women could be priestesses, and descent was traced through the mother for women and through the father for men. *See Chapters 7 through 11 for discussion of this Key Concept for Afro-Eurasia.*

4.1: Globalizing Networks of Communication and Exchange

III. Remarkable new transoceanic maritime reconnaissance occurred in this period.

After the expulsion of the Mongols, Ming Emperor Yongle sent his admiral Zheng He on a series of voyages around the Indian Ocean to reestablish lapsed tributary relations. The Chinese fleet of "treasure ships" was huge and sophisticated, dominating East Asian and Indian Ocean trade routes. However, when Yongle died, the voyages ceased. Improved naval technology and restriction of trade through Constantinople encouraged Europeans to explore the oceans in an attempt to forge new trade routes with the East. The Portuguese sponsored voyages along the coast of Africa, eventually leading to contact with Indian Ocean trade, and the Spanish sponsored Columbus, who seemingly by chance ran into the Americas while seeking Asia and forged permanent transatlantic ties.

Theme 1: Interaction Between Humans and the Environment

Some groups of people continued to follow pre-agricultural lifestyles. The inhabitants of Australia manipulated their environment by burning off brush and grass to facilitate hunting and to promote the growth of species of plants and animals they favored. Peoples such as the Chinookan, Skagit, and Tulalip of the northwest coast of North America lived in a rich environment where hunting, fishing, and gathering allowed them to build permanent villages without agriculture. Agricultural villages in what is now New York

State adopted corn and bean farming from Mesoamerica. The Aztecs brought control of their environment to a high art by draining swamps, creating floating islands, and building bridges and causeways around their capital city. The Incas had to create an empire across many ecological zones from rocky mountains to deserts and rain forests.

In China, the Ming dynasty attempted to cultivate lands ravaged by the Mongols and by plague. They rebuilt canals, reservoirs, and irrigation systems and planted an estimated one billion trees in order to reforest China.

Theme 2:
Development and Interaction of Cultures

A major goal of the Ming dynasty was to restore a pure Chinese culture following the end of Mongol rule; in many ways, China attempted to return to an idealized past or golden age. The Ming revitalized the examination system, based on Confucian learning, for choosing and promoting bureaucrats. Emperor Yongle ordered 2,000 scholars to create an encyclopedia to record or summarize all previous Chinese knowledge. Gender roles also returned to Confucian norms. The Emperor ordered the construction of a new capital and the palace complex, the Forbidden City. On the other end of Eurasia, Europeans also looked to the past, that of classical Greece and Rome, to create a new cultural movement called the Renaissance. Renaissance humanists pursued secular learning based on rational thought and empiricism, glorified the individual, and used classical models for art and architecture.

In the Islamic world (see Map 12.4, p. 517), the Turkic Safavid dynasty enforced Shia Islam, unlike the other Eurasian Islamic empires (like Ottoman and Mughal), which were Sunni. Both the Ottoman and Mughal empires also controlled large populations that were not Muslim and at times handled them with great toleration. Vijayanagara, a Hindu state south of the Mughal Empire, borrowed architectural styles from the Mughals. In the Songhay Empire of West Africa, Islam was infused with local traditions, although Timbuktu became a major center for Islamic learning.

In the Americas, the Aztec religion required sacrifices of human blood to its patron deity, Huitzilopochtli, to maintain cosmic order. Sacrificial victims were frequently prisoners of war, and the need for ever-increasing numbers to sacrifice led to continued warfare. Aztec poetry focused on the transience of human life. The Incas required their subjects to worship the major Incan deities but also allowed them to worship their own gods. While Aztec men and women worshipped deities of both sexes, Incan women worshipped the moon and men the sun.

Theme 3:
State-Building, Expansion, and Conflict

The civilizations of the fifteenth century were poised to become linked in global, instead of regional, networks (see Snapshot: Major Developments around the World in the Fifteenth Century, p. 562). A major contrast in state building existed between the centralized bureaucracy of the Ming dynasty in China, which asserted unitary rule over a large region, and the separate, often competing and warring, independent states of Europe (see Maps 12.1, p. 506 and 12.2, p. 511). Some of the individual states, especially in Western Europe, were developing more efficient bureaucracies and centralized control under their monarchs.

Other states, especially in Eastern Europe, still followed a feudal model of decentralized control with the nobles and Church exercising considerable power. The princes of Moscow freed themselves from Mongol rule and began the process of expansion that would eventually create the Russian Empire.

The Ming dynasty in China, also having thrown off Mongol rule, proceeded to establish a Confucian state. At first, there was a struggle for political power between the eunuchs, who were more innovative, progressive, and directly loyal to the emperor, and the conservative Confucian scholar-bureaucrats, who were dedicated to restoring past values and methods. The resolution of this feud can be seen in the decision to end the voyages of Zheng He (who was himself a eunuch) and the dismantling of his fleet. China looked inward, "perfecting" itself and returning to traditional virtues and concerns about its traditional pastoralist enemies in the north. Competing European states, such as Portugal and Spain, on the other hand, funded exploratory voyages, which ultimately led to European empires in the Americas and control of the lucrative Indian Ocean trade system.

The Islamic world of the Ottoman, Mughal, and Safavid empires was controlled by descendants of pastoral Turkic people (see Map 12.4, p. 517). Competition could be found between these Islamic empires; the Sunni Ottoman Empire was often at war with the Shia Safavids. Ottoman sultans claimed the title of caliph (successor to the prophet Muhammad) and asserted both secular and religious authority. The Ottomans effectively used gunpowder and cannon to defeat the last vestiges of the Byzantine Empire in 1453. They ruled a population composed of many non-Muslims, protecting (most of the time) the *dhimmi* status of Christians and Jews. The Ottoman Empire, along with China and the Incas, was one of the largest and wealthiest empires in this era. The Mughals also controlled a large non-Muslim population, composed mostly of Hindus, in southern Asia. The Empire of Songhay, successor to Mali and Ghana in controlling the gold-salt trade in West Africa, represented the further expansion of Islam in Africa.

In the Americas (see Map 12.5, p. 523), the Mexica, a semi-nomadic group in northern Mexico, gradually asserted military control over much of Mesoamerica. The new rulers claimed descent from the Toltecs in order to give themselves legitimacy and respect. They governed loosely, primarily using a tributary system bolstered by a religious justification; only the blood of sacrificed humans could keep the gods from destroying the world.

The Incas in South America, on the other hand, exercised more direct bureaucratic control. They also added religious justification in that the Inca emperor was an absolute, divine ruler. While the empire was ruled as a centralized bureaucratic state, the Incas delegated authority to local bureaucrats in regions that had previously possessed a bureaucracy and created administrative systems where none had previously existed. They exacted labor (*mita*) from their subjects to create goods, such as textiles, or to work on building projects.

In North America, the Iroquois developed a unique solution to tribal feuds and bloodshed; an agreement known as the Great Law of Peace established a confederacy where a council of clan leaders had the power to settle disputes by consensus. This creation of limited government, not imposed from the outside but mutually agreed upon, was much-admired by the creators of the United States Constitution. In Africa, the Igbo represent an agricultural society with kings; power was balanced among kinship groups, ritual experts who provided mediation, women's associations, and wealthy men. *See Chapter 13 for more detailed discussion of Eurasian empires.*

Theme 4:
Creation, Expansion, and Interaction of Economic Systems

Much of the wealth of fifteenth-century states was created by controlling commerce or by producing specialized goods, such as silk, for trade. The Afro-Eurasian trade systems were discussed previously in this unit. Changes in the fifteenth century include the Ming dynasty's decision to concentrate on internal, rather than maritime, trade networks. However, the Ming still traded across their huge internal market and with foreign merchants who came to them for the goods that China produced. In addition, much of the trade in Afro-Eurasia was under control of Muslim merchants and empires (see Map 12.6, p. 530). Malacca, located on a strategic strait (see Map 12.1, p. 506), grew into a major Muslim port and was instrumental in spreading Islam to Southeast Asia.

Another fifteenth-century landmark was the fall of Constantinople, which ended direct trade between Christian Europe and Asia. Control of the trade hub previously occupied by the Byzantines created immense wealth for the Ottomans and encouraged Europeans to begin looking to the Atlantic to find trade routes with Asia.

Beginning in the 1450s, the Portuguese funded voyages south along the western coast of Africa, seeking an alternate route into the Indian Ocean and the wealth of spices, silk, and gems that could be found there. Beginning later than the Portuguese, the Spanish sponsored Columbus's attempt to reach Asia by sailing west across the Atlantic. In the Americas, Aztec trade was under the control of the *pochteca*, an independent guild of merchants. Active markets were held in the major cities, where food and goods from throughout the region were exchanged. The Incas assumed direct control of trade along thousands of miles of roads built in the Andes, uniting the trade links between different ecological regions forged by previous cultures. *See Chapter 7 for more detailed discussion of Eastern Hemisphere trade systems.*

Theme 5: Development and Transformation of Social Structures

As discussed in previous chapters from Part Three, society remained hierarchical and most often patriarchal in most settled agricultural empires. A repeated pattern, however, was that pastoralists had fewer gender restrictions than did the agricultural peoples; as pastoral peoples assimilated into settled life, however, more gender restrictions arose (see Chapter 11).

In the Americas, women were not as subjugated to men as in Eurasia. For example, the Iroquois practiced matrilineal descent, and men lived with their wives' families. Iroquois women also were involved in selecting or deposing leaders. Aztec women could be priestesses, crafts workers, officials, traders, and teachers. In the Andes, gender parallelism (women and men operating in separate but equally valued spheres) had formed part of the culture before the rise of the Incas. For example, men worshipped the sun and women the moon with their own separate priesthoods. The *sapay Inca* (Inca ruler) and his *coya* (female consort) governed side by side, claiming descent from the sun and the moon, respectively.

Guided Reading Questions for Chapter 12

Seeking the Main Point What predictions about the future might a global traveler in the fifteenth century have reasonably made? (Page 500)

Comparison In what ways did the gathering and hunting people of Australia differ from those of the northwest coast of North America? (Page 501)

Change What kinds of changes were transforming the societies of the West African Igbo and the North American Iroquois as the fifteenth century unfolded? (Page 502)

Significance What role did Central Asian and West African pastoral-ists play in their respective regions? (Page 504)

Description How would you define the major achievements of Ming dynasty China? (Page 506)

Comparison What political and cultural differences stand out in the histories of fifteenth- century China and Western Europe? What similarities are apparent? (Page 510)

Comparison In what ways did European maritime voyaging in the fifteenth century differ from that of China? What accounts for these differences? (Page 513)

Comparison What differences can you identify among the four major empires in the Islamic world of the fifteenth and sixteenth centuries? (Page 516)

Practicing AP® Historical Thinking In what ways did the civilizations of China, Europe, and the Islamic world in the fifteenth century seem to be moving in the same direction, and in what respects were they diverging from one another? (Page 522)

Comparison What distinguished the Aztec and Inca empires from each other? (Page 522)

Description How did Aztec religious thinking support the empire? (Page 525)

Description In what ways did Inca authorities seek to integrate their vast domains? (Page 526)

Connection In what different ways did the peoples of the fifteenth century interact with one another? (Page 529)

UNIT 1
A Review of AP® World History & Ways of the World for the AP® Course, Third Edition

AP® WORLD HISTORY PERIOD FOUR
Global Interactions, c. 1450 to c. 1750

PART FOUR
The Early Modern World, 1450–1750

AP® World History Key Concepts
4.1:   Globalizing Networks of Communication and Exchange
4.2:   New Forms of Social Organization and Modes of Production
4.3:   State Consolidation and Imperial Expansion

The Big Picture:
Debating the Character of an Era

Historians have found it useful to create a descriptive label for a period, but that practice often oversimplifies or assumes that certain trends are equally valid in all parts of the world.

Chapter 13 examines the new empires of this era in Europe, the Middle East, and Asia. The globalization of trade and the economy are analyzed in Chapter 14. Chapter 15 deals with new cultural trends within religious traditions and in the newly emerging scientific worldview.

An Early Modern Era?

The term most often used to describe this period, "early modern," spotlights globalization, modernity, and the transformation of Europe into a major actor in world affairs.

■ Globalization:
  • Oceanic voyages by European explorers led to the conquest and colonization of the Americas and linked Africa to the Americas through the transatlantic slave trade.
  • Precious metals, such as silver, extracted from the Americas allowed Europeans to change the markets in Asia.
  • The Columbian exchange, the transfer of flora, fauna, people, ideas, and pathogens, altered the entire world.
  • Christianity spread to become a global religion.
  • Russia expanded east to the Pacific Ocean, China expanded into inner Asia, and the Ottoman Empire ruled from the Indian Ocean to Northern Africa to southeastern Europe.

■ Modernity:
  • The Scientific Revolution in Europe changed the way people (at least some of them) understood the world, approached knowledge, and thought about religion.

- World population doubled between 1400 and 1800; food from the Americas (such as corn and potatoes), the end of Mongol invasions, and recovery from the Black Death led to increasing population growth in Europe, China, India, and Japan. The Americas faced a catastrophic drop in the Native American population caused by the introduction of diseases from Africa and Eurasia, while African populations were limited by the transatlantic slave trade.

- Commercial, urbanizing societies developed in parts of Eurasia and the Americas; Japan, for example, was the most urbanized society in the world. In some regions, such as in China, Southeast Asia, India, and the Atlantic basin, people began to produce primarily for distant markets.

- States became stronger and more centralized; they promoted trade, manufacturing, and a common culture. Some states, particularly in Asia and the Middle East, also often incorporated local societies, using gunpowder and superior military forces to take over surrounding territories to build large empires. Some European states created overseas colonial empires.

- Population pressure and plantation agriculture led to deforestation, draining swamps, and encroachment on the traditional grounds of hunter-gatherers and pastoralists.

A Late Agrarian Era?

In 1750, it was not clear that the forces of modernization would win, as most people in the world continued to live in traditional ways. The developments of this period often seemed to be those of a late agrarian age.

- ■ IEuropean power was limited in much of Asia and Africa. China and Japan strictly limited European missionaries and merchants in their societies. African leaders set the rules under which the slave trade operated. Islam was the most rapidly growing religion. India and China were equivalent in their manufacturing output to Europe in 1750. European power might have seemed to be yet another cyclical pattern of surge and collapse.

- ■ INothing hinted that the Industrial Revolution was coming. Human and animal power, wind, and water still supplied almost all energy. Handicrafts had not been replaced by factory-based production. Landowning elites, not the middle class, still held the reins of power; rural peasants, not urban workers, made up the primary social group among the lower classes. Social inequalities were still dominant; government was predominantly in the hands of kings and landowning nobles, not parliaments or the middle class, and women were still subject to patriarchal controls.

- ■ ITraditional values prevailed, such as Confucianism, Hinduism, and the caste system.

- ■ IIslam continued to spread in Southeast Asia and Africa.

- ■ ISome individuals in Chinese, European, and Islamic societies rejected new and untried ideas and urged a return to traditional ways.

AP® Themes in Part Four:

Environment	Cultures	State Building	Economies	Social Structures
Global population growth and environmental change	Muslim/Hindu encounters in India	European conquest and empire building in the Americas	The spice trade: empires of European commerce in Asia	Class and gender in the early modern era
-	-	-	-	-
Disease and Demographic collapse: the Americas and Siberia	Muslim/Christian encounters in Ottoman realm	A Spanish colonial state in the Philippines	Asian commercial networks in Asia	Comparing colonial social structures in North and South America
-	Protestant Reformation	-	-	-
The Columbian exchange: global biological transformations	Christianity in: • The Philippines • Siberia • Spanish America • Russia • China • Japan • Mughal India	The making of a Russian Empire	Global silver trade: effects on: • Spanish America • Japan • China • Europe	Women in American colonial societies
		Peter the Great and Russia's "catching up" efforts		Emergence of mestizo/mulatto classes in the Americas
The Little Ice Age: global cooling and its consequences		A Central Asian Chinese empire	The fur trade: North America and Russia compared	The fur trade and gender roles in North America
-	African religious cultures in the Americas	The Mughals: a Muslim empire in India	The Atlantic slave trade • Origins • Operations • Outcomes	Erosion of women's roles in the colonial Philippines
Environmental effects of silver mining in Bolivia				
-	Islamic expansion in Southeast Asia	The Ottomans: a Muslim empire in the Middle East and Southeast Europe		Female merchants in Southeast Asia
Reforestation in Japan	Islamic renewal: the Wahhabi example		Plantation economies in the Americas	Erosion of pastoralism in Russian and Chinese empires
-	Neo-Confucianism, *kaozheng*, and popular culture in China	The Tokugawa state in Japan	Forced labor and the hacienda system	
Deforestation in China				Multiculturalism in China
-	Bhakti tradition in India	Japan and China: limiting European incursions	Silver-mining economy: Potosí	
Species depletion and the fur trade (in Russia and North America)			-	Women in Mughal and Ottoman empires
-	Emergence of Sikhism in India	African state building and state disintegration in the slave-trade era	Settler economies in the Americas	
Demographic history of slave trade	Emergence of modern science in Europe	Early modern state building: primary sources from Asia, the Middle East, Europe, and the Americas	Erosion of hunting and herding economies in Russian Empire	Slavery in Africa
				Gender and social change in Africa as a result of the slave trade
	The European Enlightenment			Expressing social status via trade goods
	Responses to European science: China, Japan, and the Islamic world			Women in the Scientific Revolution and the Enlightenment

NOTES:

CHAPTER THIRTEEN
Political Transformations: Empires and Encounters, 1450–1750

AP® World History Key Concepts

4.1: Globalizing Networks of Communication and Exchange

V. The new connections between the Eastern and Western hemispheres resulted in the Columbian Exchange.

VI. The increase in interactions between newly connected hemispheres and intensification of connections within hemispheres expanded the spread and reform of existing religions and created syncretic belief systems and practices.

One of the most important changes in human history was the connection of the Eastern and Western Hemispheres; it allowed people, plants, animals, technology, and culture to move freely from one part of the world to another, often with extreme consequences for the receiving region. Food (such as corn and potatoes) from the Americas allowed populations to rise in Eurasia and helped mitigate the population loss due to the slave trade in Africa. Plants and animals from the Eastern Hemisphere changed the Americas, where there were often no local competitors. In addition, the Europeans often set up plantations where single crops were grown for export, eliminating biodiversity.

More than just plants and livestock made the journey across the Atlantic; humans arrived with their diseases and their cultures. Native Americans had little immunity to Eurasian diseases such as measles or smallpox, and in some areas, nearly 90 percent of the population died within a hundred years of European arrival. Western Europeans came to settle, to get rich, or to convert natives to Christianity, often while exploiting the labor of Native Americans in mines and fields. Africans were imported as slave labor when the "great dying" left few Native Americans to work in lucrative plantations growing sugar or cotton. Europeans promoting Christianity suppressed the beliefs of Native Americans and African slaves, but in many regions (especially those with high populations before the conquest, such as Mexico and the Andes), Christianity blended some of the local traditions to create new practices. *See Chapter 12 for the discussion of the voyages of reconnaissance and exploration, and Chapter 14 for more extensive analysis of the economic implications of the global age.*

4.2: New Forms of Social Organization and Modes of Production

I. Beginning in the 14th century, there was a decrease in mean temperatures, often referred to as the Little Ice Age, around the world that lasted until the 19th century, contributing to changes in agricultural practices and the contraction of settlement in parts of the Northern Hemisphere.

II. Traditional peasant agriculture increased and changed, plantations expanded, and demand for labor increased. These changes both fed and responded to growing global demand for raw materials and finished products.

III. As new social and political elites changed, they also restructured new ethnic, racial, and gender hierarchies.

Most people still made their livings as agricultural laborers in various forms, ranging from serfdom in Russia, to peasant farmers in China, to people bound by the *encomienda* in Spanish America, to African slaves in the sugar plantations of Brazil and the Caribbean. Agricultural laborers more frequently worked to create products (such as sugar, tea, and tobacco) for global markets, not to produce food for themselves and local markets. In addition, demands for furs led to new exploitation of the environment in North America and Siberia.

In the Americas, new social orders emerged based on blending peoples from the Americas with those from Africa and Europe. For example, while pure Europeans were at the top of the social class system in Spanish colonies, people of mixed race – European and Indian or European and African – were accepted as racially mixed and identified in different groups (*mestizos* or *mulattoes*). In the British North American and Caribbean colonies, in contrast, strict racial attitudes led to people of mixed race being classified as black if they had any African ancestry. Women among the conquered indigenous people tended to fare even worse than men – in addition to harsh labor requirements, they often had to submit to the sexual advances of European men. The same was true for African women imported as slaves, but they suffered even further in that their families could be broken up and their children could be sold.

4.3: State Consolidation and Imperial Expansion

I. Rulers used a variety of methods to legitimize and consolidate their power.

II. Imperial expansion relied on the increased use of gunpowder, cannons, and armed trade to establish large empires in both hemispheres.

III. Competition over trade routes, state rivalries, and local resistance all provided significant challenges to state consolidation and expansion.

The era from 1450 to 1750 has often been called the age of gunpowder states; land-based Eurasian empires – such as the Mughal Empire, Ottoman Empire, Russian Empire, and Qing China – used their superior militaries and weapons, including cannons, to expand their empires over their neighbors. Western European states, starting with Spain and Portugal and continuing with France, England, and Holland, used superior military technology to acquire overseas empires in the Americas. These European states adapted ships to carry cannons, which allowed them to dominate sea trade, especially in the Indian Ocean. Cannon and gunpowder also helped European states overpower both the Aztec and Inca empires and more loosely populated regions in North America and Central Asia.

The conquests were also furthered by the spread of pathogens that nearly annihilated the peoples of the Americas and the small, isolated tribes in Siberia. For the first time, states ruled over vast territories that were separated by oceans from the "mother country," requiring new methods of governance. In Spanish and Portuguese colonies, rule was directly tied to the mother country. In settler colonies like British North America, somewhat more local government took place under charters granted by the king for particular groups, such as the Puritans, Catholics, or Quakers. In the Americas, indigenous governments were eradicated and replaced by European governors and European laws, conducted by European courts in European languages.

Eurasia saw the last surge of the pastoralist empires (the Mughal, Ottoman, and Qing dynasties all traced their ancestry to the steppes). At the same time, the Russian Empire, recently freed from Mongol rule, expanded into Siberia and the tundra regions to the north (as well as south and west from Moscow), subjugating nomadic hunters and herders and replacing their sparse populations with ethnic Russians. The Qing dynasty annexed the steppes from the south, as well as Tibetan and Muslim groups on the western frontiers. China and Russia thus incorporated and marginalized previously feared nomadic peoples into their empires and divided the old Silk Roads – one of the factors leading to the overland route's demise as the major east–west trade route. These empires all developed varying methods of incorporating people of different ethnic and religious groups into their empires.

Theme 1:
Interaction Between Humans and the Environment

Linking the two hemispheres of the earth in the sixteenth century created the most significant environmental consequences since beginning of settled agriculture. This link, called the Columbian exchange, was the beginning of an unprecedented movement of flora, fauna, people, and pathogens between the Eastern and Western Hemispheres. Since the Western Hemisphere had been isolated, its plants, animals, and people encountered species and diseases against which they had no natural defenses. The most obvious consequence has been called "the great dying," the death of millions of native peoples to disease borne by Afro-Eurasians. In some areas, nearly 90 percent of the pre-Columbian population died from diseases (such as measles, small pox, typhus, influenza, or yellow fever) or from starvation. This series of epidemics was one of the reasons that numerically smaller Europeans were able to conquer the Aztec and Inca empires. In addition, plants — especially food crops such as wheat, rice, sugarcane, grapes, and vegetable and fruit crops — were brought to the Americas by Europeans eager to recreate their previous diet or to farm cash crops for sale on the global market. These crops replaced local forests, grasslands, and fields at an alarming rate and required different types of agricultural labor from the digging stick technology used by Native Americans. European animals — such as sheep, goats, cattle, horses, and pigs — also had a huge impact, creating new ways of life in ranching or herding, all while destroying local habitats. Food crops from the Americas — corn, potatoes and sweet potatoes, and cassava — fueled population increases in Eurasia and ameliorated the population loss in Africa from the transatlantic slave trade. Other New World crops such as tobacco and chocolate became fashionable in European markets (as did tea from China and coffee from the Muslim world). Plantations where sugarcane, tobacco, or cotton were grown led to further environmental degradation as local flora and fauna were destroyed to create monocultures of selected, lucrative crops, often grown using forced or slave labor.

Theme 2:
Development and Interaction of Cultures

Europeans imposed their culture on conquered people in the Americas or Central Asia. Where the population was larger, as in Mexico or the Andes, significant cultural remainders endured and became part of a new syncretic culture. Where the population was small or had been relocated, "little Europes" grew. In some remote regions, traditional culture survived.

The most obvious cultural transplants were language and religion. Government was conducted in the languages of Europe, and conquered people had to adapt. In Mexico, zealous priests had most of the existing Maya and Aztec books destroyed to prevent people from returning to their old culture and religion. Christianity was also a major source of cultural transformation; Russian Orthodox Christianity spread in the newly forming empire and competed with Islam, while Roman Catholicism was brought to Spanish and Portuguese empires. In addition to being spread by conquering forces, Christianity was also spread by missionaries and Jesuit priests to China and Japan (where it later became suspect as a foreign religion). In the Americas, local beliefs became syncretized with the new faith. For example, in the Andes, sacred processions of the mummies of dead Inca kings were replaced with the processions of images of Christian saints.

Different solutions to cultural mixing occurred in the Asian empires, where much larger populations of different ethnic groups were absorbed into growing Mughal, Ottoman, and Qing empires. The Qing, hailing from Manchuria, attempted to remain separated from the conquered Han Chinese. Intermarriage was forbidden, and Manchurian dress was retained. As part of attempting to legitimize their conquest, however, the Qing adopted Confucian social and gender attitudes and bureaucracy. When they conquered Mongolia, Tibet, and Xinjiang, the Qing did not attempt to incorporate Muslim and Buddhist populations into Chinese culture (see Map 13.3, p. 579), in contrast to the practice of previous dynasties to reward assimilation to Han culture.

Mughal dynasty, Turkic Islamic rulers faced a large population of mostly Hindu Indians. Some leaders, such as Akbar, respected the cultures of local people and rewarded loyalty with government positions. Religious toleration prevailed. His heirs, such as Aurangzeb, reversed Akbar's policies and enforced Islamic law, destroyed some Hindu temples, and reinstituted the special tax (*jizya*) on non-Muslims. The art and architecture of the empire, however, continued to reflect a cultural blending of Hindu, Persian, and Arabic traditions (such as seen in the Taj Mahal, a tomb for the wife of a Mughal Shah).

Ottoman Turks also took control of a region with a large population. As they conquered the Balkans, the Ottomans did not send large numbers of Turkic Muslim settlers; instead, they gave local religious groups (such as Armenian, Eastern Orthodox, and Roman Catholic Christians and Jews) an amount of local autonomy. Non-Muslims were required to contribute children to the *devshirme*, where they were trained to become janissaries (elite Ottoman warriors) or bureaucrats. The Ottomans also welcomed Jews fleeing from expulsion in Spain and Portugal. Like the Mughals, the Ottomans were influenced by Persian culture – poetry, painting, and court rituals. *See Chapter 15 for more depth on this theme.*

Theme 3:
State-Building, Expansion, and Conflict

The possession of superior military training and technology, including gunpowder and cannons, allowed several Eurasian empires to flourish. The Russians threw off the last vestiges of Mongol rule and spread their influence to create the largest Eurasian land-based empire. Like the British in North America, they imposed their culture on the relatively sparse population of the steppes. Russia continued to be an autocracy, ruled by the tsar with the support of the Russian Orthodox Church; much of the actual power, though, rested in the hands of the large landowning *boyars* who controlled the labor of large numbers of serfs (people bound to the land). Peter the Great and Catherine the Great recognized that they were lagging behind Western Europe and began a policy of Westernization.

The Ottoman sultan claimed the title of caliph, giving him religious sanction as well as secular authority. Government was divided between regions and was, to some extent, based on local custom. Both the military and civilian bureaucracy took in young men from the *devshirme*, the tax of young boys levied on Christian communities. Court practices took their lead from the elaborate rituals of the Persians. Some women secluded in the harem also influenced the court in an attempt to promote their sons as possible future sultans.

The Qing dynasty adopted the Confucian civil service and examination system, while maintaining firm control for the Manchu elite. Han Chinese were required to wear distinctive hairstyles and clothing, and intermarriage with Manchus was forbidden. Newly conquered territories – Mongolia, Tibet, Xinjiang – were administered differently, without the usual Chinese attempt to assimilate the people into Chinese culture and without large resettlements of Chinese to the regions. In a similar manner to the Ottoman rule of its conquests, local authorities were often left in place, with Buddhist and Muslim authorities, monasteries, and nobles exempted from tax or labor obligations.

The Mughal dynasty succeeded in politically unifying most of South Asia. Akbar, who completed the conquest of this mostly Hindu region, attempted to rule in an enlightened and tolerant manner by bringing Hindus into important roles in government and military, ending the *jizya*, a special tax on non-Muslims, and ensuring religious toleration. His successors, such as Aurangzeb, reinstituted strict sharia law and the *jizya*, and destroyed some Hindu temples. Resistance by Hindu Rajputs against increasingly harsh Mughal rule weakened the empire and paved the way for British takeover.

Spanish and Portuguese colonies were ruled directly under viceroys appointed by the king and by a few *peninsulares*, men born in the Iberian Peninsula (not in the New World). The *peninsulares'* rule was aided by large royal grants (*encomienda*) giving, in addition to the land itself, control over indigenous people. This included the right to demand labor in order to produce crops or extract resources that were shipped back to the mother country. The *encomienda* often simply transferred to colonial rulers labor duties already owed to the state (such as the *mita* in Peru or labor owed to the Aztec Empire). British North American settlers came from a different environment than that of the Spanish and Portuguese; England had a limited monarchy with Parliament, a tradition of individual rights, a large and influential commercial middle class, and a history of conflicts between Catholic and Protestant (and between different Protestant groups). Attracted by readily available land, groups such as Puritans, Catholics, and Quakers came to North America. The British government paid little direct attention to the colonies in the seventeenth century, leaving the colonists to elect colonial assemblies to protect their "rights as Englishmen." Later, the colonists often resisted the governors' attempts to reassert control.

Theme 4:
Creation, Expansion, and Interaction of Economic Systems

See Chapter 14 for a full analysis of this theme.

Theme 5:
Development and Transformation of Social Structures

The Columbian exchange replaced social and political systems in the Americas with new societies that blended Native American, European, and African people. In Spanish colonies, there were relatively few European women, leading to intermingling of Europeans and Native Americans. Society distinguished between people born in Spain and those of pure Spanish ancestry born in the Americas (*peninsulares* and *creoles*), people of mixed Spanish and Native American ancestry (*mestizos*), people of mixed Spanish or Portuguese and African ancestry (*mulattoes*) and people of pure Native American or African ancestry. In general terms, these racial hierarchies also reflected social hierarchies and political control; in Peru and Mexico, *peninsulares* alone could hold the job of governor or viceroy, while creoles tended to be the large land owners and fill the top military, church, and professional roles. Mestizos mostly adopted Spanish culture and worked in skilled trades, as supervisors, and in lower-level positions in government bureaucracy, the church, or the military. Indians were at the bottom of the social hierarchy, subject to abuse and required to provide labor for the Spanish colonizers.

In the Caribbean and Brazilian sugar plantations, a similar structure developed, with enslaved Africans at the bottom of the social structure. Most of the Native Americans had either died (in the Caribbean) from European diseases or fled inland (Brazil). The populations were predominantly of African ancestry, but many were mulattoes; as many as forty groups composed of different degrees of racial mixing were identified.

In the plantation colonies of North America, different attitudes toward race prevailed; anyone with African ancestry was considered to be black, in contrast to the wide range of racial groups identified in Spanish and Portuguese colonies. Fewer slaves were freed in North America, and free blacks or mulattoes in Brazil had more economic opportunities. Settler colonies in North America had a higher ratio of

Europeans than did the plantation colonies. In addition, British colonists had access to "free" land with relatively few native inhabitants and found it easier to set up family farms and businesses, relatively free from interference by elites from Europe.

Women continued to languish under patriarchal attitudes. In the Americas, indigenous women and African women were also subjected to the same social factors as their men – conquest, forced labor, slavery – but they were also subjected to the forced sexual advances of their conquerors. Some women among the native elites married Spanish men in order to maintain some control of their ancestral lands and social status. In the Qing dynasty, rulers adopted and enforced strict Confucian attitudes toward gender roles. Under Akbar, the Mughals acted to mitigate some of the Hindu restrictions on women by forbidding child marriage or *sati* (the immolation of a widow on her husband's funeral pyre) and by allowing separate market days for women. In addition, some royal women exerted power "behind the throne." After Akbar died, his successors reinstated sharia laws. Turkic women at first enjoyed many of the liberties of pastoral women, but as the Ottomans established their empire, they adopted the more restrictive patriarchal practices of the Mediterranean world; women were secluded, veiled, and not even counted in the census.

Guided Reading Questions for Chapter 13

Seeking the Main Point In what ways did European empires in the Americas resemble their Russian, Chinese, Mughal, and Ottoman counterparts, and in what respects were they different? Do you find the similarities or the differences more striking? (Page 554)

Connection What enabled Europeans to carve out huge empires an ocean away from their homelands? (Page 554)

Change What large-scale transformations did European empires generate? (Page 562)

Change What was the economic foundation of colonial rule in Mexico and Peru? How did it shape the kinds of societies that arose there? (Page 564)

Comparison How did the plantation societies of Brazil and the Caribbean differ from those of southern colonies in British North America? (Page 568)

Comparison What distinguished the British settler colonies of North America from their counterparts in Latin America? (Page 571)

Practicing AP® Historical Thinking In what ways might European empire building in the Americas be understood as a single phenomenon? And in what respects should it be viewed as a set of distinct and separate processes? (Page 572)

Description What motivated Russian empire building? (Page 573)

Change How did the Russian Empire transform the life of its conquered people and of the Russian homeland itself? (Page 575)

Description What were the distinctive features of Chinese empire building in the early modern era? (Page 578)

Change How did Mughal attitudes and policies toward Hindus change from the time of Akbar to that of Aurangzeb? (Page 580)

Significance In what ways was the Ottoman Empire important for Europe in the early modern era? (Page 583)

NOTES:

CHAPTER FOURTEEN
Economic Transformations:
Commerce and Consequence, 1450–1750

AP® World History Key Concepts

4.1: Globalizing Networks of Communication and Exchange

I. In the context of the new global circulation of goods, there was an intensification of all existing regional trade networks that brought prosperity and economic disruption to the merchants and governments in the trading regions of the Indian Ocean, Mediterranean, Sahara, and overland Eurasia.

II. European technological developments in cartography and navigation built on previous knowledge developed in the classical, Islamic, and Asian worlds, and included the production of new tools, innovations in ship designs, and an improved understanding of global wind and currents patterns — all of which made transoceanic travel and trade possible.

See Chapter 10 for a discussion of European borrowing and innovation.

III. Remarkable new transoceanic maritime reconnaissance occurred in this period.

See Chapter 12 for a more detailed discussion of this concept.

IV. The new global circulation of goods was facilitated by royal chartered European monopoly companies that took silver from Spanish colonies in the Americas to purchase Asian goods for the Atlantic markets. Regional markets continued to flourish in Afro-Eurasia by using established commercial practices and new transoceanic shipping services developed by European merchants.

V. The new connections between the Eastern and Western hemispheres resulted in the Columbian Exchange.

See Chapter 13 for a more detailed discussion of these concepts.

VI. The increase in interactions between newly connected hemispheres and intensification of connections within hemispheres expanded the spread and reform of existing religions and created syncretic belief systems and practices.

See Chapter 15 for a more detailed discussion of this topic.

VII. As merchants' profits increased and governments collected more taxes, funding for the visual and performing arts, even for popular audiences, increased.

See Chapter 12 for a more detailed discussion about the Renaissance.

Voyages of reconnaissance and exploration (such as Columbus's to the Americas, da Gama's to the Indian Ocean, and Magellan's circumnavigation of the earth) created permanent trade networks that linked the two hemispheres for the first time. The Portuguese and Dutch in Africa and the Indian Ocean began by creating trading ports, called entrepôts; the Spanish in the Americas and the Philippines and the Portuguese in Brazil established larger colonies (see Map 14.1, p. 604). The ability of Europeans to use cannons from shipboard changed the trading patterns in the Indian Ocean, allowing the Portuguese to demand exclusive trading rights. New or improved mercantile practices allowed private trading companies, like the British East India Company and the Dutch East India Company, to prosper and enrich their shareholders, while other trade was controlled by governments (such as Spain and Portugal) under the mercantilist economic theory. At first, European presence in the Indian Ocean trade system was relatively small; European trade goods were not valued by Asians (who felt that European goods were shoddy), so European ships carried Asian trade goods from port to port for Asian merchants. Profits from this "carrying trade" could later be reinvested by European merchants in trade goods such as spices, silk, and porcelain. Eventually, silver and other bullion from the mines of the Americas became a global commodity (see Map 14.2, p. 612). Silver from the Americas poured into China, exchanged for many valued trade items such as silk, tea, and porcelain. Ultimately, the glut of New World silver led to inflation and destroyed some of the economies that first were enriched by it (such as Spain). India remained the source of cotton textiles and gems as the Portuguese, then the British, established toeholds on the subcontinent. Much of the trade in Asia remained in the hands of traditional Asian merchants (such as Southeast Asians and Indian merchant families). Europeans primarily controlled the transatlantic trade, especially the trade of African slaves to the Americas to work in profitable sugar plantations (see Map 14.4, p. 621 and Snapshot: The Slave Trade in Numbers, p. 627).

Other trading systems also emerged, such as the fur trade in North America and Siberia (see Map 14.3, p. 617), where indigenous people often trapped furs and brought them to trading posts set up by Europeans, including the French, Dutch, and British in North America and the Russians in Siberia.

The spread of Christianity was a major component of European expansion and colonization. Missionaries often followed or arrived with the explorers, carrying with them royal charters that included not only the right of landowners to use the labor of local people but also the obligation to baptize locals. In the Spanish Philippines, Christianity came up against Islam on the island of Mindanao. In both China and Japan, Christian missionaries were seen as agents of foreign powers; in Tokugawa Japan, Christian missionaries were expelled for fear that the growing movement would lead to foreign takeover, as had happened in the Philippines, while Japanese converts were executed. In the Americas, Christianity frequently became a syncretic religion. *See Chapter 15 for a more detailed discussion of Christianity in this period.*

4.2: New Forms of Social Organization and Modes of Production

II. Traditional peasant agriculture increased and changed, plantations expanded, and demand for labor increased. These changes both fed and responded to growing global demand for raw materials and finished products.

See Chapter 13 for a more detailed discussion.

III. As new social and political elites changed, they also restructured new ethnic, racial, and gender hierarchies.

See Chapter 13 for a more detailed discussion.

One of the most significant changes in labor during this period was the extension of plantation agriculture to the Americas. Most of the Native Americans in tropical coastal regions either died from European diseases and warfare or fled inland, leaving a need for labor on the sugar plantations and, in North America, cotton and tobacco plantations. This void was filled by importing Africans as slaves; the slave trade functioned with the cooperation of local African leaders who brought slaves from the interior of Africa to European trading forts along the coast where slaves were sold to European traders for weapons, luxury goods, and other goods such as pots and textiles.

In Asia, peasant agriculture also underwent changes because of globalization. In China, the influx of silver from the Americas exchanged for Chinese goods allowed the government to require that all taxes be paid in cash, not goods or labor. Therefore, peasants had to produce crops or goods for sale in order to obtain the silver needed to pay their taxes. This disrupted local agricultural customs; for example, some villages devoted themselves to growing mulberry trees on which silkworms fed, but then had to import rice for their own food from another village.

In Japan, the *daimyos* (feudal lords) and their samurai warriors fought each other and welcomed European weapons and knowledge. However, under unification by the Tokugawa shogunate, contact with Europeans was greatly restricted and the ability of daimyos to possess their own armies and weapons was eliminated. European traders, except the nonproselytizing Dutch, were banned and contact with foreign goods and ideas was carefully controlled by the government.

In some regions, such as Southeast Asia, European merchants relied on local women to conduct trade within their countries. As in the Americas, some of the European traders and trappers found it helpful to take local wives who could be their interface with the native people.

4.3. State Consolidation and Imperial Expansion

I. Rulers used a variety of methods to legitimize and consolidate their power.

II. Imperial expansion relied on the increased use of gunpowder, cannons, and armed trade to establish large empires in both hemispheres.

III. Competition over trade routes, state rivalries, and local resistance all provided significant challenges to state consolidation and expansion.

When Europeans entered Asian markets, they discovered large, ancient, and well-defended empires such as the Qing, the Mughals, and the Ottomans. In addition, trade routes were already controlled by local merchants. The European advantage lay in superior ships and cannons. These advantages allowed some European states, such as Portugal, England, and Holland, to establish empires of commerce or "trading post empires."

The Portuguese captured or bought ports along the east coast of Africa, in India, and in Southeast Asia. At first, they sold their shipping services, carrying Asian goods to Asian ports, and attempted to monopolize trade. As Portugal became overextended, other European powers challenged them for control of the lucrative spice routes.

The British East India Company and Dutch East India Company received charters from their governments granting trade monopolies, the power to make war, and the power to govern conquered peoples. Both the British and Dutch established competing trading posts. The Dutch conquered some of the small Spice Islands in what is now Indonesia, placing the remaining people under the control of Dutch planters and using slave labor to grow nutmeg, mace, and cloves. The Dutch became wealthy, but the local people were reduced to starvation because they were not given sufficient land to grow food for their families. Excluded from the Dutch-controlled Spice Islands, the British set up trading bases in India, where they purchased pepper and Indian cotton textiles. The demand for cotton turned many interior villages to the production of textiles for the British trade. Gradually, the British and Dutch transformed their trading posts into colonies. In North America, the British, French, and Dutch competed for the fur trade (see Map 14.3, p. 617), making alliances with local Native American tribes. As European empires clashed, Native Americans were drawn into British and French wars.

Spain followed a different path and took over the Philippines, which was close to trade with China and the Spice Islands. They followed a similar pattern to the one established in their American colonies by enforcing tribute, taxes, unpaid labor, and conversion to Christianity on their new subjects. The capital of the Philippines, Manila, became a major multicultural trade center — the silver from the Americas was brought there to be exchanged for goods and spices from Asia. *See Chapter 12 for the establishment of the "gunpowder empires" in the Eastern Hemisphere and Chapter 13 for the European colonial empires in the Americas.*

Theme 1: Interaction Between Humans and the Environment

Key environmental impacts followed from globalizing trade networks. First, land degradation and deforestation followed mining (such as the silver mine at Potosí in modern Bolivia) and intensive single-crop agriculture to produce exports for the world market (such as sugar, nutmeg, cotton, mulberry trees for silkworms, and tea), not only in the Americas but also in China and other regions. Movement of people — voluntary or forced — created other environmental impacts, such as the transatlantic slave trade, relocation of Native Americans from coastal regions, European colonies and trading centers, or the Dutch East India Company's transportation of large numbers of ethnic Chinese to Taiwan to grow rice and sugar for export.

Africa's population growth slowed because of the slave trade, even while new food crops from the Americas provided more nutrition. By 1900, Africa represented 6 percent of the world's population, while in 1600 it had possessed 18 percent. Along with the movement of people came the catastrophic spread of disease into regions where people had long been isolated from contact with the diseases of Eurasian agricultural people. In some cases, the death rate was near 90 percent after a century of contact. Cities grew as trade and administrative centers; one of the most spectacular was Manila, capital of the Spanish Philippines, where Spanish and Filipinos were joined by Japanese and Chinese traders, artisans, and mariners. Further environmental dislocation followed the fur trade; after depleting the populations of fur-bearing animals in Western Europe, French, English, Dutch, and Russian trappers and traders spread out into Siberia and North America, trading with local peoples, and driving many species (such as beaver, sable, and deer) nearly to extinction. *See Chapter 13 for discussion of the environmental impact of the Columbian exchange.*

Theme 2:
Development and Interaction of Cultures

See Chapter 15 for discussion of cultural transformations in this period.

Theme 3:
State-Building, Expansion, and Conflict

Europeans did not have the overwhelming political impact on the Indian Ocean basin as they had had in the Americas; they faced much more populous and organized empires, like the Mughal and Qing, and did not have the advantage of a severe local population decline due to disease. Some regions in Asia, such as parts of the Philippines, resisted Spanish attempts at mass conversion and subjugation of local people to Spanish rule. Chinese rebellions in the Philippines led to repressive responses by the Spanish, though Chinese rebellions against the Dutch in Taiwan were more successful. In Indonesia, the Dutch were more successful in controlling the local population, but not without shattering the economy and allowing thousands to die of starvation. The British were able to play upon the divisions within the Mughal Empire to secure trading bases in India. *See Chapters 12 and 13 for discussion of the political transformation in this time period.*

Theme 4:
Creation, Expansion, and Interaction of Economic Systems

Commerce in the Eastern Hemisphere had been based on trading systems that transported luxury goods from China (such as porcelain, tea, and silk), India (such as cotton textiles), and Southeast Asia (such as spices). The two main systems involved overland trade through the Silk Routes in Central Asia and maritime routes that took advantage of the monsoon winds in the Indian Ocean basin. The land routes had been divided by Qing dynasty China and the expanding Russian Empire. The maritime routes were under the control of small-scale Asian merchants.

Several factors brought Western Europeans into this trading system. First, some regions, such as the northern Italian city-states, had been involved in bringing goods from Asian markets to Europe after the goods arrived in Egypt or Constantinople. These cities had developed economies based on market exchange, private ownership, and accumulation of capital. When Muslim armies captured Constantinople, Egypt, and the Indian Ocean trade routes, European merchants had to trade at a disadvantage. The Portuguese, facing the Atlantic and not the Mediterranean, funded voyages of reconnaissance along the African coast to seek a sea route to the Indian Ocean. When da Gama arrived in the Indian Ocean in 1498, Europeans found that the East Asians did not want the inferior European goods – only silver or gold could be traded for Asian spices and silks, which created a negative trade balance for mercantilist Europeans.

The Spanish and Dutch quickly followed the Portuguese (see Map 14.1, p. 604), taking over coastal regions or establishing outposts to conduct trade. Their superior ship technology and use of shipboard mounted cannons gave them the ability to set up "trading post empires" and carry Asian goods between Asian ports. The Dutch captured land in the Spice Islands, creating a monopoly in nutmeg production and destroying the local economy. The influx of bullion, mostly silver, from Spanish-controlled mines in the Americas altered the balance between European and Asian merchants, despite the fact that Japan was also a major exporter of silver. The flow of silver into the region affected both Asian and European economies, where inflation and rising prices led to political instability and rebellions. Ultimately, Spain did not invest its profits wisely. The monarchy chose to invest in European dynastic struggles instead of commerce and industry.

In China, the need to pay taxes in silver led to increased specialization of local economies and changes in traditional peasant life; now peasants often had to import rice from other regions because they were growing cash crops such as mulberry trees. Chinese and Indian goods remained the center of the global trading system; Europeans were a conduit of American silver and competed against each other for Chinese silk and Indian cotton.

Europeans dominated the transatlantic trade, especially the slave trade. As in Asia, Europeans did not take over large territories of Africa, but instead traded European and Indian textiles, cowrie shells, metal goods, guns and gunpowder, tobacco, alcohol, and decorative items to African tribal leaders in exchange for slaves. Silver from the Americas was used to purchase the cowrie shells, some of the other decorative items, and Indian cotton, linking the slave trade with the trade in silver and textiles. European imports added to the wealth of elite groups but did not destroy local African skilled crafts.

Slavery in the Americas differed in key ways from traditional slavery: the scale of the transatlantic slave trade dwarfed earlier trade; slaves were used mostly in plantation agriculture and were treated inhumanely; the children of slaves remained slaves, with little hope of eventual freedom; and slavery in the Americas was distinctively racial. Most slaves destined for plantations in the Americas were males; however, traditional slave-trading routes controlled by Muslims continued to transport mostly female slaves across the Sahara and into the Indian Ocean.

The transatlantic slave trade affected African societies. Slaves were often taken from marginal groups, such as prisoners of war or debtors, within these societies. The gender imbalance in the slave trade meant an increase in polygamy in Africa, as well as increasing the number of female slaves in Africa itself in regions such as the kingdom of Kongo. Some women in Senegambia married European men, which provided the men with access to African-operated trade networks. In West Africa, women such as Queen Nzinga resisted Portuguese imperialism, while women in the kingdom of Kongo held lower-level administrative positions. Small, kinship-based societies often were disrupted, while Kongo and Oyo disintegrated partly because other ethnic groups gained access to European weapons and rebelled. The kingdom of Dahomey created a government monopoly in trading slaves, which contributed to its success.

Theme 5: Development and Transformation of Social Structures

See Chapter 13 for discussion of this theme.

Guided Reading Questions for Chapter 14

Seeking the Main Point In what different ways did global commerce transform human societies and the lives of individuals during the early modern era? (Page 602)

Causation What drove European involvement in the world of Asian commerce? (Page 602)

Connection To what extent did the Portuguese realize their own goals in the Indian Ocean? (Page 605)

Comparison How did the Portuguese, Spanish, Dutch, and British initiatives in Asia differ from one another? (Page 607)

Change To what extent did the British and Dutch trading companies change the societies they encountered in Asia? (Page 609)

Connection What was the significance of the silver trade in the early modern era of world history? (Page 612)

Change Describe the impact of the fur trade on North American native societies. (Page 616)

Comparison How did the North American and Siberian fur trades differ from each other? What did they have in common? (Page 620)

Practicing AP® Historical Thinking What differences can you identify in the operation and impact of the spice, silver, and fur trades? (Page 620)

Comparison What was distinctive about the Atlantic slave trade? What did it share with other patterns of slave owning and slave trading? (Page 622)

Causation What explains the rise of the Atlantic slave trade? (Page 623)

Connection What roles did Europeans and Africans play in the unfolding of the Atlantic slave trade? (Page 624)

Change In what different ways did the Atlantic slave trade transform African societies? (Page 628)

NOTES:

CHAPTER FIFTEEN
Cultural Transformations: Religion and Science, 1450–1750

AP® World History Key Concepts

4.1: Globalizing Networks of Communication and Exchange

VI. The increase in interactions between newly connected hemispheres and intensification of connections within hemispheres expanded the spread and reform of existing religions and created syncretic belief systems and practices.

As the Eastern and Western Hemispheres came into sustained contact, religions spread and adapted. Christianity underwent internal divisions and reforms in the Protestant Reformation and the Catholic Counter-Reformation (see Map 15.1, p. 648, and Snapshot: Catholic/Protestant Differences in the Sixteenth Century, p. 647) and spread to new regions (see Map 15.2, pp. 650-651), where local cultures selectively adopted and adapted the new faith. Islam also underwent a period of renewal in Arabia under al-Wahhab (see Map 15.3, p. 737) and Mughal India under Aurangzeb, even as it spread further into Africa and Southeast Asia, where local cultures often modified its practices.

China attempted to revitalize and purify traditional Chinese culture after the expulsion of the Mongols in a movement called Neo-Confucianism. In addition, syncretic religions arose, such as Sikhism, which incorporated elements of Hinduism and Islam, and Vodou or Candomble, which incorporated elements of African religions and Christianity.

Encouraged by contact with science transmitted by the Muslim world, the Scientific Revolution in Europe rediscovered texts from ancient Greece, challenged traditional beliefs, and sought to understand the natural world by employing reason, empirical observation, collection of data, experimentation, and skepticism. Many cultures practiced selective borrowing for both religious and scientific ideas that they encountered.

5.3: Nationalism, Revolution, and Reform

I. The rise and diffusion of Enlightenment thought that questioned established traditions in all areas of life often preceded the revolutions and rebellions against existing governments.

The Scientific Revolution spawned the Enlightenment in the eighteenth century. The Enlightenment attempted not only to popularize science but also to apply the principles of the scientific method and notions of progress in an attempt to find the natural laws governing human society. New ideas such as capitalism and government as a contract between the people and the rulers furthered new revolutionary thinking. In addition, many Enlightenment philosophers became deists or pantheists.

Theme 1:
Interaction Between Humans and the Environment

See Chapter 13 for discussion of the environmental impact of the Columbian exchange.

Theme 2:
Development and Interaction of Cultures

Western European Christianity fragmented beginning in 1517 when Martin Luther issued his Ninety-five Theses, condemning clerical abuses, such as corruption, immorality, luxurious lifestyles, and the sale of indulgences. Protestants also rejected the traditional Catholic belief in the authority of the Church fathers and salvation by good works. Instead, Luther proposed that man was saved by faith alone, while religious authority lay solely in the Bible. Protestants also believed that all vocations, not just monastic or religious vocations, had equal merit, which appealed to the rising urban and commercial classes. The Protestant Reformation spread rapidly because of the invention of the printing press and translations of the Bible into the vernacular, or everyday spoken language, as opposed to Latin, which was the official language of the Church but not spoken by the common people. Protestants emphasized that each person should read the Bible for him- or herself, creating an upsurge in literacy and individual thought, which also helped the Scientific Revolution.

The Catholic Church responded to the Reformation by initiating reforms, called the Catholic Counter-Reformation, and by opposing the spread of Protestantism. In addition, the Church reaffirmed the doctrines of papal authority, clerical celibacy, the veneration of saints, and the importance of church traditions and good works. Dissidents were accused of heresy and sometimes burned at the stake, and books and ideas were censored. New religious groups, such as the Jesuits (Society of Jesus), emerged, dedicated to the renewal of the Church and its spread abroad, especially to East Asia.

The missionary expansion of Christianity in the Americas and East Asia began with Spain and Portugal. Both countries conducted their voyages of discovery in the context of crusading traditions and the *Reconquista*. Catholic orders such as the Dominicans, Franciscans, and Jesuits led the missionary work, with the Portuguese focusing on Africa and Asia and the Spanish and French on the Americas. The Russian Orthodox Church followed the Russian Empire into Siberia. In these regions, new converts merged local beliefs with Christian beliefs and practices, often to the frustration of European Catholic priests who repeatedly attempted to end "backsliding" by destroying local shrines, religious artifacts and images, ancestral mummies in Peru, and books in Mexico.

Sometimes resistance to forced conversion was direct, as with the Peruvian movement known as Taki Onqoy (dancing sickness). More often, however, local people blended the new and local religious systems; for example, Aztec or Incan deities continued to be worshipped under new names, identified with Christian saints or the Virgin Mary. Syncretic religions in the Americas also formed around Africanized versions of Christianity, such as Vodou (Vodun), Candomble, Macumba, or Santeria, incorporating West African traditions such as drumming, dancing, animal sacrifice, and spirit possession.

In Asia, with its large populations and intact religious, societal, and governmental institutions, Christianity made less headway. Jesuit priests adopted the dress and language of China and chose to deal primarily with the Chinese official elite, emphasizing the similarities between Christianity and Confucian beliefs. Jesuits also passed along recent European gains in science, technology, astronomy, mapmaking, and geography, while withholding aspects such as Copernicus's heliocentric theory because it conflicted with official Church policy. Christian missionaries made few inroads in the total Chinese population for several reasons: they offered little that the Chinese needed, Christianity required converts to abandon much of traditional Chinese culture, and monogamy would require many Chinese men to abandon wives and concubines.

Islam was carried to sub-Saharan Africa by Sufi mystics, merchants, or scholars, who often intermarried with local women and did not require the total abandonment of traditional religious practices. Elites gained advisers, literacy in Arabic, the establishment of schools, and connections to the wider Islamic world. In Southeast Asia, in general, the common people also adopted a more syncretic form of Islam, while merchants aligned with stricter Middle Eastern traditions. The *bhakti* movement in India sought union with one of the Hindu deities through dance, song, prayer, and poetry; caste and gender distinctions were often set aside. The *bhakti* movement was similar to Sufi mysticism, blurring the distinction between Hinduism and Islam. Sikhism, a new syncretic religion, was developed by Guru Nanak in the Punjab region of South Asia. The new religion blended aspects of Hinduism and Islam but drew hostility from both. Among Javanese people, traditional animistic practices continued after conversion.

At the same time, Islamic renewal movements criticized what they considered to be lax Islamic practices. In West Africa, the descendants of the Fulbe led religiously based uprisings (jihads) to purify Islam. Some regions in Southeast Asia (such as the Sultanate of Acheh) attempted to enforce stricter adherence to dietary codes and alms-giving practices. In Mughal India, the emperor Aurangzeb reversed the tolerant policies of early Mughal leaders, such as Akbar. In Arabia itself, the birthplace of Islam, Muhammad ibn Abd al-Wahhab argued that the Ottoman Empire was declining because it was falling away from the pure faith of early Islam; he proclaimed that the veneration of Sufi saints and their tombs, Muhammad's tomb, or other natural sites was idolatrous and a violation of the monotheistic message of Islam. He gained the support of Ibn Saud, and they razed tombs and shrines, destroyed books on logic, and condemned using hashish, tobacco, or musical instruments.

In China, the Ming dynasty returned to Confucianism, but Neo-Confucianism incorporated insights of Buddhism and Daoism into traditional Confucian practices. In late Ming times, Wang Yangming suggested that anyone could lead a virtuous life through introspection and by studying nature, eliminating the need for traditional Confucian pursuits such as studying classical texts, intensive academic study, and constant moral striving. Later, critics argued that Wang Yangming's lax ideas were responsible for Ming decline and conquest by the Manchus. Chinese Buddhists also made their religion more accessible to laypeople. The *kaozheng* movement in China based research on evidence, paralleling the development of the Scientific Revolution in Europe. However, *kaozheng* was used more to examine old texts instead of making new scientific discoveries.

Western Europe entered a dynamic period of scientific discovery that had major long-term consequences not only for Europe but the entire world. New experimental techniques were built on Muslim science, the Hindu number system, and rediscovered Greek texts, as well as the shock to traditional patterns of knowledge caused by information from the "new" world. Fundamental views about humans' place in the universe were altered, challenging religious teachings and the authority of both the Church and cultural traditions. The Scientific Revolution — based on empirical observation, data collection, experimentation, and logical reasoning and expressed in mathematical terms — began with astronomy. Copernicus changed centuries-old beliefs by using mathematics and observation to show that the sun, not the earth, was the "center" of the universe. This observation was followed by other astronomical insights and, finally, by Newton using calculus to describe the role of gravity as the force that governs planetary motion. Medicine, anatomy, and other areas also utilized the scientific approach. Further, the interest in science led to the creation or improvement of new tools, such as the telescope, that extended human senses. In the eighteenth century, some tried to extend new scientific knowledge to broader audiences.

Building on the advancement of the Scientific Revolution, Enlightenment *philosophes* attempted to look for universal laws that governed politics and social structures. Other thinkers, such as Adam Smith, challenged the prevalent economic system of mercantilism with a new economic theory that eventually became known as capitalism. Englishman John Locke rejected the idea that government rested on the divine right of kings and suggested instead that government was a contract between the governed and the ruler. A core Enlightenment belief that continues to affect Western thought today is the idea of progress, or the belief that human society can be changed or improved by human reason and is not determined by divine plan or tradition. Other societies, such as in China and Japan, selectively chose what aspects of this new scientific movement would be allowed to enter their cultures.

Theme 3:
State-Building, Expansion, and Conflict

See Chapter 13 for discussion of political transformations in the early modern world.

Theme 4:
Creation, Expansion, and Interaction of Economic Systems

See Chapter 14 for discussion of economic transformations in the early modern world.

Theme 5:
Development and Transformation of Social Structures

Religious reforms in this period affected gender roles. For example, Protestants destroyed convents and denigrated the cloistered life, which reduced the independent power of women in these communities. Protestantism also ended the veneration of Mary and female saints. Women were still not allowed to be members of the new Protestant clergy (except in the Quaker sect) but instead were subject to male supervision and viewed first and foremost as wives and mothers. The conversion to Christianity of large numbers of people in the Americas also altered the traditional role of native women as priests, shamans, or ritual specialists, as there was no corresponding role in the male-only Christian clergy. In Southeast Asia, women, who had been rulers in Sumatra, were forbidden to govern under stricter interpretations of Islamic law. In Java, however, women continued to serve in royal courts and as merchants in local markets. In India, the *bhakti* movement appealed to women as well as lower-caste men. In Arabia, ibn-Wahhab protected some rights of women within Islam, like the right to consent to marriage and to control dowries, to divorce, and to engage in commerce. He did not require head-to-toe covering of women in public places.

Many leaders of the Scientific Revolution in Western Europe adopted restrictive attitudes toward women. Even when women were able to perform research under the protection of husbands or fathers, they had their names removed from papers and books before publication. Occasionally, women of wealth and prestige, such as Margaret Cavendish, Duchess of Newcastle, managed to force their way into meetings of scientific societies. During the Enlightenment, women were often the sponsors of salons where *philosophes* met to discuss the issues of the day but were still subject to discriminatory treatment when they tried to publish their own works. Jean-Jacque Rousseau, for example, believed that women were innately inferior to men. Mary Wollstonecraft in England challenged his views by arguing that rational education of women was essential to progress.

Guided Reading Questions for Chapter 15

Seeking the Main Point To what extent did the cultural changes of the early modern world derive from cross-cultural interaction? And to what extent did they grow from within particular societies or civilizations? (Page 644)

Change In what ways did the Protestant Reformation transform European society, culture, and politics? (Page 646)

Connection How was European imperial expansion related to the spread of Christianity? (Page 652)

Connection In what ways was European Christianity assimilated into the Native American cultures of Spanish America? (Page 652)

Comparison Why were missionary efforts to spread Christianity so much less successful in China than in Spanish America? (Page 657)

Explanation What accounts for the continued spread of Islam in the early modern era and for the emergence of reform or renewal movements within the Islamic world? (Page 659)

Change What kinds of cultural changes occurred in China and India during the early modern era? (Page 662)

Practicing AP® Historical Thinking In what ways did religious changes in Asia and the Middle East parallel those in Europe, and in what ways were they different? (Page 664)

Comparison Why did the Scientific Revolution occur in Europe rather than in China or the Islamic world? (Page 665)

Change What was revolutionary about the Scientific Revolution? (Page 667)

NOTES:

AP® WORLD HISTORY PERIOD FIVE
Industrialization and Global Integration, c. 1750 to c. 1900

PART FIVE
The European Moment in World History, 1750–1900

AP® World History Key Concepts
  5.1:   Industrialization and Global Capitalism
  5.2:   Imperialism and Nation-State Formation
  5.3:   Nationalism, Revolution, and Reform
  5.4:   Global Migration

The Big Picture: European Centrality and the Problem of Eurocentrism

The "long nineteenth century" has also been called the European century because of the dominance of Europe on the world stage. Chapters 16 and 17 explore the theme of modernity – the creation of a new form of human society following the Scientific, French, and Industrial revolutions – that envisioned social and gender equality, an end to slavery, and participation by common people in government. At the same time, through industrialization, European societies reshaped the planet in a manner paralleled only by the Agricultural Revolution. Chapters 18 and 19 explore how these modern European societies exercised their power either directly in empires or indirectly through economic penetration, missionary activity, and military intervention.

By making the prime meridian run through Greenwich, England, Europeans reformulated geography to place themselves literally at the center of the map. In addition, textbooks and historians were also Europe-centered, downplaying the contributions of other civilizations and emphasizing the role of Europe in the race for progress and modernization. With the development of the discipline of world history after World War II, the key question became: "How can we avoid an inappropriate Eurocentrism when dealing with a phase of world history in which Europeans were in fact central?" World history places the European moment, without denying its importance, in the context of continuing patterns of historical development.

■ The European moment in world history has been both recent and brief, and other societies have had long periods of regional influence, such as the Greeks, Arabs, Chinese, Mongols, Incas, and Aztecs. While Europeans were the first to exercise this influence on a global scale, events at the end of the twentieth and the beginning of the twenty-first centuries indicate an erosion of European power.

- Europe's rise occurred in a global context: the Chinese withdrew their fleet from the Indian Ocean; Native Americans lacked immunity to Eurasian diseases and were weakened by internal strife; and the Industrial Revolution was stimulated by Asian superiority in textile and pottery production and relied on New World resources and markets and the cooperation of local elites.

- Europeans faced resistance to their global dominance and were forced to modify their policies in Africa and South Asia.

- People around the world adapted European ideas and practices to local circumstances and used these ideas and practices to benefit themselves. For example, the Haitian Revolution used French ideas about the "rights of man"; European ideas of nationalism were used in anti-European, anticolonial movements in Africa and Asia. Hindus used British-introduced railroads to go on pilgrimages; and the industrial development of Japan and Russia followed a different pattern from industrial development in England.

- The rise of Europe was not the only thing happening on the world stage during the long nineteenth century. China was absorbing a huge population increase and suffered through peasant rebellions. Muslim and Hindu cultures continued to evolve in India under British rule. And African societies experienced religious wars and wars of state formation.

AP® Themes in Part Five:

Environment	Cultures	State Building	Economies	Social Structures
Industrial Revolution (IR) and: • Population growth • Energy shortage • Ecological windfall from the Americas - Environmental effects of IR - Romantic poets and early environmentalism - IR as beginning of the Anthropocene era - Changing roles of agriculture in industrial economies - Disease in the colonial world - Environmental effects of cashcrop agriculture: ex.: Burma and Vietnam - Ecological damage of Bantustan policy in South Africa - American food crops and Chinese population growth	Enlightenment ideas and revolution in the Atlantic world - Cultural expressions of nationalism - Marxist socialism as an idea and a movement - Ideologies of Imperialism - Colonial racism and racial identity - Colonial education and westernization - Missionaries and "female circumcision" - Africanization of Christianity - "Tribalism" and pan-Africanism - Hinduism :emergence of a distinct tradition in India and spread to the West - Ottoman ideologies: Islamic modernism, secularism, nationalism - Japanese westernization	Revolutions compared and connected: North American, French, Haitian, Latin American, Decembrist - Post-independence state building in U.S., Haiti, Latin America - U.S. "informal empire" in Latin America - European empires and the IR - Conquest and colonial states in Asia and Africa - Taiping Uprising in China - Opium Wars - The end of imperial China - Contraction and reform in Ottoman Empire - Meiji Restoration in Japan - Meiji Japan and women's rights - Japan as an imperial power	Revolutions compared: British, French, U.S., Russian, Japanese, Latin American - Destruction of plantation economy in Haiti - Post-slavery labor regimes in the Americas - "Dependent development": Latin America in the world economy - Colonial economies Compared: • Forced labor systems • Cash-crop production • Mining economies • Settler economies - Scarcity of colonial Industrialization - Taiping Uprising and the devastation of China's economy - Opium trade and its outcomes - Failure of Chinese Industrialization - Japan's industrial revolution	Women in Atlantic Revolutions - Early feminism - Abolition of slavery - End of serfdom in Russia - Class in colonial North America - Class and gender outcomes of French Revolution - Class, race, and social upheaval in Haiti - Absence of social change in Latin American Revolutions - Class and IR: aristocracy, middle classes, artisans, workers - Gender and IR: domesticity and return to the workforce - Patterns of migration: European, Asian, African - African women and colonial economies - New and old elites in colonial regimes - Gender policies of Taiping rebels - Tokugawa society and social change - Women and reform in Meiji Japan

NOTES:

CHAPTER SIXTEEN
Atlantic Revolutions, Global Echoes, 1750–1900

AP® World History Key Concepts

5.1: Industrialization and Global Capitalism
See Chapter 17 for more complete discussion of this key concept.

5.2: Imperialism and Nation-State Formation

II. Imperialism influenced State formation and contraction around the world.

The development and spread of nationalism as an ideology fostered new communal identities. For example, nationalism inspired the unification of Germany and Italy. Nationalism also inspired anti-imperial resistance, which led to the contraction of the Ottoman Empire as Greece and Serbia gained independence. Nationalism also encouraged the "Egypt for Egyptians" movement, which protested British and French intrusion in Egypt. As an ideology, nationalism proved quite flexible and inspired ethnic groups to revolt against the Ottoman, Austrian, and Russian empires. *See Chapters 17 through 19 for more complete discussion of this key concept.*

5.3: Nationalism, Revolution, and Reform

I. The rise and diffusion of Enlightenment thought that questioned established traditions in all areas of life often preceded the revolutions and rebellions against existing governments.

II. Beginning in the eighteenth century, peoples around the world developed a new sense of commonality based on language, religion, social customs, and territory. These newly imagined national communities linked this identity with the borders of the state, while governments used this idea to unite diverse populations.

III. Increasing discontent with imperial rule propelled reformist and revolutionary movements.

IV. The global spread of European political and social thought and the increasing number of rebellions stimulated new transnational ideologies and solidarities.

Enlightenment ideals of progress and perfectibility – the notion that society and government could be improved by rational human efforts – led to the idea of natural rights such as liberty, equality before the law, free trade, religious toleration, and republicanism. Further, Enlightenment thinkers challenged established beliefs in the divine right of kings, mercantilism, aristocratic privilege, and church authority. These ideals spread rapidly through newspapers, pamphlets, and books, not only across the Atlantic to colonies of France, Spain, Britain, and Portugal, but also to areas outside of the Atlantic world. Colonial rebellions occurred in British North America and Spain's American colonies. France went through a revolution that had far-reaching implications; not only did their revolution create a more radical society than those in the Americas, but France, through its conquering armies under Napoleon, spread its revolutionary ideals to Eastern Europe and Russia. Haiti, France's lucrative Caribbean colony, rose up in the only successful slave rebellion in history, partly basing the rebellion on Enlightenment ideas.

    Other consequences of the Atlantic revolutions and Enlightenment ideals included other liberation movements, like abolition and feminism. An unintended consequence of Napoleon's conquering armies was the spread of French ideals of liberty, equality, and fraternity and the rise of nationalism in Eastern Europe in opposition to French occupation. Nationalism involved the redirecting of individual loyalties from family, clan, and village to loyalty to a nation-state, reinforced by the government through schools, public rituals, mass media, compulsory military service, and official state languages. Ethnic nationalism became a potent force that threatened diverse empires such as the Ottoman, Russian, Austrian, and Chinese.

5.4: Global Migration

II. Migrants relocated for a variety of reasons.

Europeans continued to migrate for economic reasons to colonies or to industrializing urban centers in Europe. Following rebellions in the Americas, some people (usually elites who had "lost" in the rebellion) either migrated back to the mother country or went into exile. Indentured laborers were imported from Asia to take over work formerly performed by slaves. *See Chapters 18 through 19 for more complete discussion of this key concept.*

Theme 1:
Interaction Between Humans and the Environment

Political revolutions in the Atlantic world and Enlightenment ideals had environmental ramifications. The Haitian Revolution, the only successful slave rebellion, led to the destruction of large plantations and the division of the land into small farms for freed slaves. Instead of producing export crops such as sugar or coffee, these small farms now produced food for local consumption. In addition, the end of slavery in the Americas led to indentured servitude to supply labor for mines, construction, and plantations in the Caribbean, Peru, South Africa, Hawaii, and Malaysia. *See Chapter 17 for discussion of the consequences of the Industrial Revolution on the environment.*

Theme 2:
Development and Interaction of Cultures

The French Revolution had far-reaching effects on all parts of French society and culture. In a foment of anti-clericalism, the new revolutionary government made priests employees of the state and temporarily turned the Cathedral of Notre Dame into the Temple of Reason. Control of education shifted from church to state in order to better inculcate nationalist and revolutionary ideals. Romantic poets such as William Wordsworth (an Englishman) wrote sonnets praising the Revolution as a new beginning for humanity. Newly-awakened nationalist groups often built a sense of cultural and ethnic identity by appealing to their shared linguistic and cultural past through folktales, music, dances, and traditions (the famous Grimm's collection of fairytales are an example). Artists and writers also supported liberal social movements. Henrik Ibsen's play *A Doll's House*, for example, generated discussion on the role of women in society. *See Chapters 18 and 19 for detailed discussion of cultural interaction in this period.*

Theme 3:
State-Building, Expansion, and Conflict

The Atlantic revolutions took place in a global context, including the collapse of the Safavid dynasty in Persia, the fragmentation of the Mughal Empire, peasant revolts in Russia and China, Islamic revolutions in West Africa, and the *mfecane* movement (a series of wars and migrations) in southern Africa. However, the Atlantic revolutions were distinctive in that the wars were global rather than regional and were connected to each other, both philosophically (they were based on Enlightenment ideals like the possibility of creating a better government based on liberty, religious tolerance, equality, popular sovereignty, and free trade) and directly, through correspondence between revolutionary leaders and financial and military aid. John Locke articulated his belief that a social contract existed between the ruler and the ruled, and that if the government no longer protected the natural rights of the people, they had the right to change the government. The Atlantic Revolutions also had global impact, carrying ideas about equality, abolition of slavery, extension of the franchise, constitutional government, and nationalism around the world.

There were, however, differences in the revolutions, based on the specific circumstances of each region. The American Revolution was the first, ending in a constitution and a federal government that expanded participation to many white males and a Bill of Rights designed to protect individual rights against the power of a strong state. The Americans had benefitted from a period of benign neglect while England pursued its political affairs on the Continent; they developed a series of local assemblies dominated by local property owners and merchants and came to consider this autonomy to be part of their rights as Englishmen. With a lack of entrenched nobility and established church and with more economic opportunity and readily available land, Americans had less poverty and more social mobility than most other regions. Rebellion grew out of the sudden effort of the British to reestablish political control over the colonies and to raise revenue to pay for its struggle with France. Using Enlightenment ideas such as popular sovereignty, natural rights, and consent of the governed, the Americans rebelled. There was no major social reformation; government remained in the hands of the existing elite with a widening of the franchise to many white men, slavery was not abolished, and voting rights were not extended to women and people of color. One of the most important and globally influential aspects of the revolution was stated in the Declaration of Independence; the right of people to resort to revolution to protect natural rights. That pronouncement, along with the model of the Constitution and Bill of Rights (which set forth separation of church and state, republican government, protection of individual rights, and checks and balances) showed that Enlightenment ideals could be the basis of government.

The French Revolution a few years later was in part caused by the fiscal crisis precipitated by French support for the American rebels against England. French soldiers returned from North America filled with revolutionary ideals. When the king attempted to deal with the fiscal crisis by calling the Estates General into session, the Third Estate quickly took control and reconstituted itself as a National Assembly, which drew up the Declaration of the Rights of Man and Citizen, based on ideas from Enlightenment thinkers and the example of the Americans. This revolution was more "personal" than the Americans' rebellion against a monarch across the ocean; French nobles and the clergy had prerogatives and feudal rights that prevented the rising middle class or rural peasants from prospering, and urban workers suffered from a drop in income and rising prices for bread. The conflict between classes led to a more violent revolution and one that had profound social implications. Those representing the *ancien régime* (the old order) were overthrown or executed, including the king and queen. Church lands were confiscated and sold, priests were placed under the control of the state, and education was secularized to indoctrinate children with revolutionary ideals. French revolutionaries did not seek to restore their rights, as had the Americans, but rather to demolish the old order and create something new. They created a republic, reformed administrative structures, declared freedom of worship for Jews and Protestants, created a standing army based on universal draft, and abolished all remaining feudal obligations and social distinctions. The revolution faced military opposition from other European countries, who feared that the notion of beheading a king might catch on elsewhere. Within France, fear of antirevolutionary movements led to the Reign of Terror. As much as French men benefitted, they failed to make significant changes for women despite women's enthusiastic support for the revolution. The ideals of the revolution – liberty, equality, and fraternity – were spread by Napoleon and the French army throughout most of Europe. The society that emerged under the leadership of the Emperor Napoleon preserved civil equality, the secular legal system, and religious freedom but under a military dictatorship. Resentment of French domination created a sense of nationalism in subjected countries (such as the German states in the Austrian Empire), while military resistance from Britain and Russia ultimately led to Napoleon's defeat.

Revolutionary ideology spread to French colonies: Saint Domingue (later Haiti) was a rich sugar colony that was controlled by a small number of white planters (*grands blancs*) who wanted freedom from French control, less affluent white men (*petits blancs*) who wanted legal equality with the *grands blancs*, freedmen who wanted equality with white Haitians, and a large number of slaves, subjected to extremely brutal conditions, who wanted slavery abolished. Slaves burned plantations and killed white landowners and mixed-race people. A former slave, Toussaint Louverture, took control and resisted both the French and the landowners. The Haitian Revolution thus became the only successful slave rebellion in history. The new government became the second independent republic in the Americas and leant its support to the rebellions in the Spanish colonies on the condition that newly established governments free all slaves. All Haitians were declared equal before the law and defined as "black." Haiti's example led to the fear of other slave revolts, leading to a socially conservative elite in Latin America.

Rebellions in mainland Latin America were led primarily by elite creoles (people of pure European ancestry, born in the Americas) who resented Spain's attempts to dominate its colonies and increase revenue through high taxes and tariffs. Creole intellectuals had absorbed Enlightenment ideas of popular sovereignty, personal liberty, and republican government, but geographical obstacles and regionalism prevented the scattered rebellions from joining forces as had the thirteen North American colonies. Latin American revolutions were also more conservative because Spanish rule had been more authoritarian than British rule, class divisions were more pronounced, and white settlers were vastly outnumbered by Native Americans, African descendants, and mestizos (people of mixed Native American and European ancestry). With the conquest of Spain and Portugal by Napoleon, however, creole elites were forced into action. Latin American revolutions also included internal class struggles and were not simply rebellions against colonial rule. An alliance of the military and church with the elites provided some assurance that a social rebellion would not prevail. Nationalism was used by leaders such as Simón Bolívar as a means of getting the support of lower classes in the rebellion against Spanish rule – and many of the leaders were actually liberals with Enlightenment leanings – but little social reform actually resulted from these independence movements. *Also see Chapters 17 through 19 for discussion of imperial expansion and conflict.*

Theme 4:
Creation, Expansion, and Interaction of Economic Systems

See Chapter 17 for discussion of the Industrial Revolution and its consequences.

Theme 5:
Development and Transformation of Social Structures

The various revolutions in this period had different effects on social structures, depending in part on the causes and on the leaders of the revolution. The Haitian Revolution was the most racially and socially radical; slaves and freedmen violently overthrew French colonial rule and killed many of the detested plantation owners, all of the citizens of the new Haiti were declared to be black (even if they were of mixed European and African ancestry), and legal equality was enforced. From a nation of social and racial extremes, Haiti became a nation of small, often-impoverished farmers.

The least radical revolution socially was that of the British North American colonists. Due to long neglect by the British crown (which was more involved in its more lucrative Caribbean colonies and conflict with France), American colonists had developed a society based on "the rights of Englishmen," with a large amount of local self-government. While wealthy men such as Washington or Adams were the leaders of the rebellion, the absence of entrenched nobility or an established church and the availability of "free" land led to a society that had fewer distinctions than most others in the world at the time – for free white men, that is. When the Americans rebelled, it was not against social inequality within the Americas, but against the crown's attempt to reimpose direct rule and raise taxes. The social structure changed little because of the rebellion, only gradually widening participation in government to include all white males. Slavery remained intact in southern states, and women were not given political rights under the new Constitution. The abolition movement, both in England and the northern states, gradually gained momentum, but the actual freeing of slaves awaited the Civil War.

The rebellions of Spanish creoles against Spanish rule also had little effect on their societies; creoles simply replaced the *peninsulares* (people of European ancestry born in Spain) at the top of the social structure as the owners of land and wealth. Slaves were freed, but people of color retained their place at the bottom of the social scale.

The French Revolution was truly a revolution of social classes; the Third Estate revolted against the dual "oppressors" of the clergy and nobility. The first liberal phase of the revolution was led by the middle class (such as doctors, judges, lawyers, merchants, and bureaucrats) with some allies from the lower nobility and clergy. It was based on Enlightenment ideals and moved toward equality before the law and a society where merit determined social rank. The revolution quickly became more radical with power shifting to urban "mobs" and peasant revolts. This more radical phase of the revolution ended special taxes and feudal prerogatives and work obligations of the peasantry, confiscated and sold church land, granted toleration to Jews and Protestants, executed the king and queen, set up universal male suffrage and a republican government, and then turned to devour itself under the Reign of Terror. Napoleon took control and retained the ideal of social equality but left little individual freedom under his military rule.

Russia, inspired both by Enlightenment ideals and the desire to modernize, freed its serfs and gave them portions of the nobles' land. Most peasants, however, remained impoverished, due to the growth in rural population and the imposition of new taxes and duties. This burden added to the social unrest in late nineteenth- and early twentieth-century Russia.

While some Enlightenment thinkers favored equality for women, none of the revolutions improved women's social and legal status. In the Americas, women did not receive voting rights or the right to participate in the new governments, even though they often helped raise money and supported the revolutionary movements. The French Revolution saw profound participation by urban women – from the storming of the Bastille, to the march of women on Versailles to obtain bread for their children, to the revolutionary activities of women such as Olympe de Gouges (who proposed that women should have the same political rights as men). However, even radical revolutionaries declared that women should remain under the control of men and out of the political world. Englishwoman Mary Wollstonecraft responded with *Vindication of the Rights of Woman*, an early expression of feminist sentiment. Though the new governments did not include equality for women, the movement for equal rights grew. The Seneca Falls Conference in New York in 1848 demanded legal equality and suffrage for women, as well as equal access to schools and universities. By 1900, some women had been admitted to universities and the learned professions, but suffrage was delayed in most countries until after World War I.

Guided Reading Questions for Chapter 16

Seeking the Main Point What were the most important outcomes of the Atlantic revolutions, both immediately and in the century that followed? (Page 698)

Causation In what ways did the ideas of the Enlightenment contribute to the Atlantic revolutions? (Page 700)

Change What was revolutionary about the American Revolution, and what was not? (Page 701)

Comparison How did the French Revolution differ from the American Revolution? (Page 704)

Comparison What was distinctive about the Haitian Revolution, both in world history generally and in the history of Atlantic revolutions? (Page 709)

Connection How were the Spanish American revolutions shaped by the American, French, and Haitian revolutions that happened earlier? (Page 711)

Practicing AP® Historical Thinking Compare the North American, French, Haitian, and Spanish American revolutions. What are the most significant categories of comparisons? (Page 714)

Change What accounts for the end of Atlantic slavery during the nineteenth century? (Page 715)

Change How did the end of slavery affect the lives of the former slaves? (Page 718)

Explanation What accounts for the growth of nationalism as a powerful political and personal identity in the nineteenth century? (Page 719)

Significance What were the achievements and limitations of nineteenth-century feminism? (Page 723)

CHAPTER SEVENTEEN
Revolutions of Industrialization, 1750–1900

AP® World History Key Concepts

5.1: Industrialization and Global Capitalism

I. Industrialization fundamentally changed how goods were produced.

II. New patterns of global trade and production developed and further integrated the global economy as industrialists sought raw materials and new markets for the increasing amount and array of goods produced in their factories.

III. To facilitate investments at all levels of industrial production, financiers developed and expanded various financial institutions.

IV. There were major developments in transportation and communication, including railroads, steamships, telegraphs, and canals.

V. The development and spread of global capitalism led to a variety of responses.

VI. The ways in which people organized themselves into societies also underwent significant transformations in industrialized states due to the fundamental restructuring of the global economy.

The Industrial Revolution, the most significant change in how humans live since the beginning of agriculture, involved the switching of energy sources from wind, water, and muscle power to machines powered by steam and later electricity. Beginning with the production of machine-made textiles in Britain, factories produced large amounts of goods more cheaply than could be done by individual craftsmen. Innovation piled on innovation, rapidly changing all facets of manufacturing and also changing the way people lived.

The development of the steam engine provided new sources of power for factories and led to new methods of transportation like the steamship or railroad. These new methods of transportation allowed access to raw materials and markets around the world. Global trade fed cash crops and raw materials to the factories of Europe and North America, where manufactured goods were produced to be sold at a profit on the world market as well as to internal markets to consumers who now had more income as industrial workers, and, after an initial drop, the standard of living in industrial countries rose.

Nations pursued different paths to industrialize: Western Europe, especially Britain, had governments and legal systems largely responsive to the interests of financiers and commercial classes, growing populations, available capital (largely from overseas enterprises), raw materials, and a respect for science and technology. The United States created the most favorable climate for large corporations to emerge with little government regulation, while Russian industrialization came at the direction of an autocratic ruler. All industrializing countries saw major social reorganization – some with turmoil that was moderated with the gradual inclusion of workers' interests in government, and some with violent revolution when no such accommodation was made.

5.2 Imperialism and Nation-State Formation

See Chapters 16, 18, and 19 for discussion of this key concept.

5.3 Nationalism, Revolution, and Reform

See Chapter 16 for discussion of this key concept.

5.4: Global Migration

I. Migration in many cases was influenced by changes in demography in both industrialized and unindustrialized societies that presented challenges to existing patterns of living.

II. Migrants relocated for a variety of reasons.

III. The large-scale nature of migration, especially in the nineteenth century, produced a variety of consequences and reactions to the increasingly diverse societies on the part of migrants and the existing populations.

The global age saw global migration. Industrial states saw internal migration of displaced agricultural labor to cities, where people looked for jobs in new industries or as domestic servants. In addition, population growth in Europe led to migration to colonies, some of which became settler colonies such as Australia, New Zealand, and North America. Some Europeans also migrated to newly acquired empires (such as India or South Africa). Thriving industrial countries such as the United States, which also had vast amounts of sparsely occupied land, encouraged immigration of Europeans as well as indentured labor from Asia. Latin American countries, such as Argentina and Brazil, encouraged migration of Europeans, mostly from Spain, Portugal, and Italy. Not all of these migrants remained in the New World, and many returned to their homelands after a few years.

Theme 1:
Interaction Between Humans and the Environment

The Industrial Revolution that began in Europe, specifically in England, had such an impact on the environment that some scientists call the last 250 years the Anthropocene Age or the Age of Man. For the first time in human history, energy was not created by muscle power or renewable resources such as wood, wind, and water. On the positive side, technological innovation increased rapidly, partly spurred by population pressure and the subsequent depletion of wood as a fuel, and partly by stimulation from technological innovations such as textiles from China and India. New methods in agriculture (such as crop rotation, selective breeding of animals, higher-yield seeds, and lighter plows) and technology (such as chemical fertilizers, pesticides, mechanical reapers, and refrigeration) also helped increase the food supply while decreasing the need for rural labor. On the negative side, the extraction of nonrenewable raw materials (such as coal, iron, petroleum, copper, and tin) altered the landscape. Increased urban density, the use of fossil fuels (such as coal for steam engines and heating) and industrial waste led to water and air pollution, which in turn increased human diseases such as respiratory illness, typhoid, and dysentery.

The Industrial Revolution also contributed to population movement. Internal migration continued as displaced rural workers moved to urban areas where they hoped to find work. Western Europeans also migrated to North and South America, Australia and New Zealand, and South Africa. European Russians migrated to Siberia, largely replacing native Siberians. These migrations were caused by population pressure, poverty, the displacement of peasant farmers, the need for labor overseas, the availability of land (especially in North America), and declining costs and time involved in transportation by railroad or steamship.

Theme 2:
Development and Interaction of Cultures

See Chapters 16, 18, and 19 for discussion of this theme.

Theme 3:
State-Building, Expansion, and Conflict

Western European states, unlike Asian empires, were relatively small and decentralized. They engaged in hefty competition, both in dynastic wars within Europe and in colonial enterprises outside of Europe. Western European monarchs, especially the British, circumvented resistant land-based aristocrats and the church and instead forged ties with the commercial middle class to more efficiently obtain power and income for the costs of keeping a standing army and supplying the basic needs of government.

The government of Great Britain especially came under the control of and was favorable to the commercial class, sidelining the traditional aristocracy, although British nobles were far more likely than those in other countries to invest in lands and commerce, and later in industry. The English crown granted charters not only to cities but also to companies and corporations in exchange for much-needed cash. The government also protected inventions, sponsored scientific societies and "practical" universities where new discoveries could be shared, suppressed labor unions and strikes, set tariffs to benefit local industry or landowners, provided support for shipping by improving ports and creating a powerful navy, passed laws and regulations favorable to industry and trade, and promoted immigration of skilled craftsmen regardless of religion.

Countries such as the United States also supported the creators of industry with tax breaks, grants of land to railroads, laws favoring the formation of corporations, and patents to protect innovation. No major political party emerged in the United States to support workers, unlike in Britain and Germany where socialist and labor parties reflected the interests of the newly enfranchised working class.

Russia was the only country in Europe to be ruled by an absolute monarch. The tsars ordered creation of railroads and heavy industry but did not allow the workers to have any voice in working conditions or government. There were no legal political parties, so no labor or socialist parties could form to represent workers. Large-scale strikes erupted along with an uprising in 1905 involving workers, peasants, intellectuals, students, and the military. The revolution was suppressed. In the aftermath, a few reforms were instituted, but they were not enough to relieve the growing social unrest that led to the Russian Revolution in 1917. Russia was the only society that had a violent revolution as part of its process of industrialization.

Latin American countries were beset by internal revolts and conflicts. Conservatives, mostly large landowners allied with military officers and the church, favored centralized authority, military support, and maintenance of the status quo socially and economically. Liberals preferred federalism, attacked the power of the church, and wanted limited social reforms. Conflicts often led to military rule under *caudillos* to restore order. Constitutions were written and then discarded, only to be rewritten again. Creoles remained in charge and benefitted economically, largely from the sale of cash crops and ore. Governments protected the interests of foreign owners, such as the United Fruit Company, and became known as "banana republics." This dependency on foreign markets and investors was seen as a new form of economic colonialism. Europeans, largely displaced peasants, were also encouraged to immigrate to work the *haciendas* (plantations and ranches). Mexico endured years of dictatorial rule with violent revolts that erupted into a revolution in the early twentieth century: middle class liberals joined with workers and peasants to overthrow the dictator, Porfirio Díaz. Their new constitution created universal male suffrage, instituted land reform, limited foreign ownership, and curtailed the role of the church by removing education from its control. *See Chapters 18 and 19 for discussion of imperialism in Africa and Asia.*

Theme 4:
Creation, Expansion, and Interaction of Economic Systems

The combination of scientific and technological advances that led to the Industrial Revolution began in Great Britain and rapidly spread to Western Europe, North America, and beyond. Factors that contributed to Britain's economic development included the following:

- access to wealth from colonies in the Caribbean, North America, and India
- a highly commercialized economy favoring innovation
- a growing population
- an aristocratic class that was willing to invest in commerce and industry
- a large merchant fleet protected by the powerful British navy
- a political system that was favorable to and encouraged economic innovation, including patent laws, control of Parliament by commercial interests, checks on the power of the king, and willingness to impose protective tariffs and suppress workers' strikes
- a legal system that made it easy to form corporations
- existing infrastructure such as roads and canals
- science and learned societies that sponsored practical discoveries and "useful knowledge"
- a geographical location as an island on the Atlantic coast of Europe that protected Britain from continental wars
- possession of natural resources, especially coal and iron
- a relatively fluid social structure

The Industrial Revolution first manifested itself in the textile industry, then moved to the large-scale production of steel and steam-powered engines, including turbines, to run machines in factories as well as locomotives and steamships. The second phase of the Industrial Revolution centered on electricity as a power source, chemicals, and inventions in communication such as the telegraph and telephone. Overseas colonies were exploited for raw materials and used as markets for new manufactured goods.

Other countries followed Britain in industrializing, but each developed its own pattern. In the United States, the textile mills of New England were the first to develop, but the pace of industrial development increased rapidly following the Civil War and the development of the transcontinental railroad system. By 1914, the United States – because of its vast internal market, availability of raw materials and foreign capital, and sympathetic government regulations which allowed huge corporations such as U.S. Steel to dominate the market – produced a volume of manufactured goods equal to that of Britain, Germany, and France combined. The U.S. made its own contributions to industrialization such as mass production (using assembly lines and interchangeable parts), scientific management, and advertising.

After losses in the Crimean War, autocratic Russia sought economic improvement through top-down measures. The Russian tsar freed the serfs, supported heavy industry, invested in building railroads, and encouraged foreign capital and technological expertise.

Latin America did not undergo significant industrialization in the nineteenth century. Instead, conservative landowning elites provided raw materials and cash crops to the world market. Economic growth in Latin America was financed by foreign capital and depended on decisions made in Europe and North America, a form of economic colonialism.

Theme 5:
Development and Transformation of Social Structures

Industrialization radically changed the social structure of countries; it was the first major change of social structures since the First Civilizations developed agriculture and a stratified society based on the ownership of land. Britain was the first industrialized nation, and its class system changed with some internal turmoil, but without a revolution. The landowning aristocracy continued to control much of the land, leased to tenant farmers, and profited from the rapidly growing population's need for food. The aristocracy slowly declined, however, as wealthy urban dwellers (bankers, financiers, manufacturers, and business owners) became more dominant. By the end of the nineteenth century, business held control of the government, but aristocrats still retained high social prestige.

The middle class grew not only in numbers but in importance. It was composed of those in many professions that did not exist in prior centuries as well as more traditional university-educated men (and much later women). The upper middle class – bankers, factory and mine owners, and merchants – often assimilated or married into the aristocracy. The wealthier middle classes also often held political office and sent their sons to prestigious universities, such as Oxford or Cambridge. The more numerous "middle" middle class was made up of educated professionals, such as doctors, lawyers, engineers, scientists, teachers, journalists, and smaller business owners. Members of the middle classes often supported liberalism, characterized by support for constitutional government, private property, free trade, and moderate social reform. They also championed respectability, combining notions of social class, virtuous behavior, thrift, and hard work. Many came to believe that they prospered because of their enterprising spirit and that the poverty that others suffered was caused by laziness, intemperance, or misconduct. Wealthier middle-class women moved almost exclusively into domestic roles and became the primary arbiters of family consumption. They managed households run by servants, supervised childrearing, engaged in charitable activities, and pursued "refined" tasks such as music, embroidery, or drawing.

Lower middle-class families distinguished themselves from the laboring classes by working in service sector jobs. Many of these jobs (such as telephone operator or secretary) became the exclusive domain of women and were paid lower and had less prestige than jobs held by men. Lower middle-class women often left the workforce after marriage and certainly after having children.

The working class varied greatly, from highly skilled craftsmen at the top to unskilled laborers at the bottom. Their lives were often confined to urban slums which were overcrowded, filthy, polluted, and disease ridden. One of the major public works undertaken during the nineteenth century was the creation of sewers and clean, piped water in London. The pace and conditions of labor changed drastically for people who moved from rural areas into factories; machines set the pace, breaks were few, hours were long, working conditions hazardous, and discipline was strictly enforced by managers.

Women and children were among the first factory workers in textile mills and in the coal mines. Women were not permitted in supervisory positions, nor were they welcome in labor organizations. Those who did not work in factories often found jobs as domestic servants. Upon marriage, a working-class husband expected his wife to remain at home, but she continued to contribute to the family income by doing laundry, sewing, or taking in borders in addition to the domestic tasks she performed for her family.

Because of often intolerable working conditions, workers (especially skilled workers) sometimes responded by organizing associations or labor unions, pushing for political reform and voting rights. There were also occasional strikes and protests that at times included destroying the machines. Government forces put down strikes and violence. Reformers called for better treatment; Robert Owen created a model factory town for his workers in New Lanark, Scotland, while more radical socialists such as Karl Marx believed that a class revolt, in which workers would seize control of society from the "capitalists" who oppressed them, was imminent. The rise of labor parties and broadening of the right to vote diffused revolutionary movements among workers in Western Europe, as did improving working conditions and a higher standard of living.

Nationalism also helped diffuse class tensions by encouraging laborers to identify as German, French, or English and not as members of an international class of workers. Social equality eroded in the United States after industrialization, and some people saw the inequalities as an example of "survival of the fittest." Only in Russia did actual class revolution take place (see Chapter 21).

Guided Reading Questions for Chapter 17

Seeking the Main Point In what ways did the Industrial Revolution mark a sharp break with the past? In what ways did it continue earlier patterns? (Page 738)

Change In what respects did the roots of the Industrial Revolution lie within Europe? In what ways did that transformation have global roots? (Page 741)

Comparison What was distinctive about Britain that may help explain its status as the breakthrough point of the Industrial Revolution? (Page 744)

Change How did the Industrial Revolution transform British society? (Page 747)

Change How did Britain's middle classes change during the nineteenth century? (Page 747)

Change How did Karl Marx under-stand the Industrial Revolution? In what ways did his ideas have an impact in the industrializing world of the nineteenth century? (Page 752)

Comparison What were the differences between industrialization in the United States and that in Russia? (Page 760)

Explanation Why did Marxist socialism not take root in the United States? (Page 761)

Change What factors contributed to the making of a revolutionary situation in Russia by the beginning of the twentieth century? (Page 764)

Practicing AP® Historical Thinking What was common to industrialization everywhere, and in what ways did it vary from place to place? (Page 766)

Connection In what ways was Latin America linked to the global economy of the nineteenth century, and what was the impact of these links? (Page 768)

Comparison Did Latin America follow or diverge from the historical path of Europe during the nineteenth century? (Page 770)

NOTES:

CHAPTER EIGHTEEN
Colonial Encounters in Asia, Africa, and Oceania 1750–1950

AP® World History Key Concepts

5.1: Industrialization and Global Capitalism

I. Industrialization fundamentally changed how goods were produced.

II. New patterns of global trade and production developed and further integrated the global economy as industrialists sought raw materials and new markets for the increasing amount and array of goods produced in their factories.

III. To facilitate investments at all levels of industrial production, financiers developed and expanded various financial institutions.

IV. There were major developments in transportation and communication, including railroads, steamships, telegraphs, and canals.

V. The development and spread of global capitalism led to a variety of responses.

VI. The ways in which people organized themselves into societies also underwent significant transformations in industrialized states due to the fundamental restructuring of the global economy.

The "new imperialism" brought much of the world into global trade networks in the nineteenth century, either through direct colonial rule or through economic colonialism. New methods of transportation such as steamships, canals, and railroads greatly reduced the amount of time needed to move goods from the far corners of the earth back to the industrialized nations. Refrigeration allowed food crops to be moved long distances as well. The undersea telegraph cable allowed far-flung economic and governmental institutions to have almost instantaneous access to information.

Newly industrialized countries of Europe, Japan, and the United States sought new sources of raw materials and markets for their manufactured goods. European countries used their surplus capital to invest in building infrastructure such as railroads and canals in their colonies and in "little Europes," regions such as Argentina or the United States where native people had largely been replaced with those of European stock. Some regions, such as the African Congo under King Leopold II of Belgium, forced villagers to go into the forest to collect rubber instead of growing food crops. In Dutch-controlled Indonesia, the culture system — an economic system where landowners could require local farmers to grow export crops as a means to pay their taxes — limited people's ability to grow enough food and led to famine. The demand for cash crops spurred the growth of plantation agriculture in many colonies, displacing small subsistence farms and forcing the local people to work for low wages on these large farms. Some regions, such as British South Africa, also moved native men into mining camps to extract mineral resources under harsh conditions. Often, native people were forced onto marginal "homelands," such as Bantustans in South Africa or reservations in the United States, and were subject to restrictions on movement and limitations of rights. In South Africa, the large but still minority white population set up strict legal separation between races known as apartheid.

5.2: Imperialism and Nation-State Formation

I. Industrializing powers established transoceanic empires.

II. Imperialism influenced state formation and contraction around the world.

III. New racial ideologies, especially Social Darwinism, facilitated and justified imperialism.

Competition between industrialized nations for sources of raw materials, markets for manufactured goods, and places to invest capital brought most of Africa, India, Oceania, and parts of Southeast Asia under direct rule. Often, colonization followed trading companies such as the British East India or Dutch East India companies. New, supposedly scientific racial theories, including social Darwinism, were used to justify subjugating less technologically advanced regions as was the stated desire to spread what Europeans viewed as their superior civilization and religion. The already-weakened Mughal Empire lost control of most of India to the British. In South Africa, both the Boers, who were descendants of Dutch cape-colony farmers, and the Zulus were defeated by the British, who also established settler colonies in Australia and New Zealand. An industrializing and modernizing Japan staked out its claim to imperial status by colonizing Korea and Taiwan. Southeast Asian kingdoms, including Vietnam, lost sovereignty to the French, who also conquered large expanses of land in northern Africa. Russia and the United States continued their transcontinental territorial expansion as well, replacing and isolating indigenous people.

5.3: Nationalism, Revolution, and Reform

I. The rise and diffusion of Enlightenment thought that questioned established traditions in all areas of life often preceded the revolutions and rebellions against existing governments.

See Chapter 16 for further discussion of this key concept.

II. Beginning in the eighteenth century, peoples around the world developed a new sense of commonality based on language, religion, social customs, and territory. These newly imagined national communities linked this identity with the borders of the state, while governments used this idea to unite diverse populations.

See Chapters 16, 17, and 19 for further discussion of this key concept.

III. Increasing discontent with imperial rule propelled reformist and revolutionary movements.

See Chapter 16 for further discussion of this key concept.

IV. The global spread of European political and social thought and the increasing number of rebellions stimulated new transnational ideologies and solidarities.

Just as Napoleon's advancing French armies spurred the rise of nationalism in conquered territories of Eastern Europe, so too did New Imperialism spread reactions that ultimately led to anticolonial movements. Some local elites found that cooperation with European rulers allowed them to maintain their elite status and gave them limited autonomy. Other groups, such as the Zulu, Shona, or Ethiopians, fought colonial takeover or rebelled against colonial rule. See Map 18.1, page 795, for Asian colonies and rebellions, and Map 18.2, page 796, for African colonies and rebellions. European-educated colonial men also learned about the ideals of self-determination, constitutional government, and protection of individual rights, which led them to question why those rights did not apply to people in colonies. They later formed a cadre of liberal voices seeking independence and nationhood. Europeans often created new ethnic identities in the regions they conquered to facilitate governing, such as creating tribal units in Africa based on linguistic groups. These ethnic identities often later formed the basis of anticolonial resistance or even attempted new definitions such as pan-Africanism. *See Chapters 16, 17, and 19 for further discussion of this key concept.*

5.4: Global Migration

I. Migration in many cases was influenced by changes in demography in both industrialized and unindustrialized societies that presented challenges to existing patterns of living.

II. Migrants relocated for a variety of reasons.

III. The large-scale nature of migration, especially in the nineteenth century, produced a variety of consequences and reactions to the increasingly diverse societies on the part of migrants and the existing populations.

Several types of migration took place during the nineteenth century. The growth of cities accelerated, whether by displaced rural workers seeking employment in industry or by the migration of displaced people to colonial capitals such as Lagos, Batavia, Calcutta, or Singapore. The colonial creation of a cash economy required local people to work for wages, often living in barracks-like arrangements far from home villages to be near plantations or mines; this arrangement was especially common in South Africa. Empires also encouraged long-distance movements of people to other colonies in order to meet labor needs; for example, some Indians and Chinese were transported by the British to work in plantations in the Caribbean or Southeast Asia, sometimes replacing the labor of freed slaves. Since many of the migrants were young, able-bodied men, gender and family life in home villages was disrupted. Women often maintained traditional female tasks while also taking on previously male tasks, and polygyny (the practice of having more than one wife) increased in some regions.

Europeans also migrated to colonies whether as administrators or (to improve their standard of living) as plantation owners. Some Europeans came to settler colonies, such as Australia, New Zealand, North America, and Argentina, and largely replaced local peoples. Displaced rural peasants from countries such as Italy were invited to migrate to Latin American countries to work in agriculture; often they remained for a while and then returned to Europe. Not all migrants were welcomed by existing residents who saw this new labor source as a threat. Anti-immigrant movements formed and some governments enforced limitations on immigration from certain countries, as the United States did when it limited the number of Chinese immigrants.

Theme 1:
Interaction Between Humans and the Environment

The need of industrialized nations for raw materials and cash crops led to environmental degradation in both Africa and Asia. In the Irrawaddy and Mekong River deltas of Southeast Asia, British and French colonizers encouraged massive rice production by improving irrigation and transportation and by enacting legislation that favored small farmers. Rice production soared, providing exports to feed people in other areas, but at great environmental cost: mangrove forests and swamps were destroyed, as well as the fish they sheltered, which also cut off a source of food for local people; dikes and canals stopped the flow of nutrient-rich silt into the delta, depleting the soil; and large amounts of methane gas (linked to global warming) was released. In Africa, rich farmlands were taken over by white farmers for plantations, and Africans were often removed to less-desirable land, such as the Bantustans in South Africa. The Bantustans were overcrowded, soil fertility declined, and forests were cut from hillsides, leading to erosion.

Another environmental consequence was the massive movement of people, sometimes in search of improving their financial situation and sometimes at the behest of colonial powers. Colonial administrations demanded cash to pay taxes and fees, while at the same time, native people were removed from the richest farmland. Millions of these displaced people sought work in European-owned plantations and mines, dividing families and upsetting gender balances and roles. Sometimes workers were transported overseas; millions of Indians, Chinese, and Japanese migrated to Southeast Asia to work on plantations growing sugarcane, tea, rubber, tobacco, and sisal (used to make rope). Life was harsh, and pay was low; poverty and disease led to high death rates. British authorities also moved South Asians to the West Indies (Trinidad and Jamaica) where their labor often replaced that of freed slaves. Impoverished Chinese workers went to tin mines in Malaysia and gold mines in Australia, Peru, and California. These migrants were often subjected to discrimination. African and Asian migrants also moved to large, racially segregated cities in the colonial world, hoping to find employment and upward mobility. *See Chapter 17 for discussion of the environmental consequences of the Industrial Revolution.*

Theme 2:
Development and Interaction of Cultures

The dominance of Europeans led to cultural changes as groups absorbed European educations, responded to European missionaries, and created new identities. European education was offered in colonies, often at the hands of Christian missionaries, and was seen as a way for native people to modernize and achieve better positions in colonial society. More rarely, young men were sent to Europe for university educations and returned to form the core of doctors, lawyers, and lower-level bureaucrats in their home countries. Europeans viewed this process as a way to "civilize" the natives, bring the fruits of superior European culture, and prepare the way for "progress."

Some people in Asia or Africa embraced European culture, speaking French or English, wearing European clothes, learning about European literature, and seeing themselves as a modernizing vanguard for their societies and potentially as equal partners with Europeans. However, European racism usually prevented true upward mobility for educated colonial subjects, leading to frustration, resentment, and ultimately to anticolonial movements in the twentieth century. In India, western education led to religious reforms, revisiting and reinterpreting Brahmin texts to create a more uniform form of Hinduism out of numerous local beliefs and rituals.

Many colonial subjects received their educations, as well as health care, through missionaries spreading Christianity. Christianity was thus widely associated with modernization and education. Missionaries did create some cultural and social conflicts over gender and sexual activity as they attempted to enforce Western ideas about appropriate behavior. Christianity in Africa became Africanized, which often led missionaries to protest against "backsliding." The newly defined view of Hinduism was offered to the materialistic West as a form of spiritual renewal by Swami Vivekananda, who attended the Parliament of World Religions in 1893. In India, the British supported the Hindu renewal process, which set up future divisions in the subcontinent by Muslims who were thus seen as a separate community.

Perhaps the most profound impact of Western culture was its conception of ethnicity, begun in Europe as a form of nationalism following the revolutionary period, and a newly defined "scientific" view of race. Europeans began to define cultures in Africa and Asia by language and ethnic group, sometimes introducing those concepts for the first time to local people. It was to Europeans' advantage to denigrate African kings by calling them "chiefs" and their kingdoms as "tribes" because tribal culture was seen as less civilized and helped justify European racism and conquest. Later, Africans themselves adopted some of the new linguistic and ethnic identities. *See Chapters 16 and 19 for additional discussion of this theme.*

Theme 3:
State-Building, Expansion, and Conflict

The Industrial Revolution and the rise of nationalism sparked a new wave of European expansion known as "new imperialism." Superior factory-made weapons (such as repeating rifles and machine guns), new methods of transportation (such as steamships and railroads), new methods of communication (such as the telegraph), and new medical advances (such as quinine to treat tropical diseases) allowed European empires to acquire most of Africa and much of Asia. In addition, the nationalistic competition between European nations played itself out in the scramble to acquire colonies that might provide raw materials or markets for manufactured goods. European leaders also felt that new markets were needed to keep manufacturing and employment at a high level in order to prevent social upheavals or revolutions.

Imperial powers justified their conquests by claiming they brought progress and the benefits of civilization to lesser peoples and developed a new kind of supposedly scientific racism to further justify their claims to superiority: social Darwinism. Social Darwinism, which was not part of Darwin's theories of evolution, claimed that human cultures operated under the concept of "survival of the fittest," which implied that when technologically superior European nations took over control of other cultures, those cultures were less fit or even racially inferior. It thus became an obligation for Europeans to spread civilization to inferior peoples.

In general, Europeans preferred informal control through economic penetration rather than through direct military conquest, but the threat of European military intervention was always present. In India and Indonesia, for example, the British East India and Dutch East India companies initially took advantage of fragmented local rule to make economically advantageous agreements, only later to be followed up with direct colonial rule as needed to enforce European "rights." Some regions were colonized with little overt conflict among European powers, such as the "scramble for Africa," where European leaders agreed on which areas of the continent would be open to each country. Although resistance was strong (for example, from the Zulus and Boers), Ethiopia and Liberia were the only African countries to escape colonization. In Southeast Asia, only Siam (now Thailand) managed to retain its independence.

Certain groups perceived benefits in cooperation with colonial powers, including those who wanted to join European military forces or colonial administrations. In addition, in many areas, colonial rulers relied on local intermediaries such as Indian princes, Muslim emirs, or African rulers. Some people rebelled against colonial rule, as in the famous Indian Rebellion of 1857–1858, sometimes known as the Sepoy Mutiny. (See Map 18.1 and Map 18.2 on pp. 795-796 for examples of rebellions in Africa and Asia.)

Australia and New Zealand became British settler colonies like North America. As in North America, the native populations of Australia and New Zealand had been isolated from European diseases and so died at an alarming rate following contact, providing an opportunity for European settlers to replace them. The United States continued its imperial expansion to the west, sometimes exterminating Native Americans or moving them to reservations. Further, wars with Spain and Mexico also increased U.S. land holdings in the west and the Philippine Islands. Some freed American slaves moved to a West African territory they called Liberia and there became a colonial elite. Following European examples, Japan also became an imperial nation after undergoing its own industrialization by taking over Korea and Taiwan. Russia continued its territorial expansion in Central Asia. *See Chapters 17 and 19 for additional discussion of this theme.*

Theme 4:
Creation, Expansion, and Interaction of Economic Systems

The New Imperialism brought more regions of the world into the global economy. The search for the raw materials (such as rubber, tin, copper, sisal, cotton, cocoa, and palm oils) needed for industrial development as well as other items that had value in global markets (such as coffee, tea, cacao, sugar, gold, and diamonds) led to colonial expansion. Further, since new sources of food were needed to supply workers in colonial plantations and mines, intensive cultivation of rice and other food crops were encouraged in some regions such as Southeast Asia. Many colonial economies involved forced labor on plantations or in mines or on state projects such as road and railroad building, constructing government buildings, or transporting goods. King Leopold II's Congo colony forced locals to collect rubber under such cruel and brutal conditions that other European states objected and forced Leopold to cede the colony to Belgium. The colonial government of the Dutch-controlled East Indies (now Indonesia) required peasants to cultivate 20 percent of their land in cash crops such as sugar or coffee to pay their taxes to the state, which then sold the products at a great profit on the open market. This cultivation system contributed to famines among the peasants. In German East Africa, peasant sabotage ended the attempt to force local peoples to grow of cotton. *See Chapters 17 and 19 for additional discussion of this theme.*

Theme 5: Development and Transformation of Social Structures

Turning colonies into cash economies as well as using coerced labor or low-paid labor in plantations and mines led to massive upheaval in social and gender roles in Africa. In mining regions, men were brought in for months or years, living apart from their families in barracks. In plantation economies, men were used in the cultivation of cash crops. This left women to assume what had been traditionally male economic roles, such as herding, clearing land, or growing some types of crops, while also maintaining traditional female roles such as childrearing, food preparation, planting, weeding, and harvesting kitchen crops. In some areas, as many as 40 to 50 percent of able-bodied males were absent from rural villages because they were working in mines or on plantations. In some regions, women used this gender imbalance to their advantage, moving into small-scale trade and marketing or growing crops that had cash value and marketing them.

Men educated in Western schools, which were often church-run, formed a new group in colonized countries. Some became colonial civil servants or enlisted in the military or police; others went to Europe to obtain university educations and returned as professionals or journalists, often forming the elite in post-colonial societies. *See Chapters 17 and 19 for additional discussion of this theme.*

Guided Reading Questions for Chapter 18

Seeking the Main Point In what ways did colonial rule transform the societies that it encompassed? (Page 788)

Change In what ways did the Industrial Revolution shape the character of nineteenth-century European imperialism? (Page 789)

Change What contributed to changing European views of Asians and Africans in the nineteenth century? (Page 791)

Comparison In what different ways was colonial rule established in various parts of Africa and Asia? (Page 793)

Explanation Why might subject people choose to cooperate with the colonial regime? What might prompt them to violent rebellion or resistance? (Page 799)

Comparison What was distinctive about European colonial empires of the nineteenth century? (Page 800)

Connection How did the policies of colonial states change the economic lives of their subjects? (Page 802)

Change How did cash-crop agriculture transform the lives of colonized peoples? (Page 805)

Change What kinds of wage labor were available in the colonies? Why might people take part in it? How did doing so change their lives? (Page 808)

Change How were the lives of African women altered by colonial economies? (Page 809)

Change Did colonial rule bring "economic progress" in its wake? (Page 812)

Practicing AP® Historical Thinking In what different ways did the colonial experience reshape the economic lives of Asian and African societies? (Page 813)

Change What impact did Western education have on colonial societies? (Page 814)

Change What were the attractions of Christianity within some colonial societies? (Page 816)

Change How and why did Hinduism emerge as a distinct religious tradition during the colonial era in India? (Page 820)

Change In what ways were "race" and "tribe" new identities in colonial Africa? (Page 820)

NOTES:

CHAPTER NINETEEN

Empires in Collision:
Europe, the Middle East, and East Asia, 1800–1900

AP® World History Key Concepts

5.1: Industrialization and Global Capitalism

II. New patterns of global trade and production developed and further integrated the global economy as industrialists sought raw materials and new markets for the increasing amount and array of goods produced in their factories.

V. The development and spread of global capitalism led to a variety of responses.

Industrialization and the aggressive expansion of European states changed the Eurasian trading networks. Industrial states sought entry into the large Asia markets for their manufactured goods. At first, China, India, Japan, and the Ottoman Empire resisted these incursions. China especially refused to accept what they viewed as inferior goods in trade for traditional Chinese exports such as silk, tea, and porcelain. In the eighteenth century, China was able to forbid European merchants from entering the interior and limited their contact to a few ports along the coast. In the nineteenth century, however, following a series of rebellions and the Opium Wars, China had to submit to increasing European control of their markets.

Other Asian countries had to compete with European factory-made goods, which drove out local artisans whose work could not compete in price. By using a combination of military might and even smuggling, Europeans were able to force large Asian populations to become markets for factory-made goods and revert to becoming suppliers of raw materials to the factories of the West. While the Ottomans, Chinese, and Mughals attempted to reject, at one level or another, European control of worldwide trade networks, Japan chose to invest massively in creating its own industrial revolution and soon joined the West as a major producer and imperial power.

5.2: Imperialism and Nation-State Formation

I. Industrializing powers established transoceanic empires.

II. Imperialism influenced state formation and contraction around the world.

Asian empires, with the exception of the already fragmented Mughal Empire, did not succumb to direct colonization by Western industrial powers. Instead, they became "economic colonies" whose governments were unable to protect their people from economic exploitation. Forced to submit to unequal treaties requiring favorable trade concessions, the Qing dynasty and the Ottoman Empire were further weakened politically. Newly emerging ethnic nationalism led sections of the Ottoman Empire to revolt and break away. Japan, faced with similar threats from industrialized Western states, underwent radical political, economic, and social modernization and became an imperial state in its own right.

5.3: Nationalism, Revolution and Reform

III. Increasing discontent with imperial rule propelled reformist and revolutionary movements.

IV. The global spread of European political and social thought and the increasing number of rebellions stimulated new transnational ideologies and solidarities.

At the same time that they faced threats from Western powers, the Ottoman Empire and the Qing dynasty in China faced internal challenges as well. The Ottomans faced rebellion from ethnic nationalist groups within the empire, especially in the Balkans and Egypt, while the Qing dynasty was opposed by both peasant revolts and ethnic Chinese who saw the Qing as foreign rulers. The Japanese faced a short-lived regional revolt, but from conservative samurai and not from an ethnic nationalist movement. All three nations, when confronted with aggressive and militarily superior Western states, had to decide the extent to which they would modernize or Westernize their governments and economies. China did not respond until the nineteenth century with a self-strengthening movement, which borrowed "cautiously" from the West, but this movement was diverted by conservative landowning gentry. After the Boxer Uprising, reformists wanted to turn to Western political systems as a model, seeking limited constitutional rule and wider involvement by the people. Chinese nationalism rejected not only Western imperialism but also the foreign Qing dynasty which was overthrown in 1911.

The Ottomans also faced conservative forces such as the Janissaries and *ulama* who were opposed to Westernization and modernization. Reform-minded groups such as the Young Ottomans and the Young Turks believed that Islam was compatible with modernization. The Tanzimat reforms attempted to establish European-style secular courts and legal systems, but the sultan soon returned to autocratic rule. After a military coup, the Young Turks pushed forward with reforms along Western lines: schools and courts were secularized and political parties and elections were introduced. However, the reformers also promoted a national identity based on Turkish language and culture, which further alienated other ethnic groups outside of the Anatolian homeland.

Intense nationalism was also the source of reform in Japan when confronted with Western powers. After succumbing at first to unequal treaties, a group of samurai deposed the shogun and returned the country to rule by the young, reform-minded emperor Meiji. To achieve national unity, the role of the emperor was elevated, and the daimyo and samurai renounced their status and special privileges. A constitution was written in 1889; it was modeled on Germany's constitution, with an elected parliament that was advisory only, political parties, and democratic ideals but with power vested in the military-supported emperor and members of the oligarchy, a select group of men who controlled most decisions.

5.4: Global Migration

See Chapters 17 and 18 for discussion of global migration.

Theme 1: Interaction Between Humans and the Environment

China's population quadrupled between 1650 and 1850 without corresponding gains in agricultural production, leading to ever-smaller peasant farms as well as famine and a series of peasant uprisings. Japan, like other industrial powers, needed increased access to raw materials that could not be supplied in their tiny island nation; as a result, it colonized parts of Manchuria, Korea, and Taiwan. *See Chapters 17 and 18 for a detailed discussion of the impact of the Industrial Revolution and imperialism on this theme.*

Theme 2:
Development and Interaction of Cultures

Chinese culture, long centered on Confucian values and the conservative nature of the landed gentry, did not easily adapt to Western intrusions. As Qing society became weaker in the nineteenth century, some argued for a return to traditional Han Chinese culture (in opposition to the Qing dynasty's Manchu culture or borrowing from the West). The charismatic leader Hong Xiuquan, who believed that he was the younger brother of Jesus and supported revolutionary changes in society along with millenarian beliefs, led the Taiping Uprising (1850–1864), rejected Confucian, Daoist, and Buddhist beliefs, and called for a very different society instead of a return to an idealized past.

The Ottoman Empire also rejected much of Western culture, which it felt was inferior to Islamic culture. Both the conservative *ulama* (religious scholars) and the Janissaries rejected reforms, believing that to support modernization meant Westernization, including materialism and Christianity. The Tanzimat reforms, however, included new elementary and secondary schools that were based on European models and a more secular and less Islamic character of the state. Progressive women held salons, similar to those of Enlightenment France, where both male and female intellectuals discussed the future. In Japan, Meiji reformers did not see the need to reject core beliefs in order to embrace modernization, as had many reformers in China and the Ottoman Empire.

Japan selectively adopted Western culture and embraced its educational system, its dances and music, its movies and newspapers, and its dress and hairstyles. Shinto became an official state religion, with the Emperor, who was still viewed as the direct descendent of the sun goddess Amaterasu, at its head.

Theme 3:
State-Building, Expansion, and Conflict

Both the Qing dynasty and the Ottoman Empire in the nineteenth century endured contraction, fragmentation, and rebellion in addition to economic and political encroachment by Western industrial and imperial powers, but they maintained formal independence until the twentieth century. Japan, on the other hand, became an imperializing and industrialized nation. All of these states (as well as Persia, Ethiopia, and Siam) had to deal with European military power and the political competition between states; became intertwined with the global networks of capitalism, trade, investment, and migration set up by Western industrial powers; had to adapt to or resist Western culture and languages; and had to determine to what extent they wanted to modernize.

China, under the control of the Qing dynasty (a foreign occupying power from Manchuria), underwent an internal crisis in the nineteenth century. Centralized government gave way to control by local landowners who created their own armies to try to extract more revenue from already destitute peasants. The imperial administration showed the classic signs of a declining dynasty: failure to put down rebellions or protect from foreign incursions plus the inability to collect revenue, prevent floods, prevent corruption, protect internal trade, or ensure that enough food was grown. Peasant revolts such as the Taiping or the Boxer uprisings devastated the country, passed more power to the gentry, and were only put down with the support of Western militaries. The Opium Wars further weakened imperial rule, leading to unequal treaties that also granted territorial and trade concessions to Western powers. China was being dismembered (see Map 19.1, p. 842) and no longer controlled its own destiny.

The Ottoman Empire was similarly in decline and became known as the "sick man of Europe." Ottoman power and territory was diminished by Russian, British, Austrian, and French aggression (See Map 19.2, p. 845), but the Turks managed to avoid direct colonial rule. The Ottoman Empire also suffered from the inability to collect revenue, a loss of control to provincial warlords, and a loss of their military might. However, unlike China, the Ottoman rulers were not seen as foreigners; they were Turkic and Muslim like the core of their empire. There were several attempts to reform the empire. In the late eighteenth century, Sultan Selim III brought in European advisers and techniques to begin reforming the military, but opposition from the *ulama* and the Janissaries led to his murder. The Tanzimat reforms of the nineteenth century attempted to create a stronger, centralized state by encouraging factories, conducting land reform, creating telegraphs, steamships, and railroads, and creating new Western-style secular law codes, courts, and educational system. Further, the reforms created a new national identity, one that was not based on ethnicity or religious group, by removing distinctions between Muslims and non-Muslims. The intelligentsia, lower-level government officials, and military officers, most of whom had Western educations, were called the "Young Ottomans." They supported a democratic, constitutional government to strengthen the state from European aggression and felt that Islam could accommodate Western scientific knowledge while escaping its materialism. By the end of the century, the government had reverted to autocratic rule but was opposed by the "Young Turks," drawn from the same groups that formed the Young Ottomans. A military coup brought them to power in 1908, and they pushed for secular education, secular courts and legal system, political parties, Turkish as the official language (instead of Arabic), and the same laws regardless of religion. Turkish nationalism led to increased nationalism from other ethnic groups in the empire and led to its dismemberment after World War I.

Japan embraced modernization and Westernization. After Commodore Perry arrived with his black fleet of ships armed with cannon, the Tokugawa shogunate was forced into unequal treaties, which ended Japan's policy of isolation. The Meiji restoration, led by young, progressive samurai, restored power to the emperor in order to save Japan from foreign domination by radically transforming and Westernizing Japanese government and society. To achieve national unity, the daimyo (landowning nobility) were replaced by regional governors, and the samurai warrior class was abolished. The army was built by conscripting all social classes. All Japanese were legally commoners and equal as subjects of the emperor. "Civilization and Enlightenment" was the motto that governed far-reaching reforms; a constitution, based on Germany's constitution, was drafted with a parliament in an advisory role and ultimate power in the hands of the emperor, who was supported by the military and an oligarchy. After undergoing similar economic reforms, Japan emerged as an industrial, imperial state; it captured colonies in Korea, Manchuria, and Taiwan as well as other islands nearby. Japan's defeat of Russia in 1905 sparked rebellion in Russia and nationalistic hope in regions controlled or threatened by Europeans, such as Egypt, Aceh (Indonesia), and the Ottoman Empire. *See Chapters 16, 17, and 18 for additional discussion of this theme.*

Theme 4:
Creation, Expansion, and Interaction of Economic Systems

Backed by wealth generated by the Industrial Revolution, Western powers were aggressively seeking control of trade systems, new markets for manufactured goods, and new supplies of raw materials. At the same time, smaller or more fragmented states (such as Mughal India, the East Indies, and most of Africa) were taken over and colonized. Asian states such as the Ottoman Empire, Qing dynasty China, and Japan were faced with similar problems — how to modernize their economies and states in order to prevent European domination.

China responded slowly to the changing economic system that no longer placed it in the center and in control. As government control weakened, the ability to collect taxes also dwindled. The country was wracked by rebellion, which also disrupted the economy. The introduction of smuggled opium by the British into China not only created millions of addicts but also drained silver from the economy and created a huge trade imbalance, which was something new for the Middle Kingdom (see Snapshot: Chinese/British Trade at Canton, p. 838). The subsequent Opium Wars left Europeans in control of the economy, able to extract raw materials, enter into inland trade, and build railroads to export goods coast. Foreign goods and investments flooded into China, destroying the livelihoods of local craftsmen and preventing businessmen developing capital to fund an industrial revolution. The "self-strengthening" movement attempted modest reforms, such as repairing dikes and irrigation canals, expanding coal mining, creating a telegraph system, creating factories to make steel and textiles, and building modern arsenals and shipyards. Conservative landowning gentry feared even this limited economic progress, and much of the capital, machinery, and expertise for economic reform came from foreigners.

The Ottoman Empire, in closer contact with Europe, also launched "defensive modernization" in response to growing European economic power. As portions of the empire fell away, revenue became a problem, exacerbated by loss of control of the lucrative Afro-Eurasian commerce as Europeans used direct sea routes to East Asia. Further, Ottoman artisans were hard-hit by competition from cheap European manufactured goods. In debt, the Empire had to rely on foreign investment for any economic development, which led to foreign control of much of Ottoman revenue generation. The Tanzimat reforms encouraged infrastructure growth (such as railroads and telegraphs), steamships, a postal service, and resettlement of agricultural land. War with Russia led to reversion to older forms, and the Ottomans, like the Chinese, were unable to create an industrial economy.

Japan used state support to create a modern industrial economy – the only country outside of the West to do so in the nineteenth century. New Meiji governors replaced the daimyo and collected taxes for the state. Travel and trade were opened up again, ending Tokugawa restrictions. Studying Western science and technology was encouraged, both by sending Japanese for schooling abroad and by encouraging foreign experts to come to Japan. The government established factories (especially textiles), which it later sold to investors, created railroads, a postal system, a national currency and banking. Large firms called *zaibatsu* led in the manufacture of textiles, munitions, and industrial goods – all done without the massive foreign debt incurred by the Ottomans. By 1905, Japan's military reform and new armaments allowed it to defeat Russia in the Russo-Japanese War. *See Chapters 17 and 18 for additional discussion of this theme.*

Theme 5: Development and Transformation of Social Structures

Rapid population growth left China with an impoverished, over-taxed, and starving peasant class, which led to several rebellions, including the Taiping and the Boxer rebellions. The landed gentry was extremely conservative and prevented radical urbanizing or industrializing reforms, but the "self-strengthening" movement was able to restore social order in the countryside by supporting landlords in their repair of irrigation systems. Educated Chinese felt as though no change was possible under the empire, so they joined clubs, formed study groups, and read newspapers in an attempt to decide what reforms would help China. While traditional gender roles were maintained during this time period, some revolutionary groups such as the Taiping Rebellion allowed women to fight. Some educated women rejected traditional gender roles as part of the rejection of the Qing dynasty and the failure of traditional Chinese government and society to stand up to foreign imperialism.

Ottoman society underwent more social changes than Chinese society. As Turkish ethnic nationalism became more important to the Ottoman state, regions of the empire such as Greece, the Balkans, and North Africa redefined their own ethnic identity in opposition and began independence movements that further weakened the empire. A core issue for Ottoman modernization and Westernization became whether these reforms were compatible with the majority religion of Islam. Conservative forces within the empire, such as the *ulama* and the Janissaries, held to traditional views of the state as fundamentally Islamic and opposed secularization. Reformers such as the Young Ottomans argued that Muslim society could accept economic, social, and political reforms in a modern Islamic framework. The Young Turks restricted polygamy and permitted women to attend university, wear Western clothing, and obtain divorces.

Japanese society underwent a profound restructuring after the Meiji Restoration. The old Confucian-based social order ended. The daimyo and samurai surrendered their positions and became common citizens equal under law with all others, including the previously scorned merchant class. Many former samurai found themselves new roles in the army, government bureaucracy, or industry. All classes were conscripted into the emperor's new army. A conservative group of samurai did rebel in 1877 (also called the Satsuma Rebellion) but did little to hold back the winds of change sweeping through the country. However, rural peasants did not benefit as much from the modernization program, leading to violence in 1883–1884. Partly as a result of this rural poverty, many farmers sold or sent their daughters to work in the new textile mills under harsh conditions and low wages. Rates of rural female infanticide also grew. Women were still excluded from politics, although education was becoming even more common. *See Chapters 17 and 18 for additional discussion of this theme.*

Guided Reading Questions for Chapter 19

Seeking the Main Point What differences can you identify in how China, the Ottoman Empire, and Japan experienced Western imperialism and responded to it? How might you account for those differences? (Page 834)

Causation What accounts for the massive peasant rebellions of nineteenth-century China? (Page 836)

Connection How did Western pressures stimulate change in China during the nineteenth century? (Page 839)

Connection What strategies did China adopt to confront its various problems? In what ways did these strategies reflect China's own history and culture as well as the new global order? (Page 843)

Change What lay behind the decline of the Ottoman Empire in the nineteenth century? (Page 845)

Change In what different ways did the Ottoman state respond to its various problems? (Page 846)

Comparison In what different ways did various groups define the Ottoman Empire during the nineteenth century? (Page 848)

Practicing AP® Historical Thinking In what ways were the histories of China and the Ottoman Empire similar during the nineteenth century? And how did they differ? (Page 851)

Change In what ways was Japan changing during the Tokugawa era? (Page 853)

Change In what respects was Japan's nineteenth- century transformation revolutionary? (Page 856)

Connection How did Japan's relation-ship to the larger world change during its modernization process? (Page 859)

NOTES:

UNIT 1
A Review of AP® World History & Ways of the World for the AP® Course, Third Edition

AP® WORLD HISTORY PERIOD SIX
Accelerating Global Change and Realignments, c. 1900 to the Present

PART SIX
The Most Recent Century, 1900–present

AP® World History Key Concepts
  6.1:   Science and the Environment
  6.2:   Global Conflicts and Their Consequences
  6.3:   New Conceptualizations of Global Economy, Society, and Culture

The Big Picture: Since World War I: A New Period in World History?

World historians categorize events into periods (eras or ages) in an effort to make coherent the changes and continuities in that period that affect the lives of individuals, social groups, nations, civilizations – or the entire panorama of human history. The artificial beginning or ending dates are "imposed by scholars on a continuously flowing stream of events." AP® World History recognizes that altering the periodization can change the historical narrative, since creating periods highlights particular events, movements, cultures, or themes, and that the context in which historians write can affect their interpretations.

The "Big Picture" question, then, for Part Six of *Ways of the World* is whether the century following 1914 constitutes a separate period in world history. There are several reasons why future historians may decide that it was not:

- The period is very brief compared to thousands of years for other periods.
- Because there is so much more information in recent periods, it is difficult to determine what is really significant.
- We are too close to these events to have a historical perspective.
- The period may have already ended, and we are now in another phase of history.

Just as all for other periods, the current one is composed of continuities that have carried over from previous eras and of changes that mark distinctive events that break from the past.

Some of the continuities include:

- The world wars (Chapter 20) grew out of Europe's failure to create one regional state or civilization.
- The wars also represent a continuation of the rivalries between European states.

- The Russian and Chinese revolutions (Chapter 21) were based on long-standing division within their societies, and the ideology for those revolutions came from the nineteenth century philosophy of Karl Marx.

- The intentions of the Russian and Chinese revolutions were similar to those of the capitalists — modernization and industrialization.

- The process of disintegration of great empires (Chapter 22), such as the Ottoman, Chinese, Austro-Hungarian, Russian, or European, was merely the same pattern of rise and fall of empires going back to Assyria.

- Other movements, such as feminism (Chapter 23), began in the West in the nineteenth century but became global phenomena in the twentieth century.

- Global population growth was built on past trends such as an increased food supply derived from the spread of American crops and improvements in medicine and sanitation.

- Global industrialization represents a continuation of processes begun with the Scientific and Industrial Revolutions.

- Human environmental impact in the past may have led to extinction of Paleolithic animals.

- Globalization is an extension of past systems such as the Silk Roads, the Indian Ocean (Sea Roads), or the trans-Saharan trading networks (Sand Roads); the spread of Buddhism, Christianity, and Islam; or the Columbian exchange.

The changes for the era beginning in the early twentieth century include the following:

- The two world wars of the twentieth century were new in the extent to which entire populations were mobilized and in the destructiveness they caused.

- Both the attempt to exterminate an entire group of people (the Holocaust) and the use of atomic weapons were unprecedented.

- The Russian and Chinese Communist revolutions remade their societies from top to bottom and broke with the capitalist West.

- The cold war presented a new global division.

- Not only did the great empires disintegrate, but the idea of empire became illegitimate as both the superpowers (the United States and the Soviet Union) proclaimed anticolonial ideology.

- More than 200 nation-states, many of them in the southern hemisphere, declared sovereignty and legal equality, resulting in a new political order for the planet.

- Population exploded at an unprecedented rate, quadrupling since 1900.

- Industrial output grew fortyfold, caused by an increasing rate of scientific and technological innovation and the wide spread of industrialization.

- Industrial output and population growth created environmental impacts unprecedented in scale.

- Globalization in the past century was unparalleled in depth and involvement of nearly the entire planet.

Tentatively, there seems to be enough new about the past century to label it as a distinct era, but what happens next will determine whether or not this will be seen as a separate era, a midpoint, or the beginning of a different age altogether.

AP® Themes in Part Six:

Environment	Cultures	State Building	Economies	Social Structures
Early environmental movements in the 19th and early 20th centuries - Entering the Anthropocene era: global environmental transformations in the 20th century - Nuclear weapons and the environment Environmental issues after collapse of USSR - Climate change/global warming: origins and outcomes - Second-wave environmentalism • In the West • Role of Rachel Carson • In the communist world • In the Global South • North/South Conflict about environmental issues	Fascist ideology - Anti-Semitism and the Holocaust - Japanese nationalist Ideology - Communism as Ideology Islam and modernity: westernization in Turkey and Islamic renewal in Iran - Religion and politics in India - Critique of capitalist Globalization emerges - Global culture of Liberation - Western feminism Feminism in the Global South - Religious fundamentalism: Christian, Hindu, and Islamic - Islamic radicalism: growth, expressions, impact - Religious alternatives to fundamentalism	World Wars I and II - Authoritarian states: comparing Italy, Germany, and Japan - League of Nations and United Nations - Revolutions: comparing Russia and China - Constructing the Soviet state - The cold war - Economic reforms in communist China - End of communism in Eastern Europe - Collapse of the Soviet Union Decolonization in Asia and Africa: comparing India and South Africa - Political variations in the Global South • Democracy in India • Military rule in Africa and Latin America • Communist states in China, Vietnam, Cuba - Globalization of democracy in the late 20th century	Great Depression in • Europe • United States • The colonies • Latin America • Japan - Fascist economic Policies Marshall Plan; recovery of Europe - Communist Industrial development - Collectivization of agriculture in USSR and China - Muslim Brotherhood: goals and outcomes - Economic development in the Global South: problems, policies, and varying outcomes - Economic globalization since the 1980s: growth, instability, and inequality Globalization of industrialization in the 20th century - Debating an American empire	Social outcomes of world wars in the West - Class, gender, and fascism - Class and gender issues in prewar Japan - Social transformation in communist revolutions - Urbanization and elite privilege in the USSR - Effects of Bureaucracy and inequality in Mao's China - Communist Feminism - Women and Islam: ex.: Turkey, Iran, Morocco, Pakistan - Searching for enemies in USSR and China Global population growth and patterns of migration - Ethnicity and political conflict in the developing countries

NOTES:

CHAPTER TWENTY

Collapse at the Center: World War, Depression, and the Rebalancing of Global Power, 1900–1970s

AP® World History Key Concepts

6.1: Science and the Environment

I. Researchers made rapid advances in science that spread throughout the world, assisted by the development of new technology.

II. During a period of unprecedented global population expansion, humans fundamentally changed their relationship with the environment.

III. Disease, scientific innovations, and conflict led to demographic shifts.

The revolution in science and technology, coupled with the might of the Industrial Revolution, allowed Western powers to compete in creating massive military might. Prior to World War I, Great Britain and Germany competed to create ever-stronger navies. Other military technology of World War I included poisonous gas, machine guns, barbed wire, tanks, and airplanes. The use of barbed wire and machine guns helped eliminate sweeping infantry and cavalry movements common in previous campaigns, leading to a war that quickly settled into static trench warfare.

World War II also saw an increase in the machines of destruction such as submarines, rockets, atomic bombs, and the weapons of genocide such as poisonous gas. Loss of life in both wars was immense, but different. In World War I, while 10 million lives were lost, most of them were male, creating a gender imbalance in the surviving populations. World War II blurred the lines of combatant and noncombatant in new ways, and the death toll included many more women and children, not just because of concentration camps and the Holocaust, but also because of urban bombing (including the use of nuclear weapons at Hiroshima and Nagasaki), blockades, and starvation. *See Chapter 23 for more detailed discussion of this key concept.*

6.2: Global Conflicts and Their Consequences

I. Europe dominated the global political order at the beginning of the twentieth century, but both land-based and transoceanic empires gave way to new states by the century's end.

II. Emerging ideologies of anti-imperialism contributed to the dissolution of empires and the restructuring of states.

III. Political changes were accompanied by major demographic and social consequences.

IV. Military conflicts occurred on an unprecedented global scale.

V. Although conflict dominated much of the twentieth century, many individuals and groups—including states—opposed this trend. Some individuals and groups, however, intensified the conflicts.

By 1900, people of European ancestry controlled much of the world (see Map 20.1, p. 884-885) through direct colonization, economic influence, and projection of political power. Germany, a state created in the 1870s, was a rapidly industrializing state that competed with France, Great Britain, and Russia both economically and militarily, and for the intangible goal of "national pride." Competition between European states led to an alliance system that prepared the way for war; on one side was the Triple Alliance – Germany, Austria-Hungary, and Italy – and on the other was the Triple Entente of Russia, Britain, and France. Sparked by the assassination of the heir to the Austrian throne by a Serbian nationalist, World War I effectively launched the twentieth century. Patriotic nationalism encouraged young men to enlist in their nation's military, only to be destroyed by the new weapons of war such as gas, tanks, and machine guns. The war led to the dissolution of large empires (such as the Ottoman, the Russian, and the Austro-Hungarian empires) and to redrawing international borders, especially in Europe and the Middle East, which led to controversies between new, competing national identities. The slaughter of Armenians by the Turks at the close of the war, although not labeled genocide (a term invented for the Holocaust), is an event that is sometimes noted as the beginning of a series of attempts to exterminate an entire ethnic group, a process that became far too common in the modern era. The involvement of colonial troops in the war also reinvigorated anticolonial movements in European overseas colonies, such as India. The war helped trigger the Russian Revolution and the beginning of a communist state (see Chapter 22).

The First World War, the Great Depression beginning in 1929, and the failure of the Treaty of Versailles that ended World War I led to disillusionment with the liberal, democratic ideals of the Enlightenment. Confronted with union strikes, street protests, and the rise of communist groups, charismatic leaders such as Mussolini and Hitler introduced fascism, which was nationalistic, militaristic, authoritarian, and anticommunist. Fascism appealed to idealized national glories of the past and promised recompense for those hurt by the war and the Depression. In Germany, propaganda focused on "the other" (Jews, Communists, weak democratic leaders, and other "traitors") as responsible for the loss of pride, economic stability, and empire that followed World War I. After rising to power, both Mussolini and Hitler took steps to remove other political parties and to assume autocratic power. Both rebuilt the military and created government projects to bring about full employment. Japan's government, too, suffered from the turmoil caused by the Great Depression, and Japanese military leaders began to assert more control in the government. Japan believed that an empire was essential for national greatness and thought that attempts by Great Britain and the United States to limit Japan's expansion were hypocritical. When Japan created a puppet state in Manchuko (Manchuria, part of China), Western powers protested, leading Japan to withdraw from the League of Nations and to begin to expand into the Pacific, where it seized territory from Western colonial empires.

German territorial expansion in Austria, Czechoslovakia, and finally Poland triggered World War II in Europe. As in the First World War, alliances quickly led to the involvement of most European countries and their colonies but with a larger Pacific theater because of Japan's involvement. Lines between combatants and civilians were blurred by total war, leading to unprecedented numbers of civilian deaths, including large numbers of women and children.

As the world recovered after the war ended in 1945, colonial possessions gained independence – sometimes peacefully through treaties and sometimes after armed conflict – and Europe's position as the political, economic, and military core of Western civilization passed across the Atlantic to the United States, marking a major change in the historical development of the West. The cold war between the United States and its allies and the Soviet Union and its allies (see Chapter 21) dominated global politics until the late twentieth century. Several regional conflicts and proxy wars broke out, but the world avoided a direct confrontation between the United States and the Soviet Union. Even during the cold war and its conflicts, some states joined a movement of nonaligned nations, attempting to remain out of the conflict between superpowers. Nongovernmental organizations such as the United Nations also were formed to help prevent a future world war. *See Chapters 21 and 22 for further discussion of this key concept.*

6.3: New Conceptualizations of Global Economy, Society, and Culture

I. States responded in a variety of ways to the economic challenges of the twentieth century.

II. States, communities, and individuals became increasingly interdependent, a process facilitated by the growth of institutions of global governance.

III. People conceptualized society and culture in new ways; rights-based discourses challenged old assumptions about race, class, gender, and religion. In much of the world, access to education, as well as participation in new political and professional roles, became more inclusive in terms of race, class, and gender.

IV. Popular and consumer culture became global.

World War I was a total war that allowed states to take much more control of the economy as well as other aspects of their citizens' lives, ending the Enlightenment ideal of a free economy that regulated itself without state intervention. "War socialism" meant that strikes were suspended and wages limited, the goods produced were decided by the state, and men were drafted into the military and replaced by women in the workforce.

The war inflicted great damage on the economies of Europe, which suffered even more during the Great Depression. States responded in different ways to the postwar economic challenges. The Russian Revolution had installed a communist state, which proceeded to invest in industrial and military growth. The Soviet Union, with its state-controlled economy, suffered least from the worldwide depression. Countries that exported one or two products were hardest hit as commodity prices dropped. Many of those countries began import substitution industrialization – banning certain imports and manufacturing those products for an internal market – to attempt to regain control of their economies. Democratic socialism became a popular response in some European countries, while others turned to state-sponsored capitalism and dictatorial, fascist governments. Japan's militaristic government also became more directly involved in economic policies as the Depression cut into Japanese exports. While maintaining the *zaibatsu*, the government also subsidized strategic industries and limited profits, wages, and rents. In the United States, Franklin Roosevelt adopted the economic policies of John Maynard Keynes and attempted to set up a safety net (the New Deal), but his intervention was far short of the moderate socialism of France or Britain or the more direct control of communist or fascist states.

In the aftermath of World War II, European states had to cooperate across borders in order to receive economic aid from the United States under the Marshall Plan. The European Economic Community was established in 1957, leading to the European Union in 1994 with a common currency, the euro. Japan, under American occupation after the Second World War, was also given aid in its economic recovery. The Korean War further jump-started Japan's economic revival as the United States purchased material from Japan. The International Monetary Fund and the World Bank were also created following World War II to help emerging economies and to prevent another global depression. *See Chapters 21, 22, and 23 for further discussion of this key concept.*

Theme 1:
Interaction Between Humans and the Environment

See Chapter 23 for discussion of this theme.

Theme 2:
Development and Interaction of Cultures

Total war undermined Western faith in the ideals of the Enlightenment and the Scientific Revolution, ideals such as progress, toleration, and rationality. The horrors of war led Westerners to become disillusioned with their own civilization; some Westerners expressed these doubts and disillusionments in art and literature. An almost manic, pleasure-seeking era, sometimes known as the Roaring Twenties, immediately followed World War I. Popular culture, characterized by new music such as jazz and new celebrities such as movie stars, was disseminated globally by new media such as radio, records, and movies. *See Chapter 23 for additional discussion of this theme.*

Theme 3:
State-Building, Expansion, and Conflict

World War I effectively launched the twentieth century. The war also transformed international political life. When the Austrian-Hungarian Empire collapsed, independent Poland, Czechoslovakia, and Yugoslavia were created based on Woodrow Wilson's principle of self-determination. These new nations, however, included other ethnic minorities within their borders, leading to further conflicts by the end of the century; these conflicts took different forms, such as the violent breakup of Yugoslavia or the peaceful separation of the Czech Republic and Slovakia. In Russia, World War I triggered the Bolshevik Revolution, which led Russia to sign a separate peace with Germany. This event also launched communism onto the world stage, where it would influence world events until the end of the twentieth century. The Treaty of Versailles, signed in 1919, set the stage for another even bloodier war twenty years in the future because of the harsh reparations that were inflicted on Germany by the victorious nations. The war also ended the Ottoman Empire and created some new countries like Turkey; other former possessions of the Ottoman Empire, such as Syria, Iraq, Jordan, and Palestine, were not considered fully autonomous but were mandates of the League of Nations under the protection of either Britain or France. Conflicting promises made during the war by the British to Arab and Jewish nationalist groups regarding Palestine set the stage for an enduring struggle. In Europe's Asian and African colonies, the war set the stage for the independence struggles that followed (see Chapter 22). World War I also brought the United States to the forefront as a global power.

The Great Depression also affected state building. As the depression wore on, states took on new roles within the economic sphere. In Italy, Germany, and other Eastern European states, the Great Depression triggered disillusionment with liberal democracy and changed the politics of these newly created countries. Italy's fascist regime suspended democracy, deported opponents, and disbanded independent labor unions and peasant groups as well as all opposition political parties. As in Italy, liberal or democratic political leaders during the 1920s faced considerable hostility in Germany. Traditional elites had withdrawn from public life in disgrace, leaving the weak Weimar Republic with the unenviable task of signing the Treaty of Versailles and enforcing it. In this setting, some began to argue that German military forces had not really lost the war but that civilian democrats, socialists, communists, and Jews had betrayed the nation. In Japan, cultural modernization and the Great Depression also triggered a conservative response. In this case, it was the military who gained power even while elections and parliament continued to function on a limited basis.

The failure of the Versailles treaty to address the problems that caused World War I led to another world war just twenty years later. This war was much more destructive and much more lethal. In the aftermath of World War II, the United Nations (UN) was created to replace the ineffective League of Nations. Although the UN has had problems in enforcing its policies, it nevertheless helped prevent the cold war between Russia and the United States from becoming a hot war between superpowers. Nonetheless, numerous regional conflicts – often proxy wars – such as the Korean War or Vietnam War, still occurred. *See Chapter 22 for more discussion of anticolonial movements in the twentieth century and Chapter 23 for global interactions.*

Theme 4:
Creation, Expansion, and Interaction of Economic Systems

World War I and the Great Depression represented a fundamental change in the way capitalism was viewed. For the rich, the Great Depression meant contracting stock prices that wiped out paper fortunes almost overnight. For ordinary people, the worst feature of the Great Depression was the loss of work. Vacant factories, soup kitchens, bread lines, shantytowns, and beggars came to symbolize the human reality of this economic disaster. Just as Europe's worldwide empires had globalized the Great War, so too did economic linkages globalize the Great Depression. Cocoa prices in Ghana plunged as commodity prices dropped. Brazil destroyed an entire year's coffee crop in order to keep prices from collapsing.

In Latin America, depressed commodity prices for things such as tin and copper often led to military takeover of the state and an attempt to generate economic activity by producing goods for local markets rather than importing products. The Great Depression also sharply challenged the governments of capitalist countries and the assumption that the markets would regulate themselves and thus did not require intervention. In Britain, France, and Scandinavia, a new form of democratic socialism sought to regulate the economy and provide for a more equal wealth distribution but without total state control as in the Soviet Union or China. In Germany and Italy, fascist governments used a combination of state-sponsored tactics to provide employment; infrastructure rebuilding, control of labor unions' demands, increased production of arms and military equipment plus a violent suppression of strikes, riots, and street protests soon quieted the concerns of both the owners of industry, the middle class, and the workers. In the United States, Franklin Delano Roosevelt instituted the New Deal based on economist John Maynard Keynes's belief that government spending would ease an economic contraction. Japan was also hurt by shrinking world demand for its products during the Depression; millions of silkworm raisers were impoverished in the 1930s. Many young factory workers returned to their rural villages only to find food scarce and families forced to sell their daughters to urban brothels. Militaristic nationalism, which emphasized armament construction, helped ease the economic depression.

After World War II, international organizations such as the International Monetary Fund and the World Bank sought to ease economic burdens in developing countries. In Europe, the European Economic Community sought greater economic integration within Western Europe.

Theme 5:
Development and Transformation of Social Structures

A "warrior understanding of masculinity" dominated the first half of the century, forcing women into more traditional roles as wives and mothers. During the world wars, women had temporary opportunities to join the workforce in unprecedented numbers, but at the wars' end, they returned home to traditional roles; working in factories and farms and serving as nurses on the front lines or in auxiliary roles in the military nevertheless showed both men and women how capable women were. In Russia, some 100,000 women won military honors for their fighting at the front during World War II.

It is perhaps no coincidence that women finally won the right to vote in many countries at the end of the First World War. Along with new if somewhat limited political and economic roles, women also carved out a new social role for themselves. The flapper girls in the United States and the Japanese *moga* ("modern girls") exemplified a new era where girls and boys could enjoy each other's company on equal footing and without chaperones. Communism legalized the status of women as equals, something that upset many, including fascists who pushed back on both liberalism and feminism by forcing traditional roles onto women and praising and rewarding motherhood as woman's main role in support of the state. On the other hand, women were also deliberately targeted during World War II through rapes, forced prostitution, and the economic necessities that forced some girls and women into slavery.

Strict social class distinctions also eased as a result of the massive upheaval in the first fifty years of the twentieth century. So many men died in the two world wars that social mobility was much easier for those who survived. Because of the terrible poverty that resulted from massive job losses during the Great Depression, governments began to create safety nets for people in the form of unemployment benefits, health care assistance, and minimum wage laws. These also served to equalize the social levels in Western European countries. In communist countries, de facto social equality existed.

Genocide – the deliberate extermination of a group of people, such as the Holocaust in which 6 million Jews and other groups such as Roma (gypsies) and the disabled were killed – occurred repeatedly during the twentieth century. Nazi versions of racism and anti-Semitism relied on supposedly "scientific" racial constructs of the nineteenth century and used denial of citizenship and civil rights, public beatings, and destruction of property to whip up public acceptance of the propaganda that Jews were parasites responsible for Germany's woes. Hitler's minions used Germany's industrial expertise to create his "final solution," the extermination of all Jews in Europe. This technique of dehumanization became the model for other attempted genocides in the past century. *See Chapters 21 through 23 for more discussion of social structures.*

Guided Reading Questions for Chapter 20

Seeking the Main Point In what ways were the world wars and the Great Depression motors of global change in the history of the twentieth century? (Page 882)

Explanation What aspects of Europe's nineteenth-century history contributed to the First World War? (Page 884)

CHAPTER TWENTY-ONE
Revolution, Socialism, and Global Conflict: The Rise and Fall of World Communism, 1917–present

AP® World History Key Concepts

6.1: Science and the Environment

II. As the global population expanded at an unprecedented rate, humans fundamentally changed their relationship with the environment.

III. Disease, scientific innovations, and conflict led to demographic shifts.

The Soviet Union under Joseph Stalin and China under Mao Zedong pushed aside all concerns except rapid industrialization. They believed that the environment and nature were something to subdue. Large collective farms, huge factories, dams, and redirected rivers for agriculture all led to massive environmental degradation. *See Chapter 23 for more discussion of this concept.*

6.2: Global Conflicts and Their Consequences

I. Europe dominated the global political order at the beginning of the twentieth century, but both land-based and transoceanic empires gave way to new forms of transregional political organization by the century's end.

II. Emerging ideologies of anti-imperialism contributed to the dissolution of empires and the restructuring of states.

III. Political changes were accompanied by major demographic and social consequences.

IV. Military conflicts occurred on an unprecedented global scale.

V. Although conflict dominated much of the twentieth century, many individuals and groups—including states—opposed this trend. Some individuals and groups, however, intensified the conflicts.

Based on the theories of Karl Marx, communist revolutionaries created a new political, social, and economic order in the twentieth century that challenged the democratic, capitalist worldview of the West. However, contrary to Marx's prediction that the proletariat (working class) revolution would spontaneously arise in an industrialized state, both the Russian and Chinese communist revolutions took place in predominantly agrarian countries. Unlike European socialists, communists did not believe in pursuing reform through the political institutions of a country; revolution seemed the only solution. In addition, while most socialist parties supported patriotic nationalism, communists believed that class solidarity transcended national borders. The Bolshevik Revolution (1917) brought Lenin and his cadre of urban workers and intelligentsia to power shortly after the abdication of Tsar Nicholas II. In China, a longer struggle between the Guomindang (the Nationalists, led by Chiang Kai-shek), the Communists (led by Mao Zedong), and the invading Japanese followed the collapse of the Qing dynasty. Not until 1949 did Mao succeed in winning the power struggle. Both revolutionary movements drew on the French Revolution. They believed that an improved society could be constructed by human actions and found their vision of an ideal society in the future rather than in a past golden age. They overthrew the old elites and disposed landowners, using peasant upheavals in rural areas led by educated leadership from the cities. They differed in that the highly organized communist party wanted economic and political equality, the abolition of private property, gender equality, and the destruction of not only the elites but the middle class as well.

Following World War II, communism spread. Stalin insisted that Eastern Europe come under Soviet control as a buffer against further invasions from Germany (or France), and he used his army of occupation to install communist governments in countries such as East Germany, Poland, Romania, Hungary, and Czechoslovakia. Yugoslavia became a communist nation but independent from control of the Soviet Union. Communism spread in Asia as well, to nations such as North Vietnam, North Korea, Laos, Afghanistan, and Cambodia. The confrontation between two worldviews – the West, led by the United States and based on capitalism and democracy, and the communist bloc led by the Soviet Union – devolved into the decades-long cold war. *See Chapters 20 and 22 for more discussion of this key concept.*

6.3: New Conceptualizations of Global Economy, Society, and Culture

I. States responded in a variety of ways to the economic challenges of the twentieth century.

III. People conceptualized society and culture in new ways; rights-based discourses challenged old assumptions about race, class, gender, and religion. In much of the world, access to education, as well as participation in new political and professional roles, became more inclusive in terms of race, class, and gender.

IV. Popular and consumer culture became global.

Large agrarian states such as Russia and China that had not succeeded in modernizing or industrializing in the nineteenth century were faced with huge economic and social problems. The communist movement, based on the theories of Karl Marx, seemed to offer hope to these countries to solve the problems of rural poverty and subjugation of the peasants, the lack of industrial progress or infrastructure, and sharp class divisions. By the 1970s, nearly a third of the people in the world lived under communist regimes, characterized by the following:

- state-controlled economies
- the ousting of traditional ruling elites and the middle class
- the collectivization of agriculture
- rapid industrialization (especially in heavy industry and military material) undertaken from above in a series of five-year plans
- a commitment to social and gender equality

However, these governments also repressed political parties, instituted censorship and propaganda, and controlled movements such as women's groups or youth organizations. The early promise of a classless society soon gave way to a new Community Party elite.

The state tightly controlled cultural expression in communist countries. The state used the arts as propaganda to promote its agenda. Communist governments also suppressed religion or held it up to ridicule as part of the outdated, pre-communist past.

In the West, popular consumer culture in the second half of the twentieth century was disseminated partly by the wide availability of mass media. Much of the world listened to American music (jazz, rock and roll, and later rap), watched American movies and TV shows, and desired consumer goods popularized in America. *See Chapters 20, 22, and 23 for more discussion of this key concept.*

Theme 1:
Interaction Between Humans and the Environment

Rapid industrialization in both the Soviet Union and China led to massive environmental degradation. Government planners saw nature as an enemy to be conquered, so little was done to protect the environment. The construction of huge factories, mining operations, large collective farms, diverting waterways for irrigation, and dam construction all led to soil, water, and air pollution, erosion and salinization, loss of volume of seas and lakes, and contamination by pesticides and herbicides. In Russia today, 75 percent of the surface water is severely polluted and 70 million people live in cites with polluted air five times the acceptable level. A similar problem exists in China; for example, the level of air pollution in Beijing is so great that all factories were closed two weeks prior to the Olympics in 2008. In addition to these environmental disasters, poor government planning and collectivization of rural lands also led to massive starvation; in Russia, approximately 5 million people died, and in China 20 million died.

Theme 2:
Development and Interaction of Cultures

Communism minimized nationalism and looked forward to a movement of the working classes that would lead to international solidarity along class lines. Communists also sought to promote cultural values of selflessness and collectivism that could support a socialist society and ensure that the arts, education, and the media conformed to approved ways of thinking. Posters, plays, operas, and movies were written to extol the values and heroes of the working class and the revolution. Censorship was strong; dissenting works were published outside of the communist bloc or were printed by hand underground and distributed in secret.

In the West, consumer culture became an important distinction from communism. In many ways, Western culture became American popular culture. American music – first jazz, then rock-and-roll, and most recently, rap – have found receptive audiences abroad, particularly among the young. American movies, McDonald's restaurants, and American brand names such as Kleenex, Coca-Cola, and Jeep became common points of reference around the world. When Mikhail Gorbachev instituted *glasnost* (openness) in the 1980s, new cultural and intellectual freedoms emerged in the Soviet Union: reporters exposed the hypocrisy of communist rule; films and the arts not only examined Russian history, but also turned to forbidden models from the West; propaganda decreased; copies of the Bible and Quran were made available; and long-suppressed underground manuscripts saw the light of day.

Theme 3:
State-Building, Expansion, and Conflict

In Russia, the social upheaval caused by the First World War and the sudden abdication of Tsar Nicholas II was so strong that the Provisional Government, composed mostly of liberal middle-class and moderate socialist leaders, could not keep up. The Provisional Government would not end the war or carry out land redistribution, both of which were called for by the people. The most effective of the radical groups that entered the vacuum created by the chaos were the Bolsheviks who seized power in October 1917, claiming they would end the war, give land to the peasants, give workers control of factories, and give non-Russians self-determination. A three-year civil war followed between the Bolsheviks and an assortment of enemies including tsarist officials, landlords, disaffected socialists, regional nationalist forces, as well as troops from the United States, Britain, France, and Japan.

Once in power, the Bolsheviks worked to cement their authority over Russia. They regimented the economy, seized grain from angry peasants, and suppressed nationalist rebellions. They integrated many lower-class men into the Red Army and into the new local governments, giving many an avenue for social mobility.

Under Stalin, the Soviet Union began to turn away from the more moderate economic policies of Lenin to a more complete command economy with all decisions made by central planners. The political system was led by a small group of Communist Party members. Peasants were forced into collectivization by Soviet officials from the cities, and those who refused to give up their farms were branded as *kulaks* (wealthy peasants) and were killed or deported to gulags (work camps) in Siberia. Severe famines followed, leaving more than 5 million dead. Stalin asked the people to make sacrifices to raise the Soviet Union to economic and military parity with its Western foes in one generation, so heavy industry and military equipment were favored over consumer goods in a series of five-year plans. Mass organizations for women, workers, and students were created under tight party control.

Stalin also moved away from traditional communist values to create a return to patriotic nationalism, traditional family ties, competition, and difference in wages. Instead of collective rule by the Soviets, authoritarian rule from the top emerged. Stalin's constant vigilance for any who might disagree with his policies led to censorship, informers, and secret police, with the arrest, death, or deportation of many intellectuals and ethnic group leaders. It is estimated that millions of Russians died from famine, warfare, and purges under Stalin's rule. Stalin determined that Soviet security required friendly governments in the region to permanently end the threat of invasion from the West. Backed by the pressure and presence of the Soviet army, communism was largely imposed on Eastern Europe from outside rather than growing out of a domestic revolution, as had happened in Russia itself. The major exception to this was Yugoslavia, where a genuinely popular communist movement had played a leading role in the struggle against Nazi occupation and came to power on its own with little Soviet help. Its leader, Tito, openly defied Soviet efforts to control Yugoslav communism.

The ideas of Karl Marx were barely known in China in the early twentieth century. A small Chinese Communist Party (CCP) was founded in 1921, aimed initially at organizing the country's minuscule urban working class. Over the next twenty-eight years, that party grew enormously, transformed its strategy, found a charismatic leader in Mao Zedong (himself the son of a peasant), engaged in an epic struggle with its opponents (the Guomindang), fought the Japanese heroically during World War II, and in 1949, emerged victorious as the rulers of China. Much of the growing support that the CCP received in the countryside came from the vigor with which it waged war against the Japanese invaders. Communist forces established themselves behind enemy lines and, despite periodic setbacks, offered a measure of security to many Chinese faced with Japanese atrocities. Furthermore, in the areas it controlled, the CCP reduced rents, taxes, and interest payments for peasants; taught literacy to adults; and mobilized women for the struggle. Once in power, the CCP addressed both of China's major problems – foreign imperialism and peasant exploitation. Mao attempted to prevent people falling back into prerevolutionary modes and launched two disastrous programs: the Great Leap Forward in the 1950s (which promoted small-scale, village industrialization) and the Cultural Revolution in the 1960s (which sent the young Red Guard out into the country to purge anti-revolutionary thoughts – often among local communist party leaders and intellectuals).

The rise of communism launched a global confrontation that restructured international life and touched the lives of almost everyone, particularly in the second half of the twentieth century. The Soviet Union and the United States had become the major political and military powers, replacing the shattered and diminished states of Western Europe. They represented sharply opposing views of history, society, politics, and international relations, leading to rival military alliances (NATO and the Warsaw Pact), a largely voluntary American sphere of influence in Western Europe, and a Soviet sphere in Eastern Europe. The Soviet military put down popular attempts to liberalize the communist governments of several countries, including Hungary and Czechoslovakia. However, even in highly volatile regions such as Berlin, no shooting war occurred between the two sides in Europe. The extension of communism into Asia – in China, Korea, and Vietnam – globalized the cold war and led to its most destructive and prolonged hot wars.

Perhaps the most iconic moment of the cold war era was the Cuban missile crisis, which brought the world close to nuclear Armageddon and gave expression to the most anxiety-ridden and dangerous dimension of the cold war – the nuclear arms race. However, the leaders of the two superpowers knew that a nuclear war would produce utter catastrophe – and perhaps the end of civilization. Still, opportunities for conflict abounded as the U.S.–Soviet rivalry spanned the globe. Using military and economic aid, educational opportunities, political pressure, and covert actions, both sides courted countries emerging from colonial rule (see Chapter 22 for further discussion).

Beginning in the 1980s, the cold war ended, "more with a whimper than a bang," with the liberalizing reforms of Mikhail Gorbachev – *glasnost* (openness), *perestroika* (restructuring), and economic and governmental reforms – which led to more calls for reform than Gorbachev had perhaps intended. Eastern European satellite states took advantage of the new reforms and broke away, most vividly symbolized by the fall of the Berlin Wall in 1989. Hard-line communists in the Soviet Union attempted a failed military coup in 1991, which ended with the dissolution of the Soviet Union into fifteen new states.

In China following the death of Mao Zedong, Deng Xiaoping opened China to capitalism but retained strict control over the political system, including using the military to put down a democratic march in Tiananmen Square in 1989. Ethnic tensions led to conflicts and dissolution of states such as Yugoslavia and Czechoslovakia. Minorities, from the Chechens in Russia to the Uighurs and Tibetans in China, demanded self-determination. Traditional communist states remain on the periphery; North Korea, Cuba, and other satellites, such as Vietnam and Laos, followed China in softening economic controls. In almost all regions (with the notable exception of North Korea), consumerism grew rapidly.

Theme 4: Creation, Expansion, and Interaction of Economic Systems

Communist regimes seized landlords' estates and redistributed that land on a much more equitable basis to the peasantry. They later sought to end private property and gain greater control over the production of food needed to support urban industrialization by collectivizing agriculture. Collectivization in China during the 1950s was a generally peaceful process, owing much to the close relationship between the CCP and the peasantry. This contrasted markedly with the earlier experience of the Soviet Union from 1928 to 1933, where peasants (who received their land under Lenin) slaughtered thousands of animals rather than surrender them to collectives under Stalin. A terrible famine ensued, with some 5 million deaths from starvation or malnutrition. Although there was less violence in China, collectivization led to administrative chaos; disruption of market networks and bad weather combined to produce a massive famine that killed 20 million people between 1959 and 1962.

Although ardently anticapitalist, both the Soviet Union and China were strong modernizers and industrializers. When industrializing, both the Soviet Union and China relied on centralized planning with successive five-year plans and state ownership of all productive capacity. Priority was given to heavy industry, massive mobilization of the nation's human and material resources, and intrusive state control over the entire process. In the Soviet Union, the cold war justified a continuing emphasis on military and defense industries after World War II and gave rise to a Soviet version of the military-industrial complex. Similarly, the need for quick and often secret decision making during the cold war gave rise in the United States to a stronger presidency and a national security state in which defense and intelligence agencies acquired great power within the government and were often unaccountable to Congress. Sustaining this immense military effort throughout much of the second half of the twentieth century was a flourishing U.S. economy and an increasingly middle-class society.

Theme 5:
Development and Transformation of
Social Structures

Communist parties everywhere set out to construct socialist societies once they gained power. This meant, first of all, modernizing and industrializing, attacking long-standing inequalities of class and gender, and preventing the creation of new inequalities during the process of modern development. Mass organizations for women, workers, students, and various professional groups operated under strict party control. Global industrialization fostered a conflicting set of social outcomes: rapid urbanization, exploitation of the countryside to provide resources for modern industry in the cities, and the growth of a privileged bureaucratic and technological elite intent on pursuing their own careers and passing on their new status to their children. Thus, communist efforts to permanently eliminate differences between classes and between urban and rural life largely failed.

Communist regimes also made major efforts to liberate, educate, and mobilize women. The communist states initially declared full legal and political equality for women, including the following measures:

- Marriage became a civil procedure among freely consenting adults.
- Divorce was legalized and easier to obtain.
- Abortion was legalized.
- Illegitimacy was abolished.

Women were also actively mobilized as workers in the drive for industrialization. However, in neither the Soviet Union nor China did the Communist Party undertake a direct attack on male domination within the family. Thus, most women continued to be afflicted with the double burden of housework and child care (without many of the labor-saving devices available to their capitalist sisters) as well as work outside the home — whether in factories or on rural collective farms. Moreover, women rarely achieved the top leadership positions in either country.

Guided Reading Questions for Chapter 21

Seeking the Main Point What was the appeal of communism, both in terms of its promises and its achievements? To what extent did promises match achievements? (Page 930)

Description When and where did communism exercise influence during the twentieth century? (Page 930)

Comparison Identify the major differences between the Russian and Chinese revolutions. (Page 933)

Change Why were the Bolsheviks able to ride the Russian Revolution to power? (Page 935)

Change What was the appeal of communism in China before 1949? (Page 937)

Change What changes did communist regimes bring to the lives of women? (Page 941)

Comparison How did the collectivization of agriculture differ between the USSR and China? (Page 942)

Change What were the achievements of communist efforts at industrialization? What problems did these achievements generate? (Page 943)

Explanation Why did communist regimes generate terror and violence on such a massive scale? (Page 946)

Practicing AP® Historical Thinking How did the Soviet Union and China differ in terms of the revolutions that brought communists to power and in the construction of socialist societies? What commonalities are also apparent? (Page 947)

Connection In what different ways was the cold war expressed? (Page 949)

Connection In what ways did the United States play a global role after World War II? (Page 955)

Description What were the strengths and weaknesses of the communist world by the 1970s? (Page 956)

Change What explains the rapid end of the communist era? (Page 958)

Comparison How did the end of communism in the Soviet Union differ from communism's demise in China? (Page 961)

NOTES:

CHAPTER TWENTY-TWO

The End of Empire:
The Global South on the Global Stage, 1900–present

AP® World History Key Concepts

6.1: Science and the Environment

See Chapter 23 for a more complete discussion of this key concept.

6.2: Global Conflicts and Their Consequences

I. Europe dominated the global political order at the beginning of the twentieth century, but both land-based and transoceanic empires gave way to new forms of transregional political organization by the century's end.

II. Emerging ideologies of anti-imperialism contributed to the dissolution of empires and the restructuring of states.

III. Political changes were accompanied by major demographic and social consequences.

IV. Military conflicts occurred on an unprecedented global scale.

V. Although conflict dominated much of the twentieth century, many individuals and groups—including states—opposed this trend. Some individuals and groups, however, intensified the conflicts.

One of the major stories of the past century is the rapid change from a world controlled by large empires, both political and economic. This process can be seen as one more example of the pattern of rise and fall of empires from the second civilizations onward; however, never before did the very idea of imperialism become anathema and never before had so many states emerged in such a short period of time (see Map 22.1, p. 980). Chapter 22 deals with how the global south attempted to free itself from colonization and create new nation-states with stable political and economic systems. The ideas of nationalism and self-determination that sparked the decolonization movements were themselves products of European thought. Many of the early leaders of independence in Africa and Asia came from the European-educated elite, who brought home the idea of national self-government proposed by people such as Woodrow Wilson at the Versailles conference following World War I. In accounting for the rapid fall of European empires, some look to this internal conflict or "fatal flaw" in Western thought: how can a country support Enlightenment ideals for itself while subjugating another country? Additionally, the notion of conjuncture, that several factors came together at the same time, describes what precipitated the rapid loss of colonies after World War II. The world wars weakened Europe and discredited any stance of moral or cultural superiority while the new superpowers, the United States and the Soviet Union, both opposed colonialism and the United Nations provided a forum for anticolonial agitation.

The paths to decolonization and statehood differed. Some colonies managed to get their freedom with relatively little loss of blood; others only after prolonged conflict. Some movements were primarily secular; others were religious or Marxist or combined all three (such as Sukarno in Indonesia). Some (such as the Marxists movements in Vietnam and China) sought to transform society as well as gain freedom from foreign rule, while others (in most of Africa) focused on ending racial discrimination and gaining political independence without fostering new patterns of social inequality. Once independence was achieved, new nations had many issues to deal with, including exploding populations, extremely high expectations (often beyond what resources could provide), cultural diversity with little loyalty to the central state, and the creation of a new elite that tried to control the government for personal income or opportunities for personal enrichment. Political solutions included multiparty democracy (India and South Africa), Communist Party control (China, Vietnam, and Cuba), one-party democracy (Mexico, Tanzania, and Senegal), military rule (much of the time in most of Latin America, Africa, and the Middle East), dictatorship (Uganda and the Philippines). Sometimes systems followed each other in rapid succession as the current regime failed to achieve the goals of the nation.

6.3: New Conceptualizations of Global Economy, Society, and Culture

I. States responded in a variety of ways to the economic challenges of the twentieth century.

II. States, communities, and individuals became increasingly interdependent, a process facilitated by the growth of institutions of global governance.

III. People conceptualized society and culture in new ways; rights-based discourses challenged old assumptions about race, class, gender, and religion. In much of the world, access to education, as well as participation in new political and professional roles, became more inclusive in terms of race, class, and gender.

IV. Popular and consumer culture became global.

A major goal of the Global South was economic development — increasing production and improving distribution of wealth to raise living standards. Colonial rule had left little to build upon: low literacy rates, few people with business management experience or technological expertise, weak private economies, and transportation systems (such as railroads) built to accommodate exports instead of for national integration. In addition, these nations had little with which to bargain with transnational corporations and lacked internal investment capital. An initial concern was the degree to which state planning would help produce economic growth. Some countries followed Marxist or socialist paths, following the example of China. However, by the end of the twentieth century, confidence in these command economies had collapsed, in part due to mismanagement or corruption in many state-run enterprises, but also due to the collapse of the Soviet Union and the influence of international organizations such as the World Bank (which pushed economies in a capitalist direction).

Since many countries of the Global South were primarily exporters of cash crops or raw materials, they were vulnerable to market and commodity fluctuations. Other issues included the extent to which foreign investment and foreign aid helped or hurt in the long run. Another problem faced by emerging economies was an "urban bias"; by attempting rapid modernization and focusing on production in cities, the countryside floundered. Population growth also hurt emerging countries as well as being forced (because of limited resources and capital) to decide whether to fund large projects, such as dams or factories, or to invest in education, technical training, health care, or nutrition.

Developing countries also had to determine the extent to which modernization meant Westernization; in terms of their traditional cultures, how much of Western culture was appropriate? Feminism, consumerism, dress, music, sexual mores, religion — even democracy — became additional choices that countries and their people had to make. *See Chapter 23 for discussion of global variations in economic development.*

Theme 1:
Interaction Between Humans and the Environment

See Chapter 23 for discussion of this theme.

Theme 2:
Development and Interaction of Cultures

The postcolonial development of Turkey and Iran highlight different approaches to the question of the role of Islam in modern societies. Beginning in the later nineteenth century, Turkey, largely under the initial guidance of Mustafa Kemal Atatürk, turned toward becoming a modern, secular, national state after the collapse of the Ottoman Empire. Atatürk, similar to earlier reformers such as the Young Ottomans, wanted to bring European civilization to Turkey. He ended the caliphate and made Turkey into a parliamentary democracy with a secular law code and educational system. Women and men were expected to adopt Western dress. Polygamy was abolished. Women were granted more rights in inheritance, divorce, child custody; they also received the right to vote and to hold public office in 1934. The Quran was translated into Turkish, and the call to prayer was in Turkish instead of Arabic. Schools taught a Western-style alphabet that made literacy easier but also meant that much of Turkish literature prior to the twentieth century was no longer accessible. After Atatürk's death, many of his reforms were softened. In the early 2000s, a moderate Islamic party governed the country, and the military (staunch supporters of secularization) had less input.

Iran followed a different path. Shah Mohammad Reza Pahlavi, with the support of Western powers, led the oil-rich country in secular modernization in the mid-twentieth century, including granting women voting rights, investing in rural health care, education, and land reform. Industrial projects offered workers a chance to share in the profits. However, the *ulama* (Muslim religious leaders) as well as small-scale merchants felt threatened by the imposition of Western culture and education — as well as cheaper Western products. In addition, the shah's use of the secret police and military (often trained by the West) to maintain power angered many. Led by Ayatollah Ruholla Khomeini, Shi'ite religious leaders called for the shah's removal. A cultural revolution followed, one that reversed the secularization and Westernization under the shah. Iran became an Islamic republic, using Islamic law with a parliament and constitution; in practice, a group of clerics called the Council of Guardians exercised control over the constitution, elections, and legislation to ensure that all was compatible with their vision of Islam. Schools and universities were closed; when they reopened, the books, curricula, and teachers had been purified of "non-Islamic influences." Women returned to wearing hijab, sexual segregation in public was enforced, and family rights (such as the legal age for marriage) were altered to reflect sharia law. However, voting rights remained intact, and the number of women in universities increased to 60 percent. After Ayatollah Khomeini's death, his reforms were somewhat lessened, similar to what happened in Turkey following Atatürk's death.

In Iran and Turkey, both secularization and Islamicization could be measured by the effects on women's dress. In Turkey, Atatürk's aggressive Westernization led women to shed their veils and head coverings and adopt Western-style clothing. As Islamic political parties became more powerful, many women returned to more modest dress and covered their hair. The Shah of Iran, like Atatürk, encouraged women to adopt Western dress as a sign of modernity; after the Cultural Revolution and restoration of Islamic law, women once again donned the hijab.

Theme 3:
State-Building, Expansion, and Conflict

Two examples of political struggles to throw off colonial domination are India and South Africa. Before the British, Indian cultural identities were local – dominated by family, caste, and village – but the British promoted a sense of Indian identity and never attempted to assimilate into Indian society, which strengthened Indians' awareness of themselves as a separate group. British colonial infrastructure, administrative and legal bureaucracy, and the use of English in the educational system and journalism all helped to link India's diverse population. This growing sense of national identity was expressed in the Indian National Congress (INC) and its leader Mohandas K. Gandhi. Like many early anticolonial movements, the INC was composed of Western-educated elites from regionally prominent, higher-caste families. At first they hoped to gain greater inclusion in the colonial government and military, not independence, but the British consistently failed to accept their demands.

After World War I, the British promised greater self-government, but following a series of repressive acts, Gandhi was able to mobilize larger segments of the population through his use of *satyagraha* (truth force), a nonviolent but confrontational approach to political action employing boycotts, strikes, and marches. He appealed to Indians to include greater rights for untouchables as well as Muslims in a secular state, which he envisioned as self-sufficient villages grounded in Indian principles of duty and morality. Not everyone in the INC shared his vision; Jawaharlal Nehru embraced modern technology and Muhammad Ali Jinnah favored separate Hindu and Muslim states. After independence, the subcontinent was divided into India (Hindu and secular) and Muslim Pakistan (see Map 22.2, p. 987).

South Africa had achieved political independence from Britain in 1910. It was a settler colony whose 20 percent white population included both economically powerful English and politically powerful Afrikaners, Dutch settlers conquered by the British in the Boer War (1899–1902). Both British and Afrikaner groups depended for their economic success on the labor of black Africans, so any movement toward majority rule was bitterly contested. Pass laws limited the movement of Africans, and the creation of separate Bantustans (native reserves) kept Africans separated along tribal lines. Similar to the INC, the African National Congress (ANC), founded in 1912, was led by Western-educated, professional, middle-class males who at first did not want to overthrow the system but appealed to the white settlers' stated liberal, humane, and Christian values to be accept as "civilized men." They pursued peaceful strategies such as petitions and delegations sent to appeal to authorities, while denying women full membership until 1943. However, women protested the pass laws, used rural churches to organize, and joined union demands for better wages for domestic servants.

In 1948, the Afrikaner National Party came to power in South Africa on an apartheid (racial separation) platform. The ANC launched boycotts, strikes, and demonstrations against the new government, using tactics created by Gandhi during his stay in South Africa, only to be met with harsh repression, including the Sharpville massacre of unarmed demonstrators in 1960. The ANC was banned, and its leader, Nelson Mandela, was imprisoned. Nationalist groups moved underground and turned to armed struggle, as in the Soweto rebellion. Radicalization and urban violence led to a state of emergency. International pressure to end apartheid included sanctions, exclusion from sporting events, economic boycotts, and the withdrawal of foreign investment funds. This combination of external and internal pressure ultimately led to national elections in 1994, bringing the ANC to power. Similar to the INC in India, the nationalist movement was divided, but not along religious lines. Instead, division arose among the ANC, which saw itself as an alliance of everyone opposed to apartheid (even whites); the Pan Africanist Congress, which limited its membership to black Africans; and the Inkatha Freedom Party, composed of separatist-leaning Zulus. This internal division, however, did not lead to a division of the country, as had happened in India (see Map 22.3, p. 992).

Some countries, especially in Africa and Latin America, experienced military coups. In Chile in 1972, Marxist politician Salvador Allende was elected by a slim margin. He began to move the country peacefully toward socialism by ordering wage increases and by freezing prices; by nationalizing major industries including banks, copper, coal, and steel; and by seizing large estates to redistribute land. Landowning elites, the military, the church hierarchy, wealthy businessmen, and the bureaucracy – as well as some small businessmen and middle-class people – organized a strike in 1972. The U.S. government as well as many of the affected corporations actively supported the overthrow of Allende. Headed by General Augusto Pinochet, the military overthrew Allende and instituted a repressive regime known for torture and the "disappearance" of thousands. The constitution was suspended, and political parties were outlawed. A free market economy was restored, and foreign investments were encouraged. Wealth increased, but so did rural poverty and landlessness, and wages for urban workers fell. During the 1980s, many military regimes (including Pinochet's) collapsed amid a series of global economic downturns and a movement toward the spread of democracy.

Theme 4:
Creation, Expansion, and Interaction of Economic Systems

Improved economic development and quality of life were goals of all emerging nations. However, hampered by the effects of colonial rule (see Key Concept 6.3) and a world economy dominated by capitalist countries and transnational corporations and faced with sharp internal divisions along lines of class, ethnicity, gender, and religion, emerging economies struggled to fulfill the expectations that came with political independence.

Following the example of the Soviet Union, many countries expected the state to take control of their new economies, with some success in China and Cuba. In other areas, such a Turkey, India, South Korea, and much of Africa, the state provided overall planning as well as protective tariffs, licenses, loans, and subsidies but left most of the production capacity in private hands. However, as communist state-run economies collapsed (see Chapter 21), many countries have turned to market economies and privatized their state-run enterprises. Pressure from the West through international organizations such as the World Bank or International Monetary Fund pushed countries to pursue capitalist economies. This approach often led to economic growth, as in India and China, but also produced increased social inequalities. In the twenty-first century, many nations (such as China, Brazil, Russia, and Saudi Arabia) turned to state capitalism, allowing state-owned companies to buy and sell stocks on the open market, seeking a balance between market forces and state management.

In response to the Great Depression, many Latin American countries tried to shield themselves from the global economy by using their resources to make their own consumer goods and protecting their fledgling industries with tariffs, a process known as import substitution stabilization. Brazil pursued this course, leading to the rapid industrialization called the "Brazilian miracle" in the 1970s. Massive infusions of foreign capital and the accumulation of huge foreign debts, cycles of inflation, and high levels of poverty accompanied the "miracle." In the 1980s and 1990s, Brazil became more integrated into the global market by exporting automobiles, steel, aircraft, and computers. Several Asian economies (such as South Korea, Taiwan, Hong Kong, and Singapore) also chose to produce products for export, such as textiles, electronics, and automobiles.

Theme 5: Development and Transformation of Social Structures

Accompanying the rejection of empire as a political construct, nationalist movements rejected race as a basis for social or political rights. However, independence often led to new ethnic and religious rivalries and often did not overturn long-standing economic class differences, especially the poverty of rural peasants. Class conflict, rural poverty, and massive migration to urban slums led to challenges against the postcolonial educated elite who had access to high-paying jobs and privileged positions in government bureaucracies or who controlled the productive capacity of the country. In Latin America and Africa alike, these conflicts sometimes devolved into guerrilla warfare, attempted genocide, or military coups.

Nationalist movements often began with men who were part of the local elite and who had received European educations, such as Atatürk, Gandhi, Nehru, Nkrumah, Mandela, and Sukarno. Some of these leaders pursued independence as their first priority rather than embracing social reform. As in the case of Latin American independence movements in the nineteenth century, many twentieth-century independence movements at first simply removed the foreign occupiers, allowing landowners and the educated urban middle class to assume dominant roles in the new nations. Nationalist movements led by communists, such as in Vietnam and China, promised major social transformations but often led to the creation of new, party-based elites instead of a classless society. Some independence leaders such as Gandhi sought to create a society where religious, class (or caste), and ethnic divisions were diminished or eliminated. His vision was rejected by Hindus and Muslims alike.

The men who led independence movements often did not accept women into national party politics. Women, however, still contributed through strikes, boycotts, and marches. Women continued to be much affected by rural poverty, lack of education, and high birth rates in much of Africa and Latin America. However, some leaders, such as Atatürk, placed a high value on modernity, including removing educational, social, and legal inequalities for women, symbolized by their adoption of European clothing and the removal of veils. Other leaders, such as Gandhi, retained traditional gender roles at home while actively recruiting women in his *satyagraha* movement because he saw them as more naturally able to follow the discipline required of nonviolent civil disobedience. *See Chapter 23 for discussion of global feminism.*

Guided Reading Questions for Chapter 22

Seeking the Main Point In what ways did the experience of the "Global South" during the past century register on the larger stage of world history? (Page 976)

Comparison What was distinctive about the end of Europe's African and Asian empires compared to other cases of imperial disintegration? (Page 978)

Change What international circumstances and social changes contributed to the end of colonial empires? (Page 979)

Description What obstacles confronted the leaders of movements for independence? (Page 982)

Change How did India's nationalist movement change over time? (Page 983)

Change What was the role of Gandhi in India's struggle for independence? (Page 985)

Description What conflicts and differences divided India's nationalist movement? (Page 986)

Comparison Why was African rule in South Africa delayed until 1994, when it had occurred decades earlier elsewhere in the colonial world? (Page 988)

Change How did South Africa's struggle against white domination change over time? (Page 990)

Practicing AP® Historical Thinking How and why did the anticolonial struggles in India and South Africa differ? (Page 993)

Change What led to the erosion of democracy and the establishment of military government in much of Africa and Latin America? (Page 995)

Change What obstacles impeded the economic development of third-world countries? (Page 1001)

Change How and why did thinking about strategies for economic development change over time? (Page 1002)

Comparison In what ways did cultural revolutions in Turkey and Iran reflect different understandings of the role of Islam in modern societies? (Page 1005)

NOTES:

CHAPTER TWENTY-THREE
Capitalism and Culture:
The Acceleration of Globalization, since 1945

One of the major characteristics of the world since 1945 is globalization – not the imperial reach of the nineteenth and early twentieth centuries, but the "increasingly dense web of political relationships, economic transactions, and cultural influences." Chapter 23 explores the spread and consequences of three of these globalizations: neoliberal capitalism, liberation, and environmentalism.

AP® World History Key Concepts

6.1: Science and the Environment

I. Researchers made rapid advances in science that spread throughout the world, assisted by the development of new technology.

II. During a period of unprecedented global population expansion, humans fundamentally changed their relationship with the environment.

III. Disease, scientific innovations, and conflict led to demographic shifts.

Science and technology led to rapid economic growth as well as population growth. In addition, because of population growth and increased consumption, humans impacted the environment in new and rapidly accelerating ways, which led to pollution, global warming, and the loss of biodiversity. Environmentalism began as a reaction to industrialization in England and developed into a movement to protect wilderness by creating national parks in the United States. A new wave of environmentalism began in the 1960s, first in the West as a means of protecting wild nature, and then spreading to the third world where it was seen as a means for securing food security, health, and basic survival. Developing countries came to believe that environmentalists' desires to cut back on industrial pollution and address global warming meant that the North/South industrial gap would be preserved. By the late twentieth century, environmentalism had become a global concern, stimulated by UN and other international conferences. Global environmentalism has helped to further the idea of "one world," the recognition that some issues transcend the artificial boundaries of nation-states. Environmentalism also challenged the idea of continued unconstrained growth, a foundational idea of modernity, substituting ideas of sustainability and restraint.

6.2: Global Conflicts and Their Consequences

See Chapters 20, 21, and 22 for more discussion of this key concept.

6.3: New Conceptualizations of Global Economy, Society, and Culture

I. States responded in a variety of ways to the economic challenges of the twentieth century.

II. States, communities, and individuals became increasingly interdependent, a process facilitated by the growth of institutions of global governance.

Following World War II, there was concern that the global economy might again suffer the disastrous fate that followed World War I and led to the Great Depression. In 1944 at Bretton Woods, New Hampshire, capitalist countries, led by the United States, created a number of agreements designed to promote free trade.

By the 1970s, state-controlled (command) economies were struggling, and many leading capitalist countries (such as the U.S. and the United Kingdom) turned to a philosophy called neoliberalism (a reference to classical liberalism of the nineteenth century, which had advocated laissez faire capitalism) and viewed the world as a single, integrated market. Neoliberalism advocated an end to government controls on the economy, privatization of state-run enterprises, reduced tariffs, free global movement of capital, a mobile and temporary workforce, and cuts in taxation and government spending. The International Monetary Fund (IMF) and World Bank (created at the Bretton Woods conference in 1944) imposed these pro-business policies on emerging countries in need of loans.

By the late twentieth century, economic globalization led to increasingly rapid circulation of goods, capital, and people in the form of labor migration. The impact of economic globalization has led to the rapid creation of immense wealth, which has in turn led to increased life expectancies, declining infant mortality, increased literacy, and declining poverty. However, economic globalization also created instability and uneven distribution of wealth both globally and within nations. In the early years of the twenty-first century, the lack of regulation led to a global economic contraction started by the housing bubble and lending crisis in the United States.

The United States, often seen as an informal empire similar to the ones that Europeans projected onto China and the Middle East in the nineteenth century, used economic penetration, political pressure, and periodic military action to influence other countries to create societies and governments compatible with neoliberal values and interests. These policies have led to increasing global and internal opposition.

III. People conceptualized society and culture in new ways; rights-based discourses challenged old assumptions about race, class, gender, and religion. In much of the world, access to education, as well as participation in new political and professional roles, became more inclusive in terms of race, class, and gender.

IV. Popular and consumer culture became global.

Ideas also went global in the twentieth century, including the idea of liberation: communism promised liberation from capitalist oppression, nationalism promised liberation from imperialism, and democracy promised liberation from authoritarianism. The 1960s saw a variety of liberation and protest movements around the world. In the United States, protests covered civil rights, the counterculture, and antiwar movements; in France, students protested university conditions, to which the state responded with police brutality; the Prague Spring shook Eastern Europe and the Soviet Union, which also responded with military force. In addition, political and social activists in developing countries promoted a "third world" ideology, claiming to be creating new models of economic growth, grassroots democracy, and cultural renewal.

Another liberation movement was women's liberation, or feminism. Although feminism began in the West, in the twentieth century, women's issues went global. For example, communist governments attacked many of the aspects of traditional patriarchy in order to gain women's support. Feminism underwent a revival in the West beginning in the 1960s, and women's movements spread globally. However, the demands of Western women for sexual and occupational equality did not resonate with women in the third world for whom the more immediate issues were ending political and economic exploitation. Differences also appeared along religious and cultural lines within the women's movements. The UN declared 1975 International Women's Year.

Intellectuals since the Enlightenment had predicted the decline of religion in the face of modernity, science, communism, or globalization. The scientific community asserted that only empirical realities should be considered, those that were measurable through scientific techniques. However, major trends in the last century refute those assumptions. World religions have continued to spread and have taken on new forms; they have become a political source of community identity and conflict, while fundamentalist movements have opposed elements of secular and global modernity. *See Chapter 22 for more discussion of this key concept.*

Theme 1:
Interaction Between Humans and
the Environment

The twentieth century, especially after the 1960s, saw a new awareness of humanity's growth and ability to impact the environment. Future generations may well see environmental awareness as the most fundamental change of the twentieth century. The foundation of the environmental transformation rested on three factors. First was the huge growth in human population, a quadrupling in just a century, caused by advances in medical science and technology that lowered the death rate and the Green Revolution, which dramatically increased the supply of food through genetically modified seeds and fertilizers. Second was the unprecedented ability to use energy (coal in the nineteenth century and petroleum in the twentieth, but also natural gas, hydroelectricity, and nuclear power) to increase production. Third was accelerating economic growth as science and technology increased the production of goods and services.

While human activity has altered the natural world in the past, the effects have been primarily local, not on the global scale of the modern era; cropland doubled, forests and grasslands contracted, and erosion (and desertification) increased at alarming rates. Population growth has led to huge urban complexes. Shrinking natural habitats have also rapidly increased the rate of extinction of many species, while humans have remade the ecosystem to increase the plants and animals useful to them. Ninety percent of the environment today has been shaped by humans. Additionally, the global spread of industry with its use of fossil fuels has led to air pollution so bad that it is estimated that 35,000 people die from it in Mexico City every year. In the former Soviet Union, 20 percent of the population lives in regions that have been deemed "ecological disasters," and half of the rivers are severely polluted. However, global warming (caused by human activities that release "greenhouse gases" such as burning fossil fuels) is perhaps the most threatening aspect of environmental transformation. While the rate of warming is debated, consequences such as the melting of glaciers and polar ice caps, rising ocean levels, thawing permafrost, extreme storms such as hurricanes and typhoons, and increased species extinction have already been observed.

Environmentalism as a mass movement began in the 1960s with the publication of Rachel Carson's *Silent Spring* (which exposed the effects of chemical contamination on birds), the Club of Rome's publication in 1972 of a report called *Limits to Growth* (which warned of resource exhaustion and the collapse of modern, industrial-based society), and the formation in the 1980s of the Green Party in Germany, which was based on opposition to nuclear fuels. Environmentalism spread to the third world in the 1970s and 1980s, but unlike the primarily middle-class movement in the West, which called upon individuals to change their values, turn away from materialism, and appreciate the natural world, third-world environmentalism was more local and limited, more concerned with food security, health, basic survival, and social justice than with wilderness protection. For example, in India, the Chikpo (tree-hugging) movement wanted to prevent deforestation in order to preserve the livelihoods of local people; others focused on stopping construction on the Narmada River dam, which would displace many local people (in contrast, anti-dam movements in the U.S. were primarily concerned with protecting wildlife such as salmon). Many industrializing countries viewed the West's call to limit development that produced pollution and greenhouse gases as a way of perpetuating the economic divide between Global North and Global South by curtailing economic development in emerging economies. The West has argued that new industrial giants such as China and India must agree to limits on greenhouse gases if drastic climate change is to be avoided. By 2011, delegates from 194 countries to the Durban, South Africa, conference agreed to move toward a climate change treaty.

Migration has also become increasingly global. War, revolution, political repression or genocide, and the end of empires led to vast numbers of refugees.

Theme 2:
Development and Interaction of Cultures

While religious belief declined sharply in countries such as the Soviet Union, France, and the Netherlands, the global expansion of Buddhism, Christianity, and Islam continued in the twentieth century. Buddhist ideas such as meditation found new expression in the West; Christianity spread to non-Muslim parts of Africa, South Korea, parts of India, and China and found 62 percent of its adherents in Asia, Africa, and Latin America; migrants from the Islamic world expanded Islam to the West.

However, religious fundamentalism (militant piety – often defensive, assertive, and exclusive) also grew. The scientific and secular focus of global modernity conflicted with the "unseen reality" that was the focus of religious belief. Traditional class, family, and gender relationships were upset by social upheavals associated with capitalism, industrialization, and modernization, often brought by Western intrusion through colonial rule, military conquest, or economic dependency. Fundamentalisms have looked to the past for models of spirituality and selectively rejected cultural aspects of global modernity but have often used the technology and sought the prosperity associated with the modern world. Education and propaganda, political mobilization, social welfare programs, and sometimes violence have been used to achieve goals. Conservative Christians emerged as a significant factor in American politics, while Hindutva (Hindu nationalism) became a major political force in India in the 1980s. The most prominent late twentieth-century religious fundamentalism took place in Islam. Earlier Islamic renewal movements, such as the Wahhabis, focused on internal problems in Muslim societies, while those of the twentieth century also reacted to Western imperialism, cultural penetration, and secularism. The UN's creation of the state of Israel in 1948 was regarded as a Western cultural outpost in the heart of Islam, which also led to the displacement of large numbers of Arab Palestinians; the Six-Day War in 1967 left the holy city of Jerusalem as well as other Arab territories under the control of Israel.

The search for Islamic alternatives to Western modernity was grounded in the belief that the Quran and sharia could provide a guide for political, economic, and spiritual life not dependent on Western ideas. Figures such as Mawlana Mawdudi in India and Sayyid Qutb in Egypt said that only a return to the "straight path of Islam" would create a revival of Muslim societies. They labeled this return to Islamic principles a *jihad* (or struggle to please God) to achieve an authentic Islamization of social and political life and to defend Islam against Western intrusions. In 1928, Hassan al-Banna created the Muslim Brotherhood in Egypt, advocating that the government act in accordance with Islamic law and principles. By the last quarter of the twentieth century, Islamic renewal was expressed in several ways. On the personal level, people became more religiously observant and participated in Sufi practices (although in some places Salafist groups rejected Sufi mysticism as non-Islamic). Many women returned to modest dress and the veil. Political leaders began to use Islamic rhetoric to maintain legitimacy. Countries such as Sudan and Pakistan adopted Islamic law. Islamic renewal movements created organizations to provide social services, took part in unions and professional organizations, and tried to use modern science and technology appropriately within Islamic culture. Some movements sought to overthrow governments, such as Iran in 1979, Afghanistan in 1996, and parts of northern Nigeria in 2000.

Hamas in Palestine and Hezbollah in Lebanon targeted Israel with uprisings, suicide bombings, and rocket attacks. The Soviet invasion of Afghanistan led to the creation of a new group, al-Qaeda ("the base" in Arabic) under Osama bin Laden. After bin Laden returned to Saudi Arabia, he became disillusioned by his country's acceptance of U.S. troops in Islam's holy land and returned to Afghanistan to plan the attack on the World Trade Center in 2001. Other al-Qaeda groups launched attacks on Western interests in East Africa, Indonesia, Spain, Great Britain, Yemen, and Saudi Arabia itself to fight "irreligious" Western modernity, American imperialism, and American-led economic globalization.

Aside from militant and revolutionary fundamentalism, there were other religious alternatives to growing disenchantment with globalization and secular modernity. Islamic political parties made strong electoral showings in the 1990s and early twenty-first century in places such as Turkey, Egypt, Jordan, Iraq, Palestine, Morocco, Tunisia, and Lebanon. Debate continued about the proper role of the state and the possibility of democracy in Islamic countries, the difference between religious law and human interpretations of it, and women's rights. In Turkey, the Gulen movement, claiming to be "faith-based but not faith limited," sought to bring Sufi mystical ideas to solve some of the problems of modern society through interfaith dialogue, multiparty democracy, nonviolence, and modern, scientifically based education for both boys and girls. Christian groups, such as the liberation theology movement in Latin America, also examined the ethical issues and growing inequality arising from globalization. In Asia, "socially engaged Buddhism" advocated social reform, educational programs, health services, and peacemaking activities. The UN designated the first week in February 2011 as World Interfaith Harmony Week.

Theme 3:
State-Building, Expansion, and Conflict

See Chapters 20, 21, and 22 for more discussion of this theme.

Theme 4:
Creation, Expansion, and Interaction of Economic Systems

By the late twentieth century, neoliberal economic policy and new technology that lowered transportation costs and provided almost instantaneous communication led to a "reglobalization" of the world economy that was characterized by increasingly rapid circulation of goods, capital, and people. World trade went from $57 billion in 1947 to $16 trillion in 2009, while foods and products from around the world flooded into consumer markets. Transnational corporations (TNCs), such as Mattel, Royal Dutch Shell, Sony, or General Motors, produced goods or delivered services simultaneously in many different countries. By the 1960s, some TNCs had grown so large that their assets and economic power exceeded that of many countries. Neoliberal economics allowed them to move quickly from place to place looking for the cheapest labor and lowest taxes or regulation.

Economic globalization with its reduction of controls has also created instability, such as the OPEC-generated oil crisis and stock market crash of 1973–1974 (which hurt countries in Latin America that had to choose between fuel for their new economies or repayment of their international debt) or the Asian financial crisis of the late 1990s (which caused the collapse of businesses, political turmoil, and unemployment in Indonesia and Thailand). Recently, the lack of regulation created a global economic contraction. The housing bubble in the U.S. led to foreclosures, unemployment, tightening of credit, and reduced consumer spending. Lack of global regulation transmitted this crisis to such distant places as Iceland, where the stock market dropped, three major banks failed, and its currency lost 70 percent of its value, and Africa, where the drastic demand for exports hurt countries such as Sierra Leone. China's economic slow-down has increased urban unemployment, causing a movement back to already overcrowded and poor rural regions. Unemployment in the U.S. meant that workers from Central America and the Caribbean couldn't send money back home. Contracting economies in Europe (such as in Greece, Italy, and Spain) threaten the European economic integration and the euro.

Unequal distribution of wealth is another product of economic globalization: following industrialization, the difference in income between the top and bottom 20 percent of the world was three to one in 1820; but by 1991, it was eighty-six to one, worsening the gap created by the Industrial Revolution between the Global North and the Global South (see Snapshot: Global Development and

Inequality, 2011, p. 1031). The needs of the Global South are not uniform; disparities exist between the oil-rich states and agricultural producers and rapidly industrializing Asian countries (such as China, India, and South Korea) and poor African countries. Unequal distribution also occurs within nations; the offshoring of manufacturing jobs in the U.S. has forced many factory workers to move into lower-paying service-sector jobs, while other workers in high-tech industries are doing well. In Mexico, the northern part of the country has access to business and manufacturing linked to the United States, while the southern section is largely agricultural. China has a growing difference between the poorer rural areas and the cities, where income is three times higher.

Critics of neoliberal globalization, such as political activists, scholars and students, trade unions, women's rights organizations, and religious and environmental groups, have come from both rich and poor countries. They seem to agree that global free trade has favored rich countries and large corporations while it has prevented poor countries from protecting their vulnerable economies, lowered labor standards, disregarded human rights, ignored local cultures, led to environmental degradation, and increased global inequality. These critics organized protests against the World Trade Organization beginning in late 1999 and formed their own World Social Forum in 2001 to share strategies, experiences, and ideas.

From the 1980s, the U.S. has faced growing international competition, first from Europe and Japan, and later from South Korea, Taiwan, China, and India. While the U.S. share of world production was 50 percent in 1945, it had fallen to just 8.1 percent in 2008, accompanied by a growing trade imbalance. Military ventures (for example in Korea, Vietnam, Iraq, and Afghanistan) were costly and led to resistance at home. Even allies such as France resented U.S. influence and withdrew from NATO in 1967. Intellectuals feared American "cultural imperialism." The United States refused to take part in some international organizations, such as the World Court, or to sign treaties, such as the Kyoto protocol on the environment, which led to more resistance to American cultural and economic domination.

Theme 5:
Development and Transformation of Social Structures

Feminism in the West went into decline after suffrage was achieved following World War I. It revived in the turbulent 1960s with the publication of *The Second Sex* by Simone de Beauvoir and *The Feminine Mystique* by Betty Friedan. The new movement in the U.S. became known as the women's liberation movement, aligning it with other liberation movements of the time. Instead of just focusing on voting and legal rights, the liberation movement attempted to counter millennia of patriarchal attitudes and behavior, seeking equality in the workplace, freedom from the purely domestic role, and a change in traditional ideas of beauty and femininity. The advent of the birth control pill also allowed women to more freely express their sexuality. Women of color, however, did not have the same goals; most already worked outside the home and shared with men the larger issues of racism and poverty.

In the Global South, gender was also not the key issue; independence, poverty, economic development, and political oppression were more important. Women played key roles in all these movements, without being allowed by men to be members of the parties themselves. African feminists often saw Western feminists' goals as too individualistic, too focused on sexuality, and not concerned enough with motherhood, marriage, and poverty. They resented Western feminists' culturally charged attitudes on female genital mutilation and polygamy and perceived these attitudes as a new form of colonialism. Instead of focusing on the sexual issues that concerned Western women, women's movements in Africa focused on self-help groups attempting to meet the needs of their communities. In Muslim North Africa, women focused their attention on Family Law Codes that still defined women as minors and did not permit them to initiate divorce or obtain custody of children. In Chile, the women's movement was part of the larger movement against military oppression, torture, and "disappearance" and was a significant part of the return to democratic government in the 1990s.

By the later twentieth century, women's rights became a global focus: "women's rights are human rights" became the motto, and the UN declared 1975 as International Women's Year as well as sponsoring conferences for the next twenty years.

The international spotlight revealed several issues. First, who had the right to speak for women from patriarchal societies — those appointed by the government or more radical members of nongovernmental groups (NGOs)? Secondly, North/South divides appeared; women from the U.S. wanted to focus on political and civil rights, while others from third world or communist countries wanted to focus on economic justice, decolonization, and disarmament. Finally, Muslim women opposed equal inheritance laws because they differed from the Quran, but African women saw support of these laws as a matter of survival in countries ravaged by AIDS. Some women, such as Phyllis Schlafly, felt that the agenda of feminism undermined family life, while many in Muslim countries saw claims of gender equality and open sexuality as morally offensive, leading to a backlash that forced many women to wear veils and lead more restricted lives. In other words, "not all women share identical interests."

Guided Reading Questions for Chapter 23

Seeking the Main Point To what extent has globalization fostered converging values and common interests among the world's peoples? In what ways has it generated new conflicts among them? (Page 1024)

Change What factors contributed to economic globalization in the second half of the twentieth century? (Page 1024)

Connection In what ways has economic globalization more closely linked the world's peoples? (Page 1026)

Connection What new or sharper divisions has economic globalization generated? (Page 1029)

Comparison What distinguished feminism in the industrialized countries from that in the Global South? (Page 1038)

Change In what respect did the various religious fundamentalisms of the twentieth century express hostility to global modernity? (Page 1043)

Change From what sources did Islamic renewal movements derive? (Page 1044)

Comparison In what different ways did Islamic renewal express itself? (Page 1046)

Practicing AP® Historical Thinking How might you compare feminism and fundamentalism as global movements? In what ways did they challenge earlier values and expectations? To what extent were they in conflict with one another? (Page 1052)

Change How can we explain the dramatic increase in the human impact on the environment in the twentieth century? (Page 1053)

Comparison What differences emerged between environmentalism in the Global North and that in the Global South? (Page 1056)

UNIT 2
A Review of AP® World History & Ways of the World for the AP® Course, Third Edition

Preparing for the AP® Exam

This section includes two complete AP® World History practice exams. You should take the tests toward the end of your AP® course and evaluate your weaknesses and strengths. If you can do well on these practice tests, we are confident you will do well on the AP® Exam in May.

As mentioned in the preface, this guide does not include answers to the exam questions. This is because some teachers like to use these practice exams for credit. Your teacher has access to the practice exam answers (for essays: what good answers will include), and can provide them to you, depending on his or her plans for utilizing this book in class. If your teacher gives you the answer key and allows you to practice the exams on your own, do not just get your score and leave it at that. Take the time to look over each question carefully and read the explanations of what makes a good essay response. Make a list of what you got wrong. Are there topics in which you were particularly weak as indicated by a high proportion of wrong answers? Are there certain types of questions that you often got wrong? Did you struggle with your essays? Once you have a better sense of what you need to work on, you can prepare better for the actual AP® Exam. Do not be shy about asking your teacher, too; he or she is likely to be able to make recommendations about where to focus your energies.

Registering for the Exam

Most likely your school will be taking care of this for you, but if not, make sure that you register in time, sometime during the month of February. If you are homeschooled, you need to contact AP® Services at the College Board by March 1 to find out the name of an AP® coordinator near you; you will have two weeks to make contact and locate a school near you where you can take the examination. If you qualify for extra time or are a student with a disability, make sure that all your paperwork is in order and that the AP® coordinator at your school is aware of your special needs. The coordinator will have to submit an SSD form by mid-February if documentation is needed or early March if it is not. Check the AP® Web site early for exact dates.

If your family is struggling to pay the full examination fee, it can be reduced by the College Board through your school, so look into this early. Not only does the College Board provide a subsidy, but many states also help underwrite the cost of exams for low-income students. Qualification information is available on the College Board Web site (http://apcentral.collegeboard.com) in February, through your school's AP® coordinator, or via your state's department of education Web site. There is also a useful downloadable Bulletin for AP® Students and Parents at the site. If you have questions, e-mail apexams@info.collegeboard.org or call AP® Services at 609-771-7300 or 888-225-5427.

Familiarizing Yourself with the Exam

If your teacher has not given you AP® Exam questions or old AP® Exams as practice, you should look closely at these two practice tests in this book. You can also go to the AP® Web site (http://apcentral.collegeboard.com) and review the many past exams that have been posted there.

The AP® World History Exam is three hours and five minutes long and consists of two parts. The first part of the exam consists of two sections. Part A will be multiple-choice and Part B will be short-answer questions. You will have 55 minutes to complete 55 multiple-choice questions in Part A. Each question contains four answer options. Part A will account for 40% of your total score. Part B will consist of four short-answer questions and you must answer each question. You will have 50 minutes for Part B which will account for 20% of your score. The second section of the exam will also have two parts. Part A will be a document-based question. It will include seven documents followed by an essay question and will account for 25% of your score. You will have 55 minutes to complete Part A. It is recommended that you spend the first 15 minutes of that time reading the documents and planning your essay. Part B will be the long-essay question. You will be offered two long-essay questions but only answer one. Both long-essay questions will test the same historical thinking skill. Part B will account for 15% of your grade and you will have 35 minutes to complete it.

Setting Up a Review Schedule

Your teacher will almost certainly organize review sessions or review in class, but often that is insufficient to feel really ready for the exam. You might want to reread the textbook to prepare, but for most students, that's impossible because of time constraints. Thus, a study guide like this one is an excellent way to prepare, as it crystallizes the information in the textbook and allows you to hear a fresh voice. See those Guided Reading Questions in the Section 1 of this guide—they are a helpful review.

You should schedule three weeks of review time in order to prepare for the exam, but in most cases, your teacher will still be trying to teach the rest of the course in April. For this reason, you will have to begin reviewing while you are still learning new material. What is the best way to do this?

Ideally, take the three weeks leading up to the exam and read one chapter of the study guide a night, which, if you remain focused, should be about a half-hour's work. Since there are twenty-three chapters, this works out to a little over three weeks of review. If this plan doesn't work for you, try to set up a schedule before the end of April in which you complete two or three chapters a night. On the exam, time periods 3 to 6 each comprise 20 percent of the multiple-choice questions, while periods 1 and 2 combined make up the remaining 20 percent, so you can't afford to neglect any part of the year's curriculum during your preparation.

The time before the AP® Exams is often very hectic for students. If you are on an athletic team, you may have playoffs or championship games, and the workload in all your classes may be getting intense as the year is coming to its conclusion. You do not want to let your other responsibilities get in the way of earning a 5 on the exam, so an absolute key to success is time management. While this is always useful, it is crucial in the period before AP® Exams. Otherwise, you will not prepare much and have to rely on your innate abilities and your memory. In most cases, such "preparation" will not bring you to a score higher than 3. If you want the 5, you will need to spend the week or two before the AP® Exam preparing for the test instead of socializing or focusing on your other activities.

Is it worth it? Absolutely! In almost every college, a score of 5, and in some places a 4, will bring you three or more credits. Even if you do not receive college credit, you might be placed directly into advanced-level history courses. *Since you are very likely taking this exam as a sophomore, garnering a good score is something you can include on your college applications. It will help set you apart as a good college candidate.*

The AP® Exam is physically grueling—about an hour's worth of multiple-choice questions and two hours of writing. If you are not used to writing by hand, be sure to practice in the weeks before the exam, otherwise your hand might cramp up or get tired. Be sure to eat well, stay away from junk food, and get enough sleep the night before the exam so that your body will be an ally and not a detriment to you. Be sure to have a good and healthy breakfast before the exam so your energies will not flag in the last hour. Do not drink too many liquids; you don't want to lose valuable exam time making frequent bathroom visits. Take a snack in with you to the exam for the break if that's allowed, wear comfortable clothes and shoes, and bring a sweater or jacket in case the room is cold. You do not want anything to interfere with your ability to concentrate on the exam. Most importantly, bring a watch! *You will not be able to use your cell phone to help you with timing.* You need a good, reliable timepiece that will accurately tell you how much time is left. *Do not assume there will be a clock in the room.*

Your examination proctor will certainly remind you of this, but in any case, leave all cell phones and other electronic devices outside the examination room. If you are involved in a breach of security, your examination will likely be canceled, and there could be other consequences at your school. It's simply not worth it to take such a chance.

How the Exams Are Scored

It helps to know how the exams are scored so that you can understand how to earn the highest score. The multiple-choice question answers are scored electronically, but the essays and short answer questions are read by people.

In June more than 1,000 readers–university professors and high school AP® World History teachers –meet for a week in a central location to read and score the essays and short answer questions. Readers are organized into groups of eight at a table, chaired by a table leader who is responsible for quality control. The exams are scored in June, and the scores are sent out in July. You can call for your score after July 1 if you cannot wait to get it in the mail. For a fee, you can get your score by phone.

You should not need this, but just in case: if the exam proves to be a disaster–which it certainly should not–you can cancel the score in writing by mail or fax to AP® Services by June 15, before you get your score. You can also have AP® Services withhold a score from being sent to a college.

AP® World History Exam Strategies

If you are well prepared, you will be successful on the AP® Exam; however, there are key test-taking skills that will all but guarantee that you get the score that your level of mastery should bring you.

The single most common problem is not reading the question carefully or ignoring parts of a question. For the essays, read the question carefully, think about what the question is asking, and answer every part. Students sometimes answer the question they know or the one they wish had been asked, rather than the one that has been asked; this is particularly true on the essays but can be true on multiple-choice questions, too. Do not rush and assume you understand the question before you read it carefully.

Types of Multiple-Choice Questions

There are eight types of multiple-choice questions that appear on the AP Exam. All questions will be grouped in sets of 2-5 questions and will refer to a provided stimulus, such as a primary or secondary text, a map, photograph, or work of art. The questions will test your ability to interpret the stimulus and relate it to your own knowledge of world history. The questions below are included as examples of how multiple choice questions test your historical thinking skills.

Causation

Causation questions will ask you to look at the relationship between causes–either short term or long term–and effects.

Example:

Which of the following was the most immediate cause of the success of the Chinese Communist Revolution in 1949?

(A) The survival of the Chinese Communist leadership during the Long March
(B) The outbreak of the Cold War
(C) The escape of the Nationalist government to Taiwan
(D) The weakening of the Chinese Nationalist government during the war against Japan

Answer: D

Chronological Reasoning

Chronological reasoning questions will test your understanding of changes and continuities within or between time periods.

Example:

Which of the following was an important continuity in Eurasian history from 1000 C.E. to 1500 C.E.?

(A) Hindu political dominance of the Indian subcontinent and Southeast Asia
(B) The importance of the Silk Roads in cultural exchanges across Eurasia
(C) The Abbasid Caliphate as the dominant power in Southwest Asia
(D) The military superiority of Western Europe over other regions of Eurasia

Answer: B

Comparison

Comparison questions ask you to compare related historical developments and processes across geography, chronology, or different societies, or within one society.

Example:

Which of the following is the basis for nearly all boundaries of today's sub-Saharan African states?

(A) Postcolonial conquests of one African state by another
(B) Fragmentations of countries after they achieved independence from Europe
(C) Decisions by European powers during the process of colonization
(D) Precolonial linguistic groupings

Answer: C

Contextualization

Contextualization questions test your ability to recognize how historical phenomena or processes connect to broader regional, national, or global processes.

Example:

"Never believe, as I have never believed, that the British are going to fail. I do not consider them to be a nation of cowards. I know that before they accept defeat every soul in Britain will be sacrificed.

They may be defeated and they may leave you just as they left the people of Burma, Malaya and other places, with the idea of recapturing lost ground when they can. That may be their military strategy. But supposing they leave us, what happens to us? In that case Japan will come here.

The coming in of Japan will mean the end of China and perhaps Russia, too. In these matters, Pandit Jawaharlal Nehru is my guru. I do not want to be the instrument of Russia's defeat, nor China's. If that happened I would hate myself."

Mohandas K. Gandhi, speech to the All-India Congress, August 7, 1942

Gandhi's speech is best understood in which of the following contexts?

(A) Calls for violent resistance to British rule in India
(B) Disputes within the Indian independence movement over whether to support the British war effort
(C) Divisions within the Indian independence movement between Hindus and Muslims
(D) British offers of autonomy to India in return for help in the war against Japan

Answer: B

Historical Argumentation

Historical argumentation questions require you to identify the answer choice that best supports a conclusion or assertion from a historical argument.

Example:

Which of the following best supports the conclusion that Africans played a key role in acquiring slaves for the transatlantic slave trade between 1500 and 1800?

(A) Europeans seldom ventured into the interior of Africa in this period.
(B) Most slaves acquired in this period were intended for labor on plantations in the Americas.
(C) Large-scale slavery was uncommon in sub-Saharan Africa before 1500.
(D) Most African slaves were purchased with goods produced in Europe.

Answer: A

Historical Interpretation

Historical interpretation questions ask you to critique various historical interpretations of a specific event.

Example:

The fourteenth-century Arab historian Ibn Khaldun described pastoral peoples in the following way: "It is their nature to plunder whatever other people possess." Which of the following evidence would counter the view of pastoral societies expressed by Ibn Khaldun?

(A) The Xiongnu Empire extorted tribute payments from Han dynasty China.
(B) Nomadic Bedouin Arabs regularly raided nearby agrarian societies.
(C) Mongol rulers offered merchants 10 percent or more above their asking price.
(D) The Seljuk Turks spread Islam throughout the Middle East by military conquest.

Answer: C

Periodization

Periodization questions require you to pick the best model of periodization for the question. Usually, the stem will argue that one date is better than another date at emphasizing a particular phenomenon.

Example:

Historians who maintain that the approximate date 500 C.E. is the best choice for the transition between two major periods in world history and historians who maintain that the approximate date 600 C.E. is a better choice for that transition are most likely to disagree on the relative importance they assign to which of the following?

(A) The emergence of the classical Maya civilization
(B) The role of technological change in world history periodization
(C) The decline of polytheism in the Mediterranean and the Middle East after the fifth century C.E.
(D) The fall of the Western Roman Empire

Answer: D

Use of Evidence

In this question, students are expected to analyze one type of historical evidence: audience, purpose, point of view, format, or argument.

Example:

> "Although many people might think it crazy, the development model of the global economy has a marked relation to gender. . . . Women in every household are suffering every day as a result of impoverished economies, and those who are exposed to the effects of foreign debt are women. . . . The adoption of austerity measures mean a curtailment of the state's commitment to social services. . . . Women keep the smallest portion of the meager family income. . . . As a result malnutrition among women is increasing at an alarming rate."
>
> *Gladys Acosta, Peruvian feminist*

In the excerpt above, Acosta's main purpose is to point out that

    (A) women in developing countries have tended to be largely responsible for financial decisions made by their families

    (B) malnutrition results from increases in the prices of basic goods

    (C) foreign debt and consequent austerity measures have had disproportionately negative consequences for women in developing countries

    (D) because women keep the smallest portion of the family income, they are least affected by foreign debt

Answer: C

Strategies for Multiple-Choice Questions (MCQ)

1. **Pace yourself.** You are expected to answer the questions in one minute per question, so do not spend a long time on any one question. If you are struggling to select the correct answer, leave it and return to it at the end of the allotted time. On the other hand, do not rush. Get to know how long a minute is. Time yourself often so you know the rhythm of the exam.

2. **Make sure that you fill in your answers accurately and in a timely fashion.** If you skip a question, be sure that you skip an answer on the answer sheet. Periodically check that you are filling in the circles on the correct line. You do not want to find at the end of the exam that you have filled in the wrong circles for your answers, as you may not have time to correct the errors. If you like working questions in your test booklet and THEN bubbling in the answers, make sure you leave plenty of time to do so. Once time is called, you will not be able to fill in the bubbles. Anything in your multiple-choice test booklet will not be scored.

3. **About guessing:** until 2011, there was a penalty of one-quarter of a point off for each wrong answer, but this has been eliminated for AP® Exams in all subjects. As there is no longer a guessing penalty, answer every question, even with a wild guess. You have nothing to lose and a 25 percent chance of getting the answer right.

4. **Some questions will be straightforward and easy,** so don't assume that they are trying to trick you. The fifty-five questions will vary in difficulty; a number of them are easy and will be answered correctly by the vast majority of students. Similarly, there will be a few multiple-choice questions that are really tough, and only a small percentage of students will get them right.

5. **The higher you score on the multiple-choice section,** the greater the likelihood of a high score on the exam. Remember, the multiple-choice section counts for 40% of your final score.

6. **Read each question and its answer choices carefully** and be sure to notice if the question is an "except" question. Use the process of elimination as you read the choices (you can write on the exam booklet), crossing out the choices you know for sure are wrong. General rules of thumb: absolute answers—"all of the above" or "none of the above"—are usually wrong. Remember, the correct answer for a multiple-choice question should be the best answer of the four options. Typically, one potential answer will be clearly and definitively wrong, two might be correct or partially true, while the remaining one is the most accurate or complete answer to the question.

Strategies for Short-Answer Questions (SAQ)

Each short answer question will be graded on a scale of 0-3. Typically an SAQ will have three parts, each of which will be worth one point. As indicated earlier, each SAQ will test at least one of the historical thinking skills. Some of the SAQs will be based on a stimulus, but not all of them will be. To answer each of the questions you will need to be able to interpret the stimulus but also to incorporate prior knowledge of world history. Not surprisingly, the stimulus is intended to stimulate your thought memory and thought processes, you will not be able to infer from it all the information you will need to answer the question.

You will be provided with an answer sheet for each Short Answer Question. Your answer sheet will contain a box. You must write your answer within the box and you cannot use additional space. This will force you to keep your answer succinct.

Strategies for the Document-Based Question (DBQ)

The DBQ tests your abilities with multiple skills: argumentation, analyzing evidence, contextualization, and synthesis. It requires that you develop an argument based on primary documents, cite the documents specifically as evidence, interrogate the documents by analyzing the author's point of view or purpose, incorporate relevant context and evidence from beyond the documents, synthesize the argument by extending it to other time periods or regions or by incorporating information from other fields of study.

While this may sound like a tall order you should remember many successful essays will be able to accomplish some but not all of the tasks mentioned above. Furthermore, readers understand that you are under time pressure and are trained to regard your essay as a first draft. Consequently, neither grammatical errors nor occasional factual errors will detract from your score.

Core Scoring

The basic premise of core scoring is that there are specific and identifiable skills that can be articulated as demonstrations of competence in DBQ essay writing. Three of these skills can earn you up to two points, while the synthesis skill will earn you one. The maximum score you can receive on a DBQ, therefore, will be seven points.

   The seven core points are:

1. **Thesis and Argumentation (2 points).** One point will be awarded for a thesis that makes a historically defensible claim, consists of one or more sentences, and is located in the first or final paragraph of the essay. A second point will be awarded to an essay which recognizes historical complexity by indicating the relationship among the documents. The best way to do this is to state the argument in the thesis and support it consistently with evidence from the documents. In the course of supporting an argument the essay should analyze the ways in which the documents corroborate or contradict each other, or ways in which they qualify the thesis.

2. **Document Analysis (2 points).** One point will be awarded for and essay which utilizes at least six of the seven documents. The phrases "utilizes" means the essay goes beyond demonstrating basic understanding. It must show how the document supports the thesis. A second point will be awarded for an explanation of the relevance of the author's point of view, purpose, historical context, and/or audience for at least four documents. To earn this point students must be able to explain why such factors may help us better understand the document. Merely repeating the source line, or accusing a document's author of "bias" will not be sufficient.

3. **Using evidence beyond the document (2 points).** One point will be awarded for contextualization. To earn this the student must utilize information not contained in the documents to explain relevant historical events or processes. "Contextualization" in this case refers to an explanation of a larger historic process or development which sets the context for the argument of the essay. Setting the historical context for merely a single document will not earn this point. It is recommended that you include this in the introduction, in the same paragraph as the thesis, or in the conclusion. A second point will be awarded for a discussion of specific relevant evidence not found in the documents. The bar for these points is high. Students must explain, usually with multiple sentences, what the context or evidence is and why it is relevant. There is no "double-dipping:" evidence which received other rubric points cannot receive credit under this point.

4. **Synthesis (1 point).** This point is awarded to an essay that extends the argument in one of three ways: by relating developments discussed in the essay to developments in a different region of the world or from a different time period, by relating the argument in the essay to course themes that are not a part of this essay (eg., political or cultural history), or by utilizing information from other academic disciplines such as economics, art history, political science, or anthropology. The bar for this is also high. To receive the point the synthesis must be satisfactorily explained. A mere phrase or passing reference will not earn the point.

Other DBQ Essay-Writing Tips

1. **Pay attention to the wording of the question.** It is crucial that your essay directly responds to the prompt. If the question asks for a comparison, for example, you must show similarities and differences. If the questions asks you to address causes, you must address causes and/or effects. Note also that if the prompt includes pluralized words (eg., causes, responses, results, relationships), you must discuss more than one.

2. **Do not repeat the historical background.** Each DBQ begins with a question, followed by a paragraph called historical background, which is designed to give you key information you need to understand and analyze the documents. You may use or refer to it, of course, but do not waste your time repeating it. The readers already know it well.

3. **There are no intentionally misleading or trick documents.** You should use every document. Even though you are allowed to use only six out of seven, using all seven provides you with some insurance in case you misinterpret one of the documents. Think of this like a jigsaw puzzle: every document has a place in the narrative you are creating.

4. **Do not simply paraphrase or summarize a document.** In fact, given the time constraints, it is not recommended that you provide lengthy quotations from any of the documents. The point is to show that you can use the documents to support a historical argument, not merely that you know what they say. If you use quotations, keep them brief, and make sure you provide a context for such quotations in your own words.

Be sure to examine the DBQs, the essays, and the generic rubrics available to you on the College Board Web site for students, www.collegeboard.com/testing. While you will not be provided with a copy of the rubric as you take the test, the essential requirements of the DBQ will be provided to you at the beginning of the question.

Strategies for the Long-Essay Question (LEQ)

There will be two long-essay questions on your test and you will choose one. Each will test the same historical thinking skill: comparison, causation, continuity and change over time, or periodization. While each essay choice will address the same skill, they may refer to different regions and/or time periods.

Core scoring

The LEQ will be scored on a 0-6 scale.

1. **Thesis (1 point).** One point will be awarded for a thesis which presents a defensible claim and address all parts of the question (eg., change *and* continuity, similarities *and* differences, causes *and/or* effects, or why a particular event or time period should or should not be characterized as a turning point). The thesis may be one or multiple sentences and may appear in the first paragraph or in the conclusion.

2. **Using the historical thinking skill (2 points).** One point will be awarded for accurately addressing the tested skill: comparison, change and continuity, causation, or periodization. It is important

to recognize that both comparison and change and continuity have two parts. For comparison the essay must address similarities and differences. For change and continuity the essay must address both change and continuity. A second point will be awarded to essays that contain deeper analyses. For comparative essays this point will be awarded for an explanation of the reasons for the similarities and differences. (Tip: to earn this point you must show *why* the similarity and difference occurred, not simply describe the similarity and difference in detail). For causation essays the second point will be awarded for explanation of the reasons for the causes and/or effects discussed in the essay. For the change and continuity essay the second point will be awarded for an explanation of the causes of the changes and continuities discussed in the essay. For periodization essays the second point will be awarded for a fuller explanation of the extent to which the historical development under discussion was different from and similar to events that preceded and/or followed it. (If the question asks you to evaluate whether or not a particular event or development was a turning point, then you must address similarities and differences to both events that preceded it and followed it).

3. **Evidence (2 points).** One point will be awarded for incorporating relevant evidence. A second point will be awarded for effective use of evidence to substantiate the thesis or a relevant argument. To earn this second point you will need a sentence or two to show how the evidence you cited supports your argument.

4. **Synthesis (1 point).** One point will be awarded for an essay which explains the connections between the arguments in the essay and ONE of the following: a development in a different time period or geographic era, a course theme or approach to history that is not the focus of the question (eg., political, economic, or cultural history), a different academic discipline (eg., economics, political science, anthropology, art history).

Interpreting your results on a Practice Exam

1. First, look at the multiple-choice score. It is a fair indicator of what your overall score will be. How many out of fifty-five did you get right?

2. Check to see if you got too many wrong answers for the goal you have set for yourself. Examine the ones you got wrong to see if you got them wrong because you did not know the answer or because you guessed poorly. Look at those questions closely to see what you might have missed that would have helped you make a better choice.

3. Examine your essay scores. What strengths and weaknesses do you find? If you did not do as well as you would have liked, try to focus on whatever problems you had in writing the essays. Was it your thesis statement, use of evidence, errors, or lack of organization? Once you identify your difficulties, you can focus your attention on addressing them.

4. Set a realistic goal for yourself. 60% of your score will be based on your written responses so it pays to write well. The more you can strive to become a well-rounded student, the more likely it is that you will be able to earn a 5 on the AP® Exam.

5. Make it happen!

NOTES:

PRACTICE EXAM 1

SECTION I

Total Time – 1 hour, 45 minutes

Part A: Multiple-Choice Questions

Time: 55 minutes

Questions 1-3 refer to the map below.

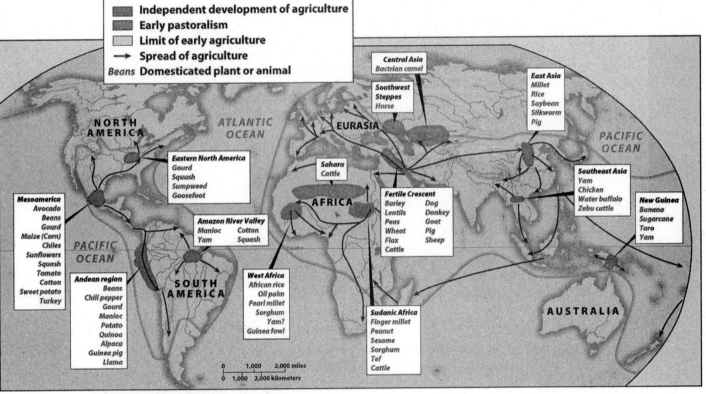

Map 1.3 The Global Spread of Agriculture and Pastoralism
Chapter 1, *Ways of the World: A Brief History,* Second Edition and
Ways of the World: A Brief Global History with Sources, Second Edition
Copyright © 2013 by Bedford/St. Martin's
Page 28 (page 28, *With Sources*)

1. Which of the following interpretations is supported by the information shown in the map?

   (A) Agriculture developed independently in different parts of the world.
   (B) Agriculture emerged at the same time in the Americas and Afro-Eurasia.
   (C) Agriculture spread from the Mediterranean to the Americas.
   (D) Agriculture led to the emergence of new social structures.

2   What type of evidence most likely forms the basis for the information presented in the map?

(A) Climactic evidence of changing global temperatures
(B) Documentary evidence of tribute collected in different societies
(C) DNA evidence of early plant domestication
(D) Paleolithic cave paintings of animal hunts

3.   Modern historians attribute the growth of agriculture to which of the following factors?

(A) Population pressures leading to increased demand for food.
(B) Technological innovations reducing the labor time needed for production.
(C) The emergence of belief systems which emphasized humans' relationship to the land.
(D) The diffusion of language systems which allowed for the spread of knowledge about farming.

Questions 4-6 are based on the excerpt below.

"The fourfold division of castes was created by me according to the appointment of qualities and duties ... The duties of Brahmins, Kshatriyas, and Vaisyas, and of Sudras, too ... are distinguished according to the qualities born of nature. Tranquility, restraint of the senses, penance, purity, forgiveness, straightforwardness, also knowledge, experience, and belief in a future world, this is the natural duty of Brahmins. Valor, glory, courage, dexterity, not slinking away from battle, gifts, exercise of lordly power, this is the natural duty of Kshatriyas. Agriculture, tending cattle, trade, this is the natural duty of Vaisyas. And the natural duty of Sudras, too, consists in service.

...Listen, now, how one intent on one's own duty obtains perfection. Worshipping, by the performance of his own duty ... a man obtains perfection. One's duty, though defective, is better than another's duty well performed. Performing the duty inscribed by nature, one does not incur sin."

Source: Tashinath Trimbak Teland, trans., *The Bhagavad Gita,* in *The Sacred Books of the East,* edited by Max Mueller (Oxford: Clarendon Press, 1879-1910).

4.   The passage cited above most likely served which of the following purposes?

(A) The establishment of a clerical hierarchy
(B) Imperial conquest and empire building
(C) The promotion of ancestor veneration
(D) Justification of social hierarchy

5.   The *Bhagavad Gita's* promise that even lower caste members can achieve perfection was likely a response to

(A) Confucian principles which protected the rights of the lower classes
(B) The emergence of Buddhism which rejected the caste system
(C) The rise of peasant revolts demanding improvement in the lives of Vaisyas
(D) Efforts by the Gupta state to rally popular support

6.   A Hindu follower of the teachings of the Bhagavad Gita would most likely have rejected which of the following aspects of contemporary Chinese society?

(A) The practice of state collection of tribute from peasant villages
(B) The inferior status of women in Confucian teachings
(C) The use of the civil service examination system in state administration
(D) Conflicts with pastoral peoples along the borders of the Han Empire

Questions 7-9 refer to the excerpt below.

"The Way of husband and wife is intimately connected with Yin and Yang and relates the individual to gods and ancestors. Truly it is the great principal of Heaven and Earth, and the great basis of human relationships ...

If a husband be unworthy, then he possesses nothing by which to control his wife. If a wife be unworthy, then she possesses nothing with which to serve her husband. If a husband does not control his wife, then the rules of conduct manifesting his authority are abandoned and broken. If a wife does not serve her husband, then the proper relationship between men and women and the natural order of things are neglected and destroyed..."

Source: Nancy lee Swann, trans., *Pan Chao: Foremost Woman Scholar of China* (New York: Century, 1932).

7. In this passage Ban Zhao was most likely influenced by

    (A) the Confucian emphasis on the maintenance of a stable social order
    (B) the Buddhist desire to seek a path to nirvana
    (C) Shinto practices designed to maintain harmony between people and nature
    (D) Legalist strictures crafted to preserve state authority

8. Ban Zhao's purpose in citing *Yin* and *Yang* was most likely

    (A) to root gender inequality in Buddhist teachings
    (B) to appeal to women of the merchant class
    (C) to convince readers that gender differences were an immutable aspect of the universe
    (D) to incorporate teachings imported from South Asia

9. First century Chinese teachings on gender roles came under challenge in subsequent centuries because

    (A) women led successful peasant revolts and demanded a greater role in society
    (B) pastoral tribes invaded and imposed less strict limits on women's roles
    (C) NeoConfucian scholars rejected the classical distinction between public and private gender roles
    (D) the growth of South East Asian trade routes encouraged women to serve as record keepers

Questions 10-11 refer to the excerpt below.

"It is true that we are called a democracy, for the administration is in the hands of the many and not of the few."

Source: Pericles, a funeral oration delivered c. 430 B.C.E.

10. In the quote above, Pericles is describing the government of

    (A) Athens
    (B) India
    (C) Persia
    (D) Sparta

11. Which of the following would weaken Pericles' claim that "the administration is in the hands of the many and not of the few"?

    (A) The extension of access to public office to a wider group of men
    (B) The exclusion of women, slaves, and foreigners from citizenship
    (C) The participation of all citizens in the Assembly
    (D) The compensation paid to all who held public office

Questions 12-15 refer to the map below.

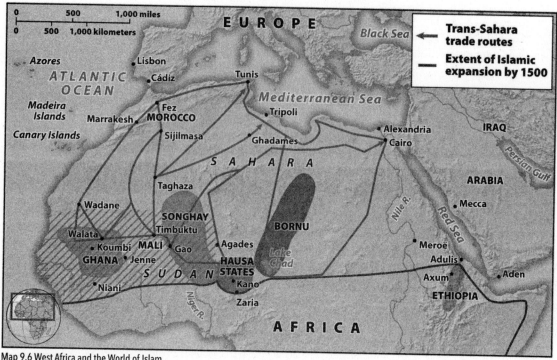

Map 9.6 West Africa and the World of Islam
Chapter 9, *Ways of the World: A Brief Global History with Sources,* Third Edition
Copyright © 2016 by Bedford/St. Martin's
Distributed by Bedford/St. Martin's/Macmillan Higher Education strictly for use with its products; Not for redistribution.

12. The information shown in Map 9.6 supports all of the following conclusions EXCEPT

    (A) The trans-Saharan trade facilitated the spread of Islam
    (B) Islam entered North Africa through military conquest and forced conversions
    (C) The presence of Islam was strongest in the empires of West Africa
    (D) Commerce and Islam connected West Africa to the Islamic world

13. Which of the following represents an accurate difference between the spread of Islam in North Africa and the spread of Islam in West Africa prior to the 16th century C.E.?

    (A) In North Africa the spread of Islam brought few changes in language while in West Africa the spread of Islam led to Arabization
    (B) In North Africa Islam was brought by Turkic tribes while in West Africa Arab tribes spread Islam.
    (C) In North Africa the spread of Islam led to Arabization while in West Africa Arabic never became the common spoken language
    (D) In North Africa the spread of Islam promoted the growth of urban centers of religious learning while in West Africa no such centers emerged.

14 Which of the following global events most likely facilitated the spread of Islam in Africa after 600 C.E.?

    (A) The decline of the Gupta empire in South Asia
    (B) The growth of Byzantine power in the Mediterranean
    (C) The Mayan Golden Age in Mesoamerica
    (D) The Decline of Roman power in the Mediterranean

15. Which of the following aspects of Islam helps to explain its rapid spread in Africa after the 7th century?

  (A) Its polytheism allowed the incorporation of local deities
  (B) Its emphasis on salvation through prayer appealed to the lower classes
  (C) Its establishment of monasteries allowed an alternative path for women
  (D) Its universalism encouraged converts from a variety of cultures

Questions 16-18 refer to the image below.

Kushan pendant from the fourth century. The figure depicted is Hariti, a Hindu goddess.

A pendant from the Kushan Empire
Victoria & Albert Museum/V&A Images/Art Resource, NY
Chapter 3, *Ways of the World: A Brief Global History with Sources,* Third Edition
Copyright © 2016 by Bedford/St. Martin's
Distributed by Bedford/St. Martin's/Macmillan Higher Education strictly for use with its products; Not for redistribution.

16. The pendant shows the influence of all of the following cultures EXCEPT

  (A) Greek
  (B) Olmec
  (C) Indian
  (D) Buddhist

17. All of the following help to explain the cultural cosmopolitanism of the pendant EXCEPT

  (A) The official language of the Kushan Empire was derived from India.
  (B) The Kushan Empire was linked to the Silk Road trading network.
  (C) Parts of the Kushan Empire had once been part of the empire established by Alexander the Great.
  (D) The Mongols were descendants of the founder of the Kushan Empire.

18. The pendant most clearly reflects which of the following historical processes?

    (A) Syncretism
    (B) Isolationism
    (C) Religious fundamentalism
    (D) Humanism

Questions 19-22 refer to the excerpt below.

> "[T]he networks and webs of the premodern millennium differed sharply from those of more recent centuries. Most people still produced primarily for their own consumption rather than for the market, and a much smaller range of goods was exchanged in the marketplaces of the world. Far fewer people then were required to sell their own labor for wages, an almost universal practice in modern economies. Because of transportation costs and technological limitations, most trade was in luxury goods rather than in necessities. In addition, the circuits of commerce were rather more limited than the truly global patterns of exchange that emerged after 1500."
>
> Source: Robert W. Strayer, *Ways of the World for the AP® Course*, Third Edition, (Boston: Bedford/St. Martins, 2016).

19. Which of the following represents a valid continuity in inter-regional trade from the period prior to 1500 to the modern world?

    (A) The predominance of wage labor in manufacturing.
    (B) The dependence of most people on the market for the purchase of basic goods.
    (C) The existence of transcontinental networks of exchange.
    (D) The dominant role of imperial states as controllers of key trade routes.

20. Which of the following describes how the preference for luxury items in the Silk Road trade affected ordinary people?

    (A) People from the lower classes could live the lifestyles of the powerful and wealthy.
    (B) Artisans in India began mass-producing wool and linen textiles to satisfy local demand.
    (C) Peasants in China shifted from the cultivation of crops to the production of silk, porcelain, and iron tools.
    (D) Merchants focused on local trade where the volume was higher, the profits more predictable, and the risks minimal.

21. A historian interested in investigating Strayer's thesis about the types of items traded would be most likely to examine which of the following types of evidence:

    (A) Merchant records found in cities along the Silk Road in western China
    (B) Ibn Battuta's records of his travel throughout the Islamic world
    (C) Archaeological evidence of homes and pottery along the Swahili coast of East Africa
    (D) Mongol legal documents which regulated commerce along the Silk Road

22. The limited volume of trade Strayer describes for the period 600 C.E. to 1450 C.E. nonetheless encouraged all of the following EXCEPT

    (A) The growth of powerful city-states and kingdoms
    (B) Trans-Atlantic merchant voyages
    (C) The diffusion of religion along existing trade routes
    (D) The spread of crops within the Americas

Questions 23-25 refer to the excerpts below.

"[Columbus was a] pioneer of progress and enlightenment. . . ."

from a U.S. presidential address, 1892

"Columbus was a perpetrator of genocide. . . ."

Winona LaDuke, president of the Indigenous Women's Network, 1992

23. What accounts for the different view of Columbus by the late twentieth century?

(A) The discrediting of imperialism
(B) The pseudo-scientific basis of racism
(C) The resurgence of European dominance
(D) The rejection of the Columbian exchange

24. How would the speaker of the first quote portray Columbus's arrival in the Americas in 1492?

(A) As marking the beginning of the Enlightenment
(B) As signaling the moral decline of the West
(C) As paving the way for greater tolerance and equality
(D) As initiating an era of American achievements

25. How would the speaker of the second quote portray Columbus's arrival in the Americas in 1492?

(A) As proof of European dominance
(B) As a sign of Native American resistance
(C) As an invasion
(D) As a blessing

Questions 26-27 refer to the image below.

Visual Source 12.3 was painted in the late fifteenth century by an Italian painter to serve as the front piece for a volume containing a Latin translation of Aristotle's writings along with commentaries by the twelfth-century Muslim scholar Ibn Rushd. Both men are depicted at the top, with Ibn Rushd on the left and Aristotle on the right.

Source 12.3 Aristotle and Averroes
Illumination attributed to Girolamo da Cremona and assistants, Venice, 1483/The Pierpont Morgan Library/Art Resource, NY
Chapter 12, *Ways of the World: A Brief Global History with Sources,* Third Edition

26. What does the image suggest about the relationship between Aristotle and Ibn Rushd?

    (A) Aristotle convinced Ibn Rushd to convert to Christianity.
    (B) Ibn Rushd rejected the secular elements of Aristotle's thoughts.
    (C) Aristotle made Ibn Rushd's works available to later generations.
    (D) Ibn Rushd made Aristotle's works available to later generations.

27. The illuminated page in Visual Source 12.3 offers evidence that would support which conclusion?

    (A) Europeans sought to reconcile Greek rationalism with Christian humanism.
    (B) Renaissance artists sought inspiration from the Greco-Roman and Islamic civilizations.
    (C) Italian thinkers sought to purge all Muslim influence from the writings of Aristotle.
    (D) Muslims sought to break the European intellectual monopoly on natural philosophy.

Questions 28-30 refer to the map below.

Map 12.1 Asia in the Fifteenth Century
Chapter 12, *Ways of the World: A Brief Global History with Sources,* Third Edition
Copyright © 2016 by Bedford/St. Martin's
Distributed by Bedford/St. Martin's/Macmillan Higher Education strictly for use with its products; Not for redistribution.

28. Which of the following conclusions is supported by the information in Map 12.1?

    (A) Ming dynasty China reached the Americas a century before the Europeans.
    (B) The voyages of Ming dynasty China were undertaken to conquer new territories.
    (C) The Chinese maritime expeditions facilitated long-distance trade in the Indian Ocean basin.
    (D) China lost control of most of the trade routes in the Indian Ocean after the European arrival.

29. Which of the following cities shown on Map 12.1 emerged as an important trading port in the fifteenth century as a result of the growing communities of Muslim merchants in the Indian Ocean region?

    (A) Beijing
    (B) Baghdad
    (C) Delhi
    (D) Malacca

30. Of the civilizations shown on Map 12.1, which represents the last significant military conquest of pastoral societies from Central Asia?

    (A) Ming dynasty China
    (B) Timur's empire
    (C) Delhi Sultanate
    (D) Vijayanagara

Questions 31-33 refer to the excerpt below.

"The Chinese, Mughal, and Ottoman empires continued older patterns of historical development, while those of Europe represented something wholly new in human history – an interacting Atlantic world of Europe, Africa, and the Americas. Furthermore, the European empires had a far greater impact on the peoples they incorporated than did other empires. Nowhere else did empire building generate such a catastrophic population collapse as in the Americas. Nor did Asian empires foster the kind of slave-based societies and transcontinental trade in slaves that were among the chief outcomes of Europe's American colonies."

Source: Robert W. Strayer, *Ways of the World for the AP® Course*, Third Edition, (Boston: Bedford/St. Martins, 2016).

31. Which of the following best explains the difference between the European empires which emerged after 1500 CE and the Asian empires Strayer cites?

    (A) The European armies utilized gun powder technology which the Asian powers did not have.
    (B) The Europeans built maritime empires while the Asian empires were land-based.
    (C) European empires facilitated inter-regional trade while Asian empires were increasingly isolationist.
    (D) Christian teachings permitted slavery while Islamic law prohibited it.

32. What accounts for the demographic collapse in the Americas which Strayer describes?

    (A) The collapse of indigenous armies in the face of Spanish and Portuguese military technology
    (B) Spanish policies of shipping Amerindians to Europe for slave labor
    (C) The spread of diseases to which Amerindians were immune
    (D) Disruptions in reproductive patterns due to the excessive use of female labor

33. Which of the following is valid evidence of an interaction between an Asian empire and an Atlantic empire?

    (A) The development of a secular empire in China
    (B) The establishment of Islamic sultanates in central Asia
    (C) The incorporation of the potato into the northern European diet
    (D) The introduction of new rice varieties in East Asia

Questions 34-36 refer to the excerpt below.

". . .a class of laborers, who live only so long as they find work, and who find work only so long as their labor increases capital. These laborers, who must sell themselves piece-meal, are a commodity, like every other article of commerce, and are consequently exposed to all the vicissitudes of competition, to all the fluctuations of the market."

Source: Karl Marx and Frederick Engels, *The Communist Manifesto*, 1848. Authorized English Translation. (Chicago: Charles H. Kerr & Company, 1906).

". . .the skilled workman, unless trained in good habits, may exhibit no higher a life than that of the mere animal; and the earning of increased wages will only furnish him with increased means for indulging in the gratification of his grosser appetites. . . . This habitual improvidence . . . is the real cause of the social degradation of the artisan."

Source: Samuel Smiles, Thrift, (Toronto: Belford Brothers, Publishers, 1876).

34. Which of the following statements captures the explanations for the poverty of the working class offered by the writers above?

(A) The first passage blames the capitalist system, while the second passage blames the workers' habits.
(B) The first passage blames increasing demand for unskilled labor, while the second passage blames declining wages.
(C) Both agree that industrial capitalism will ultimately improve the lives of the working class.
(D) Both agree that the government should establish a minimum wage for workers.

35. The class of laborers described in the quote above emerged as a result of the

(A) French Revolution
(B) Agricultural Revolution
(C) Industrial Revolution
(D) Scientific Revolution

36. Karl Marx and Friedrich Engels advocated which of the following as a solution to the problem they outlined?

(A) government reforms to ameliorate the conditions of the lower classes
(B) revolutions to replace the capitalist system with a socialist one
(C) technological improvements to increase total national wealth
(D) education to give laborers alternatives to factory work

Questions 37-39 refer to the map below.

Map 18.2 Conquest and Resistance in Colonial Africa
Chapter 18, *Ways of the World: A Brief Global History with Sources,* Third Edition
Copyright © 2016 by Bedford/St. Martin's
Distributed by Bedford/St. Martin's/Macmillan Higher Education strictly for use with its products; Not for redistribution.

37. The map above reflects the outcome of which of the following?

  (A) The scramble for Africa
  (B) The great dying
  (C) The Middle Passage
  (D) The African National Congress

Questions 45-46 refer to the image below.

"The Eternal Jew," Germany 1937

Nazi Hatred of the Jews
akg-images
Chapter 20, *Ways of the World: A Brief Global History with Sources,* Third Edition
Copyright © 2016 by Bedford/St. Martin's
Distributed by Bedford/St. Martin's/Macmillan Higher Education strictly for use with its products; Not for redistribution.

45. The ideas expressed in this poster can best be categorized as

   (A) Communist
   (B) Anti-Semitic
   (C) Imperialist
   (D) Anarchist

The purpose of the poster was most likely to

   A) Promote fear of a Jewish-Soviet conspiracy
   3) Justify German ambitions in Czechoslovakia
   ') Oppose the growth of Zionism in Europe
) Justify the renunciation of the Treaty of Versailles

Questions 47-48 refer to the excerpt below.

"To many historians, that century [the twentieth], and a new era in the human journey, began in 1914 with the outbreak of World War I.

... this most recent century both carried on from the past and developed distinctive characteristics as well. Whether that combination of the old and new merits the designation of a separate era in world history will likely be debated. . ."

Source: Robert W. Strayer, *Ways of the World for the AP® Course*, Third Edition, (Boston: Bedford/St. Martins, 2016).

47. In contrast to the view expressed in the first quotation, the second quotation
    (A) challenges the notion that the twentieth century represented anything new
    (B) insists that the twentieth century constituted a new period
    (C) questions the significance of World War I as an epoch-marking turning point
    (D) argues that World War I dramatically transformed the world

48. Which historical development would support the thesis that World War I was NOT a turning point in world history?
    (A) The creation of the League of Nations after the Treaty of Versailles
    (B) The Russian Revolution and the growth of Communist movements around the world
    (C) The role of the United States as a global economic power in the 20th century
    (D) European colonial rule in Africa in the 1920s and 1930s

Questions 49-51 refer to the image below.

Women Can Hold Up Half the Sky; Surely the Face of Nature Can Be Transformed," China 1975.

Source 21.3 Women, Nature, and Industrialization
Courtesy, University of Westminster Poster Collection, London
Chapter 21, *Ways of the World: A Brief Global History with Sources,* Third Edition
Copyright © 2016 by Bedford/St. Martin's

49. Which of the following statements most accurately reflects the message of this poster?

    (A) Women work under difficult and grueling conditions.
    (B) Progress depends on human mastery over nature.
    (C) China still lacks modern technology
    (D) China is dependent on foreign investment

50. The purpose of the poster was most likely to

    (A) Encourage women to abandon traditional roles for the national good
    (B) Warn of the environmental risks of rapid industrialization
    (C) Promote the cult of Mao Zedong
    (D) Mobilize the youth for military service

51. Which historical event established the context for this poster?

    (A) The Long March
    (B) The War of Liberation
    (C) The Cultural Revolution
    (D) The Tiananmen Square protests

Questions 52-55 refer to the excerpts below.

"I believe that Islam within it provides justice and equality for women, and I think that those aspects of Islam which have been highlighted by the *mullas* [religious scholars] do not do a service to our religion ...But ... as more and more people in Muslim countries, both men and women, achieve education and begin to examine the Qur'an in the light of their education, they are beginning not to agree with the *mullas* on their orthodox or reactionary version of Islam.

Let us start with the story of the Fall. Unlike Christianity, it is not Eve who tempts Adam into tasting the apple and being responsible for original sin. According to Islam – and I mention this because I believe that Islam is an egalitarian religion – both Adam and Eve are tempted, both are warned, both do not heed the warning, and therefore the Fall occurs."

Source: Benazir Bhutto, "Politics and the Muslim Woman," transcript of audio recording, April 11, 1985, in *Liberal Islam: A Sourcebook*, ed. Charles Kurzman (New York: Oxford University Press, 1998).

52. Bhutto's purpose in making this statement was most likely to

    (A) Challenge the authority of emerging religious leaders in Central Asia and South Asia
    (B) Champion an increased role for Islam in public life
    (C) Limit the power of the Pakistani military within her country's government
    (D) Encourage western powers to lift trade embargoes on Pakistan
    Answer: A

53. The purpose of Bhutto's reference to the Islamic version of the Adam and Eve story was to

    (A) Demonstrate that Islam is superior to other religions
    (B) Urge Christians to adopt a more liberal interpretation of the story of the Fall
    (C) To provide a scriptural justification for gender equality
    (D) To encourage public school students to study the Qur'an

54. Bhutto's emphasis on justice and equality is most similar to ideas found in which other religious trend in world history?

    (A) Early Hinduism in South Asia
    (B) The Protestant Reformation in Western Europe
    (C) Liberation Theology in Latin America
    (D) Zen Buddhism in Japan

55. Which of the following historical development most likely provided the context for this speech?
    (A) The growth of nationalist movements in 20th century Egypt and Turkey
    (B) Escalating conflicts between Pakistan and India over control of disputed territories
    (C) Increasing violence in the West Bank against Israeli occupation
    (D) The growth of extreme religious movements in Afghanistan after the Soviet invasion

3. Use the two passages below and your knowledge of world history to answer all parts of the question that follows.

   Source 1:

   One historian's view of the origins of the Boxer Rebellion in China, 1899-1900:

   "Disaster, moreover, had manufactured rebellion throughout Chinese history. ... Thus officials were hardly surprised when flood distress fused with perceptions of foreign conspiracy to produce a significant local uprising ...

   "Joining the Boxers, moreover, was a sure way of filling one's belly. Everywhere the movement was active it patriotically cajoled or, if necessary, simply expropriated surplus food from merchants and rich peasants.... [T]he radical slogan of 'equal division of grain' was central to the explosive growth of the Boxer uprising."

   Source: Mike Davis, *Late Victorian Holocausts: El Niño Famines and the Making of the Third World* (2001) pps. 182-184.

   Source 2:

   Anonymous Boxer poem:

   "The Gods assist the Boxers,
   The Patriotic Harmonious corps.
   It is because the 'Foreign Devils' disturb the 'Middle Kingdom,'
   Urging the people to join their religion ..."

   Source: Louis Snyder, Marvin Perry, and Benjamin Mazen. *Panorama of the Past* (1966).

   a. Identify and explain ONE way the anonymous poem supports Davis' analysis of the roots of the Boxer Rebellion.

   b. Identify and explain ONE way the anonymous poem might complicate Davis' analysis of the roots of the Boxer Rebellion.

   c. Identify ONE change *OR* ONE continuity in the patterns of Chinese rebellions in the first half of the twentieth century.

4. Answer all parts of the question that follows.

   Identify and explain THREE ways in which social movements have challenged traditional gender roles in the 20th century. Your answer must refer to specific global regions.

SECTION II

Total Time–1 hour, 30 minutes

Part A: Document-Based Question

Suggested reading and writing time: 55 minutes

It is suggested that you spend 15 minutes reading the documents and 40 minutes writing your response.

Note: You may begin writing your response before the reading period is over.

Directions: Question 1 is based on the accompanying documents. The documents have been edited for the purpose of this exercise.

In your response you should do the following.

- ■ **Thesis:** Present a thesis that makes a historically defensible claim and responds to all parts of the question. The thesis must consist of one or more sentences located in one place, either in the introduction or the conclusion.

- ■ **Argument Development:** Develop and support a cohesive argument that recognizes and accounts for historical complexity by explicitly illustrating relationships among historical evidence such as contradiction, corroboration, and/or qualification.

- ■ **Use of the documents:** Utilize the content of at least six of the documents to support the stated thesis or a relevant argument.

- ■ **Sourcing the documents:** Explain the significance of the author's point of view, author's purpose, historical context, and/or audience for at least four documents.

- ■ **Contextualization:** Situate the argument by explaining the broader historical events, developments, or processes immediately relevant to the question.

- ■ **Outside Evidence:** Provide an example or additional piece of specific evidence beyond those found in the documents to support or qualify the argument.

- ■ **Synthesis:** Extend the arguments by explaining the connections between the argument and ONE of the following
  - A development in a different historical period, situation, era, or geographical area.
  - A course theme and/or approach to history that is not the focus of the essay (such as political, economic, social, cultural, or intellectual history)
  - A different discipline or field of inquiry (such as economics, government and politics, art history or anthropology).

1. Using the documents provided and your knowledge of world history, analyze changes and continuities in the responses of the Chinese imperial government (Qing dynasty) to British trade from 1750 C.E. to 1900 C.E.

Document 1

Source: Chinese Qing dynasty Emperor Qianlong, "Message to King George III," a letter to the British monarch, 1793. From E. Backhouse and J. O. P. Bland, *Annals and Memoirs of the Court of Peking* (Boston: Houghton Mifflin, 1914).

"Your request for a small island . . . where your merchants may reside and goods be warehoused, arises from your desire to develop trade. . . . Consider, moreover, that England is not the only barbarian land which wishes to establish relations with our civilization and trade with our Empire ...This also is a flagrant infringement of the usage of my Empire and cannot possibly be entertained. . . .

"If, after the receipt of this explicit decree, you . . . allow your barbarian merchants to proceed to Zhejiang and Tianjin, with the object of landing and trading there, the ordinances of my Celestial Empire are strict in the extreme ... Should your vessels touch the shore, your merchants . . . will be subject to instant expulsion. Do not say that you were not warned in due time! Tremblingly obey and show no negligence!"

Document 2

Source: Xu Naiji, a senior official and advisor to Qing Emperor Daoguang, "An Argument for Legalization," 1836. "Memorial from Heu-Naetse," in *Blue Book–Correspondence Relating to China* (London, 1840).

"Formerly, the barbarian merchants brought foreign money to China; which being paid in exchange for goods, was a source of pecuniary advantage to the people of all the sea-board provinces. But lately, the barbarian merchants have clandestinely sold opium for money, which has rendered it unnecessary for them to import foreign silver. Thus foreign money has been going out of the country, while none comes into it.

It is proposed entirely to cut off the foreign trade, thus to remove the root, to dam up the source of the evil. The Celestial Dynasty would not, indeed, hesitate to relinquish the few millions of duties arising therefrom. But all the nations of the West have had a general market open to their ships for upward of a thousand years, while the dealers in opium are the English alone; it would be wrong, for the sake of cutting off the English trade, to cut off that of all the other nations. Besides, the hundreds of thousands of people living on the sea-coast depend wholly on trade for their livelihood, and how are they to be disposed of?"

Document 3

Source: British company records, 1835–1836.

Chinese/British Trade at Canton, 1835–1836 (values in Spanish dollars)

British exports to Canton		British imports from Canton	
Opium	17,904,248	Tea	13,412,243
Cotton	8,357,394	Raw silk	3,764,115
All other items	6,164,981	All other items	6, 676,541
Total:	32,426,623	Total:	23,852,899

Document 4

Source: Lin Zexu, a senior official sent by Qing Emperor Daoguang to suppress the illegal opium trade, "A Moral Appeal to Queen Victoria," 1839. From Alexander Murray, Doings in China: Being the personal narrative of an officer engaged in the late Chinese Expedition, from the Recapture of Chusan in 1841, to the Peace of Nankin in 1842 (London: Richard Bentley, New Burlington Street, Publisher in Ordinary to Her Majesty, 1843), pl. ii/Visual Connection Archive.

"Let us ask, where is your conscience? I have heard that the smoking of opium is very strictly forbidden by your country; that is because the harm caused by opium is clearly understood. Since it is not permitted to do harm to your country, then even less should you let it be passed on to the harm of other countries – how much less to China! Of all that China exports to foreign countries, there is not a single thing which is not beneficial to people: they are of benefit when eaten, or of benefit when used, or of benefit when resold: all are beneficial. Is there a single article from China which has done any harm to foreign countries? . . . [O]ur Celestial Court lets tea, silk, and other goods be shipped without limit and circulated everywhere without begrudging it in the slightest. This is for no other reason but to share the benefit with the people of the whole world . . .

We have heard heretofore that your honorable ruler is kind and benevolent. Naturally you would not wish to give unto others what you yourself do not want . . .

Therefore in the new regulations, in regard to those barbarians who bring opium to China, the penalty is fixed at decapitation or strangulation. This is what is called getting rid of a harmful thing on behalf of mankind . . .

Document 5

Source: The Treaty of Nanjing, ending the First Opium War between Britain and China, 1842. From "Treaty Between Her Majesty and The emperor of China." Signed, in the English and Chinese Languages, at Nanking, 29th August, 1842.

"II.
His Majesty the Emperor of China agrees, that British subjects, with their families and establishments, shall be allowed to reside, for the purposes of carrying on their mercantile pursuits, without molestation or restraint, at the cities and towns of Canton, Amoy, Foochowfoo, Ningpo, and Shanghai. . . .

III.
It being obviously necessary and desirable that British subjects should have some port whereat they may [maintain] and refit their ships when required, and keep stores for that purpose, His Majesty the Emperor of China cedes to Her Majesty the Queen of Great Britain, &c., the Island of Hong-Kong. . . .

IV.
The Emperor of China agrees to pay the sum of 6,000,000 of dollars, as the value of the opium which was delivered up at Canton in the month of March, 1839, as a ransom for the lives of Her Britannic Majesty's Superintendent and subjects, who had been imprisoned and threatened with death by the Chinese High Officers. . . .

VI.
The Government of Her Britannic Majesty having been obliged to send out an expedition to demand and obtain redress for the violent and unjust proceedings of the Chinese High Authorities towards Her Britannic Majesty's officer and subjects, the Emperor of China agrees to pay the sum of 12,000,000 of dollars, on account of the expenses incurred. . . .

Document 6

Great powers of the day (from left to right: Great Britain's Queen Victoria, Germany's Kaiser Wilhelm, Russia's Tsar Nicholas II, a female figure representing France, and the Meiji emperor of Japan) sit around the pie of China while a Chinese figure stands behind them.

Carving Up the Pie of China
The Chinese Cake, from *Le Petit Journal,* 1898, lithograph by Henri Meyer (1844–1899)/Private
Collection/Roger-Viollet, Paris, France/Bridgeman Images
Chapter 19, *Ways of the World: A Brief Global History with Sources,* Third Edition
Copyright © 2016 by Bedford/St. Martin's

Document 7

Source: Emperor Guangxu, "Edict on Education," 1898. Issued during the "Hundred Days of Reform." From J. Mason Gentzler, *Changing China* (New York: Praeger, 1977), 88-89; Isaac Taylor Headland, *Court Life in China* (New York: F.H. Revell, 1909).

"We soon see how weak we are. Does anyone think that our troops are as well drilled or as well led as those of the foreign armies? Or that we can successfully stand against them? Changes must be made to accord with the necessities of the times…. We must substitute modern arms and western organization for our old regime; we must select our military officers according to western methods of military education; we must establish elementary and high schools, colleges and universities, in accordance with those of foreign countries …"

Part B: Long-Essay Question
Time–35 minutes

Directions: Choose EITHER Question 2 or 3.

In your response you should do the following:

- ■ **Thesis:** Present a thesis that makes a historically defensible claim and responds to all parts of the question. The thesis must consist of one or more sentences located in one place, either in the introduction or the conclusion.

- ■ **Application of historical thinking skills:** Develop and support an argument that applies historical thinking skills as directed by the question.

- ■ **Supporting the argument with evidence:** Utilize specific examples of evidence to fully and effectively substantiate the stated thesis or a relevant argument.

- ■ **Synthesis:** Extend the argument by explaining the connections between the argument and ONE of the following:

  - A development in a different historical period, situation, era, or geographical area.
  - A course theme and/or approach to history that is not the focus of the essay (such as political, economic, social, cultural, or intellectual history).
  - A different discipline or field of inquiry (such as economics, government, and politics, art history, or anthropology).

2. Compare the effect on social structures of TWO of the following belief systems before 600 CE.
   - ■ Hinduism
   - ■ Confucianism
   - ■ Buddhism
   - ■ Christianity

OR

3. Analyze similarities and differences in trade dynamics between the Indian Ocean trading system and the Trans-Saharan trade routes from 600 CE to 1450 CE.

PRACTICE EXAM 2

SECTION I

Total Time–1 hour, 45 minutes

Part A: Multiple-Choice Questions

Time: 55 minutes

Questions 1-3 refer to the excerpt below.

"My main conclusion was that societies developed differently on different continents because of differences in continental environments, not in human biology. Advanced technology, centralized political organization, and other features of complex societies could emerge only in dense sedentary populations capable of accumulating food surpluses – populations that depended for their food on the rise of agriculture that began around 8,500 B.C. But the domesticable wild plant and animal species essential for that rise of agriculture were distributed very unevenly over the continents. The most valuable domesticable wild species were concentrated in only nine small areas of the globe, which thus became the earliest homelands of agriculture. The original inhabitants of those homelands thereby gained a head start toward developing guns, germs, and steel. The languages and genes of those homeland inhabitants, as well as their livestock, crops, technologies, and writing systems, became dominant in the ancient and modern world."

Source: Jared Diamond, commenting on the original thesis he developed in his landmark book. From Jared Diamond, *Guns, Germs, and Steel: The Fates of Human Societies.* (New York: W.W. Norton & Company, 2005). The AFTERWORD.

1. Jared Diamond's argument would best explain

   (A) The differences between the Chinese and Roman writing systems which emerged in the ancient period
   (B) The differences between historical developments in the Americas and Eurasia prior to the Columbian Exchange
   (C) The similarities among different Slavic languages after the first millennium
   (D) The impacts of language diffusion on central African agricultural societies

2. Which type of evidence did Diamond most likely utilize?

   (A) Diaries of early herders and agriculturalists
   (B) Cave drawings showing the prevalence of large mammals
   (C) Genetic evidence showing the evolution of plant and animal species
   (D) Religious myths describing early settlement patterns

3 Diamond's most likely purpose in writing this passage was to

   (A) Utilize environmental differences to explain different patterns of human development
   (B) Emphasize the primacy of culture to explain uneven levels of agricultural development
   (C) Highlight the role of language diffusion in shaping where technologies emerged
   (D) Identify the specific regions in which agriculture first emerged.

Questions 4-6 refer to the map below.

Map 3.5 Classical China
Chapter 3, *Ways of the World: A Brief Global History with Sources,* Third Edition
Copyright © 2016 by Bedford/St. Martin's
Distributed by Bedford/St. Martin's/Macmillan Higher Education strictly for use with its products; Not for redistribution.

4. What was the most likely purpose of the Great Wall depicted in Map 3.5?

   (A) To keep the Xiongnu and other nomadic peoples from the northern steppes out of China
   (B) To keep the Chinese from conquering the northern steppes in Central Asia
   (C) To honor the emperors of the Qin and Han dynasties
   (D) To protect travelers and merchants along the Silk Road

5. Map 3.5 suggests that the city of Xi'an (previously known as Chang'an) was an important center of

   (A) warfare
   (B) defense
   (C) religion
   (D) commerce

6. Map 3.5 suggests that Chinese expansion northwards was checked by the
   (A) lack of infrastructure
   (B) bandits along the Silk Road
   (C) Xiongnu Confederation
   (D) Qin and Han empires

Questions 7-10 refer to the excerpt below.

"Here I want to consider how a few historians have periodized their narratives of Japan's earliest recorded epoch …

In textbooks and general overviews, one frequently finds periods named after the venue of the monarch's court and capital: there are the Asuka (592-710), Nara (710-794), and Heian (794-1185) periods.

But much of the postwar historiography written in Japanese divides history into four epochs … This scheme is generally paired with a Marxist model of socioeconomic development that sees society developing from the primitive communalism of kin groups … into a slave-based society in the ancient age, into a serf-based society in the medieval age, and then into a capitalist society in the modern age."

Source: Joan R. Piggot, "Chapter 3: Defining Ancient and Classical," Karl Friday, ed, *Japan Emerging.* (Boulder, CO: Westview Press, 2012).

7. In this passage historian Joan R. Piggot points out that
   (A) The Marxist model offers the best framework for understanding Japanese history
   (B) Attempting to divide a nation's history into distinct periods leads to faulty conclusions
   (C) Japan's history was driven by shifts in monarchical power
   (D) Historians political views often influence how they define historical periods

8 In the postwar historiography which Piggot describes which of the following events might have marked a turning point into the "modern age"?
   (A) the Japanese defeat of the Mongol invasions in the 12th century
   (B) The establishment of the Tokugawa shogunate in the 17th century
   C) The Meiji Restoration of the 18th century
   (D) The emergence of Japanese imperialism in the 20th century

9. Which of the following would best describe the "earliest recorded epoch" (592-1185 CE) to which Piggot refers?
   (A) A period of warring clans in which no stable monarchy developed
   (B) A period of cultural consolidation and the emergence of the emperor
   C) A period of rejection of Chinese influences and the beginning of isolationism
   (D) A period in which no nobility could survive because of the decline of agricultural production.

10. Critics of the periodization of Japan which Piggot attributes to postwar historians would contend that the division of history into those four periods is better suited to the history of
    (A) Western Europe
    (B) China
    (C) South Asia
    (D) The Americas

Questions 11-13 refer to the map below.

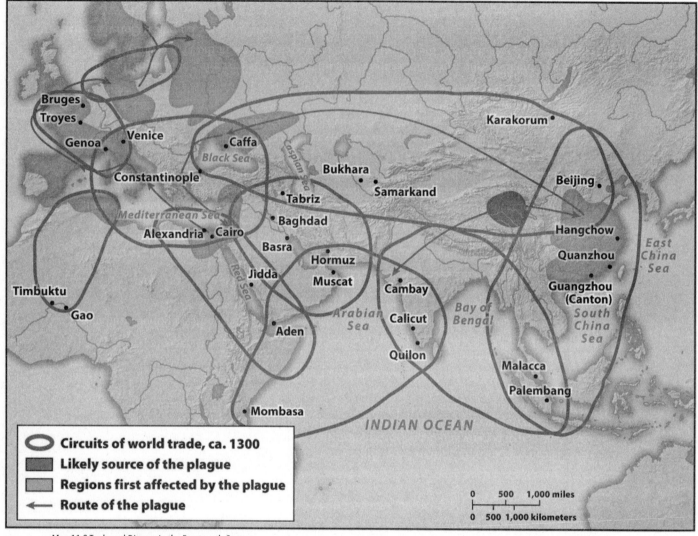

Map 11.2 Trade and Disease in the Fourteenth Century
Chapter 11, *Ways of the World: A Brief Global History with Sources,* Third Edition
Copyright © 2016 by Bedford/St. Martin's
Distributed by Bedford/St. Martin's/Macmillan Higher Education strictly for use with its products; Not for redistribution.

11. The spread of the plague was facilitated and accelerated by the networks of exchange created by the empire established by the

    (A) Europeans
    (B) Xiongnu
    (C) Mongols
    (D) Uighurs

12. Which of the following can be inferred based on the information shown in Map 11.2?

    (A) Central Asia was protected from the spread of the plague because of its marginalized position in the circuits of world trade.

    (B) The trade circuits of the fourteenth century linked Europe to the long-established trading networks of Eurasia.

21. The relationship between Marco Polo and Kubilai Khan depicted in the painting was most likely reflective of which aspect of Mongol rule?

 (A) IWhile adopting Confucian values the Mongols imposed harsh restrictions on the Chinese
 (B) Mongol khans often adapted to the dominant religions of the regions they ruled
 (C) Mongol values allowed a more substantial role for women than had many other empires at the time
 (D) The Mongols in China often employed Muslims and Europeans in the royal court.

Questions 22-24 refer to the excerpt below.

"When Moctezuma had finished, Doña Marina translated his address into Spanish so that the Captain could understand it. Cortés replied in his strange and savage tongue 'Tell Moctezuma that we are his friends. There is nothing to fear …'

When Moctezuma was imprisoned [by the Spanish, the Aztec nobles] … all went into hiding. They ran away to hide and treacherously abandoned him!"

Source: Anonymous. Aztec illustrated histories translated from the Nahuatl language. From Miguel Leon-Ortilla, Lysander Kemp, trans. *The Broken spears: The Aztec Account of the Conquest of Mexico*, 1500s C.E. (Boston: Beacon Press, 2006).

22. Which of the following best describes the Anonymous author's likely purpose in writing this account?

 (A) To express fascination with the Spaniard's technological superiority
 (B) To highlight the critical role played by Doña Marina in promoting cultural interaction
 (C) To express disgust for the dishonesty of the Spaniards and the cowardice of Aztec nobles
 (D) To warn other Amerindian leaders to prepare for battle with the Spanish.

23. Which of the following events was the most likely immediate cause of the events described in the passage?

 (A) The reunification of Spain after centuries of Muslim rule
 (B) The establishment of the Catholic Church as a powerful institution in Latin America
 (C) The fall of the Mayan city-states leading to a power vacuum in Mesoamerica
 (D) The introduction of Eurasian diseases to the Americas by Spanish conquerors.

24. Which of the following was an immediate consequence of the events described in the passage?

 (A) The rapid collapse of the Aztec empire
 (B) The growth of silver as a global currency
 (C) Spanish competition with Great Britain over American shipping lanes
 (D) The development of the Atlantic slave trade

Questions 25-28 refer to the table below.

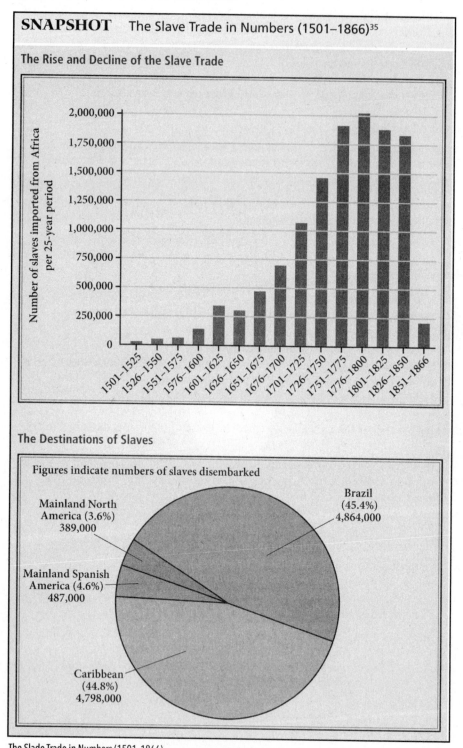

25. The data on the destination of African slaves can best be explained by
    (A) The development of the cotton gin and growth of cotton plantations
    (B) The global demand for sugar and the development of sugar plantations
    (C) The increasing use of slaves as soldiers and advisors
    (D) A gender imbalance in west Africa due slave raiding

26. The changes reflected in the data for the 19th century depicted in the bar graph resulted from
    (A) Slave revolts in the Americas which made slavery unpopular
    (B) Trends toward abolition of the slave trade in most of the Americas
    (C) The collapse of plantation agriculture following the industrial revolution
    (D) Competition from Egyptian and Indian cotton producers which reduced U.S. Cotton sales

27. The African slave trade most likely contributed to which of the following developments?
    (A) The development of African leadership in many independence movements in the Americas
    (B) Substantial poverty and the delay of industrialization throughout the Americas
    (C) The development of indentured servitude drawing laborers from Asia
    (D) Demographic transition in the Americas and emergence of new social hierarchies

28. Which of the following best explains the data for the 16th and 17th centuries?
    (A) The decline of the indigenous populations led to the demand for a new labor source
    (B) The rise of North American industry created the need for low-wage laborers
    (C) European colonialism in most of Africa enabled European powers to begin population transfers
    (D) Independence for the United States led to a boom in the slave trade

Questions 29–31 refer to the excerpt below.

"Having on one occasion asked my father the reason why he had forbidden anyone to prevent or interfere with the building of [Hindu temples], his reply was … 'With all of the human race, I am at peace … Neither is it to be forgotten, that the class of whom we are speaking … Are usefully engaged, either in the pursuits of science or the arts, or of improvements for the benefit of mankind, and have in numerous instances arrived at the highest distinctions in the state, there being, indeed, to be found in this city men of every description, and of every religion on the face of the earth.'"

Source: Jahangir, Mughal emperor, early 17th century, recalling a conversation with his father, Akbar the Great. From *Memoirs of the Emperor Jahangir*, translated from the Persian by Major David Price (London: Oriental Translation Committee, 1829).

29. Which of the following represents a substantial difference in the governing policies of the Mughal emperors of South Asia and the Christian rulers in Western Europe in the 17th century?
    (A) While the Mughals avoided military conflicts with their neighbors, the European Christian rulers fought many wars for territory
    (B) While the Mughal armies were armed primarily with swords, Christian European armies utilized gun powder and rifles
    (C) While Mughal emperors often practiced religious tolerance, European Christian rulers imposed Christianity
    (D) While Mughal rulers imported products exclusively via land-based trade networks, European Christian leaders relied increasingly on sea-based trade systems.

30. One likely goal of Jahangir's statement was to

    (A) Encourage Hindu conversion to Islam
    (B) Establish a separation between religion and state
    (C) Maintain Muslim control of Indian Ocean trade ports
    (D) Sustain Hindu loyalty to a Muslim state

31. Which feature of the Mughal empire represented a change from most South Asian states that had preceded it?

    (A) The Mughal empire ruled over peoples of varying languages and religions
    (B) Under Mughal rule South Asia was primarily agrarian but had thriving commercial ports
    (C) The Mughals united the majority of South Asia under a single state
    (D) During the Mughal period the majority of Hindus and Muslims converted to a new syncretic religion

Questions 32-34 refer to the excerpt below.

"Preamble.

1. Woman is born free and remains equal to man in rights. Social distinctions may be based only on common utility.

2. The purpose of all political association is the preservation of the natural and imprescriptible rights of woman and man. These rights are liberty, property, security, and especially resistance to oppression.

3. The principle of all sovereignty rests essentially in the nation, which is but the reuniting of woman and man. No body and no individual may exercise authority which does not emanate expressly from the nation."

Source: Olympe de Gouges, The Declaration of the Rights of Woman (France, September 1791). From *The French Revolution and Human Rights: A Brief Documentary History,* translated, edited, and with an introduction by Lynn Hunt (Boston: Bedford/St. Martin's, 1996).

32. Which of the following ideological developments likely had the greatest influence on Olympe de Gouges?

    (A) Socialism
    (B) The Englightenment
    (C) Laissez-faire
    (D) Nationalism

33. The purpose of this document was most likely to

    (A) Pressure French Revolutionary leaders to address gender inequality
    (B) Prevent the restoration of the French monarchy
    (C) Challenge the influence of the Catholic clergy over the French government
    (D) Limit suffrage in the new revolutionary society

34. A long-term impact of de Gouges' work on the Atlantic world was to

    (A) Limit the effectiveness of independence movements
    (B) Encourage abolitionist movements
    (C) Support constitutional republics
    (D) Contribute to the development of women's movements

Questions 35-37 refer to the excerpt below.

"[W]e are, moreover, neither Indian nor European, but a species midway between the legitimate proprietors of this country and the Spanish usurpers. In short, though Americans by birth we derive our rights from Europe, and we have to assert these rights against the rights of the natives, and at the same time we must defend ourselves against the invaders."

Source: Simon Bolivar, "The Jamaica Letter," 1815. Letter written to an English gentleman during Latin America's wars for independence.

35. Which of the following visions of a Latin American future does Bolivar implicitly advocate in this passage?
    (A) A society based on racial equality that is independent from Spain
    (B) A society that is independent from Spain but ruled by those of European descent
    (C) A society that is still part of the Spanish empire but with greater control over its own affairs
    (D) A society in which Amerindians are restored to power

36. Bolivar likely wrote this letter in order to

    (A) Convince indigenous peoples to join the independence cause
    (B) Convince the Spanish crown to grant Latin American independence
    (C) Persuade Spain's European rivals to support Latin American independence
    (D) Prevent the United States from intervening in Latin American affairs

37. Which of the following represents a difference between the results of the South American independence movement led by Simon Bolivar and the Haitian independence movement led by Toussaint L'Ouverture?

    (A) While most of South America won independence from Spain in the 19th century, Haiti remained a French colony for most of the 19th century
    (B) While Haiti isolated itself from foreign trade for most of the 19th century, South America became a major supplier of goods to Great Britain
    (C) While slavery was abolished in Haiti immediately following independence, most South American countries did not abolish slavery until the mid-19th century
    (D) While Whites of European descent continued to play a leading role in Haitian politics, people of indigenous descent played an increasingly important role in South American governments.

Questions 38-39 refer to the image below.

"Cecil Rhodes, 19th century British businessman and politician"

THE RHODES COLOSSUS

STRIDING FROM CAPE TOWN TO CAIRO.

Map 18.3 From the Cape to Cairo
Chapter 18, *Ways of the World: A Brief Global History with Sources,* Third Edition

38. The artist's purpose in creating "The Rhodes Colossus" was to

   (A) Warn Africans of the danger of European imperialism
   (B) Celebrate the role of Europeans as modernizers
   (C) Depict the process of European colonization
   (D) Persuade Europeans to oppose imperialism

39. Which of the following historical developments most likely set the context for this image
    (A) The rise of Apartheid in South Africa
    (B) The rise of Swahili city-states in East Africa
    (C) The Morocco crisis of 1905
    (D) The "Scramble for Africa"

Questions 40-41 refer to the chart below.

A late 19th century chart depicting a European view of racial categories.

European Racial Images
The Granger Collection, NYC–All rights reserved
Chapter 18, *Ways of the World: A Brief Global History with Sources,* Third Edition
Copyright © 2016 by Bedford/St. Martin's
Distributed by Bedford/St. Martin's/Macmillan Higher Education strictly for use with its products; Not for redistribution.

40. The purpose of this chart was to
    (A) Utilize new scientific theories to justify social inequality
    (B) Celebrate the diversity of 19th century Europe
    (C) Encourage open trade between Europe, Africa, and Asia
    (D) Discourage Asian and African migration to Europe

41. One impact of European theories of racial difference as it developed in the 19th century was to
    (A) heighten competition between France and Germany for global power
    (B) Encourage European imperialism in Africa and Asia
    (C) Discourage independence movements in Latin America
    (D) Stimulate trade and exploration

Questions 42-43 refer to the chart below.

Long- Distance Migration in an Age of Empire, 1846-1940

ORIGINS	DESTINATION	NUMBERS
Europe	Americas	55-58 million
India, southern China	Southeast Asia, Indian Ocean rim, South Pacific	48-52 million
Northeast Asia, Russia	Manchuria, Siberia, Central Asia, Japan	46-51 million

42. Which of the following best explain the patterns of Indian and Southern Chinese migration described in the chart?

   (A) The industrial revolution created a demand for low-wage factory workers
   (B) The age of imperialism led to mass expulsions from South and East Asia
   (C) Many migrants left their homelands seeking religious freedom
   (D) The abolition of the African slave trade created a demand for a new source of labor

43. Which of the following was a long-term impact of the long-distance migrations of the late 19th and early 20th centuries?

   (A) Increasing competition among European powers for colonies and trade routes
   (B) The development of diaspora communities in many regions of the world
   (C) Increasing resistance to colonialism in Africa and Southeast Asia
   (D) The spread of pathogens which wiped out indigenous populations

Questions 44-46 refer to the image below.

1911 poster published by the Industrial Workers of the World, a radical U.S. labor union. In subsequent years the poster would be translated into several languages and displayed throughout the world.

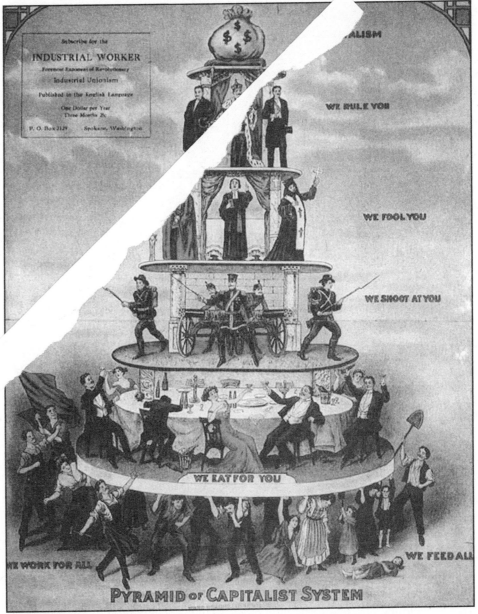

The Socialist Outlook
From *Pyramid of Capitalist System,* issued by Nedelkovich, Brashick and Kuharich, Cleveland (International Publishing Company, 1911)/photo: IAM/akg-images
Chapter 17, *Ways of the World: A Brief Global History with Sources,* Third Edition

44. Although this poster first appeared in the United States its ideas were most compatible with those of

    (A) The Nationalist movement in China
    (B) Emiliano Zapata's revolutionary movement in Mexico
    (C) The Bolshevik (Communist) Party of Russia
    (D) The Fascist Party of Italy

45. The poster was likely created in response to conditions created by which of the following historic events?

    (A) The Industrial Revolution
    (B) Latin American independence
    (C) The Opium Wars
    (D) The French Revolution

46. The poster is illustrative of which of the following differences between the Industrial Workers of the World and most labor unions in the United States and Western Europe after World War II?

    (A) While the Industrial Workers of the World advocated the overthrow of capitalism, most post-World War II unions merely advocated improvements in their members' wages and working conditions
    (B) While the Industrial Workers of the World admitted females to full membership, most post-World War II unions remained almost exclusively male
    (C) While the Industrial Workers of the World advocated broader social and legal changes, post-World War II unions tended to focus on bargaining for contracts
    (D) While the Industrial Workers of the World advocated a return to an agrarian society, most post-World War II unions celebrated the growth of industry

Questions 47-50 refer to the excerpt below.

> "The various ideological and social evils of present-day Japan are the result of ignoring the fundamental and running after the trivial … and this is due to the fact that since the days of *Meiji* so many aspects of European and American culture, systems, and learning have been imported, and that too rapidly…. [T]he foreign ideologies imported into our country are in the main ideologies of the [European] Enlightenment…. [T]hese lay the highest value on, and assert the liberty and equality of, individuals…
>
> We have already witnessed the boundless Imperial virtues. Wherever this Imperial virtue of compassion radiates, the Way for the subjects naturally becomes clear. The Way of the subjects exists where the entire nation serves the Emperor united in mind."
>
> *Source:* "Cardinal Principles of the National Entity of Japan," 1937. Pamphlet published by the Japanese Ministry of Education. From J.O. Gauntlett, trans., and R.K. Hall, ed., *Kokutai No Hongi* (*Cardinal Principles of the National Entity of Japan*) (Cambridge, MA: Harvard University Press, 1949).

47. The pamphlet's reference to the aftermath of the Meiji period was likely a critique of

    (A) Japanese government-sponsored industrialization programs in the 19th century
    (B) The growth Japanese imperialism in East Asia
    (C) The importation of western fashions and political systems
    (D) The increasing power of the emperor in Japanese politics

48. Which development in early 20th century Japanese history most likely influenced the decision of the Ministry of Education to publish this pamphlet?

    (A) The growth of strikes and Japanese trade unions
    (B) The emergence of militarist and nationalist political groups
    (C) The weakening of the monarchy following the death of the Meiji emperor
    (D) Mechanization and the growth of new industrial technologies

49. The references to the "Way of the subjects" were likely designed to
    (A) Provide a religious basis for an appeal to national loyalty
    (B) Provide political justification for Japanese expansion
    (C) Appeal to foreign audiences concerned about Japanese expansion
    Sway the Japanese parliament to improve educational opportunities

50. Which of the following accurately describes a change in the role of the emperor in the aftermath of World War II?
    (A) the emperor seized power from the military rulers who had led Japan to war
    (B) The emperor endorsed the terms of surrender and had less influence in post-war politics
    (C) The emperor became a secular ruler and no longer claimed divinity
    (D) The emperor renounced the throne and became an ordinary citizen

Questions 51-53 refer to the excerpts below.

Source 1:

"The Muslim religion includes freedom of religious opinion … Will not every grown-up person in the new Turkish state be free to select his own religion? … When the first favorable opportunity arises, the nation must act to eliminate [religious law] from our Constitution …"

Source: Turkish leader Mustafa Kemal Ataurk, "Speech to the General Congress of the [Turkish] Republican Party," 1927. From *A Speech Delivered by Ghazi Mustapha Kemal, October 1927* (Leipzig: K.F. Kochler, 1929).

Source 2:

"After having studied the ideals which ought to inspire a renascent nation on the spiritual level, we wish to offer … Some practical suggestions …

2nd. To reform the law in such a way that it will be entirely in accordance with Islamic legal practice…

9th. Government will act in conformity to the law and to Islamic principles; … The scheduling of government services ought to take account of the hours set aside for prayer …"

Source: "Toward the Light." Statement of the Muslim Brotherhood of Egypt, 1936. Hasan al-Banna, "Towards the Light," in Robert Langdon, *The Emergence of the Middle East* (Van Nostrand, 1970).

51. Which of the following statements best reflects the differences between the political views of the Egyptian Muslim Brotherhood and the Turkish Republican Party?
    (A) The Egyptian Muslim Brotherhood advocated parliamentary democracy while Ataturk's Republicans supported military rule
    (B) The Egyptian Muslim Brotherhood advocated a state based on religious principles while the Turkish Republican Party supported the outlawing of religion
    (C) The Egyptian Muslim Brotherhood advocated independence from colonial rule while the Turkish Republican Party sought restoration of a Turkish empire
    (D) The Egyptian Muslim Brotherhood advocated shari'a, or religious law while the Turkish Republican Party advocated a secular state.

52. Which of the following historical event most directly established the context for Ataturk's statement?
    (A) The Balfour Declaration which promised a homeland for the Jewish people in Palestine
    (B) The collapse of the Ottoman Empire following World War 1
    (C) The creation of the Mandate system in which European powers obtained influence in the Middle East
    (D) The establishment of a strict Islamic state in Saudi Arabia

53. Which of the following represents a long-term influence of the Muslim Brotherhood in the 20th century?

(A) the sustained presence of "Political Islamic" organizations such as al-Qaeda, Hammas, and ISIS
(B) Pan-Arabist movements such as those of Gamal Abdel Nasser in Egypt or the Palestine Liberation Organization
(C) The continued work of the Arab League which represents Arab governments in the Middle East
(D) The growth in the mid-20th century of the Communist Parties of Egypt, Iraq, and Syria

Questions 54-55 refer to the map below.

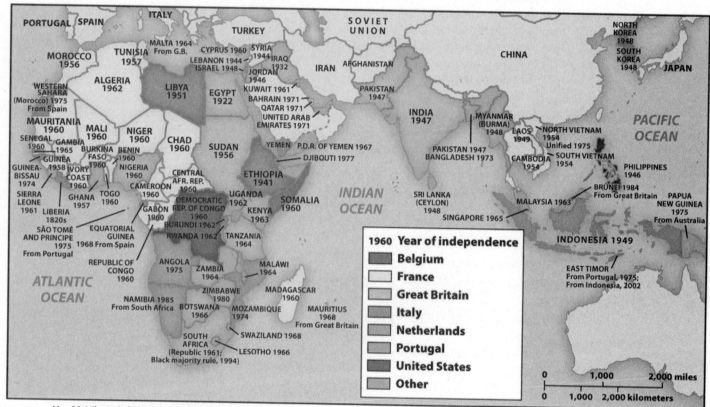

Map 22.1 The End of Empire in Africa and Asia
Chapter 22, *Ways of the World: A Brief Global History with Sources,* Third Edition
Copyright © 2016 by Bedford/St. Martin's
Distributed by Bedford/St. Martin's/Macmillan Higher Education strictly for use with its products; Not for redistribution.

54. Which of the following historical developments had the most immediate impact on the wave of decolonization depicted in the map?

(A) The United States dropping of the atomic bomb on Japan in 1945
(B) The Cold War and the emergence of competing military alliances
(C) The weakness of European powers due to damages caused by World War II
(D) The Islamic, Hindu, and Buddhist religious revivals which followed World War II

55 One critical difference between the independence movements in South East Asia and the independence movements in West Africa was that

(A) West African independence movements relied on non-violent protests while Southeast Asian independence leaders led military revolts

(B) West African independence movements were based primarily on religious goals while Southeast Asian independence movements pursued secular objectives

(C) West African independence movements won full independence from European powers while Southeast Asian independence movements remained part of larger European-led "Commonwealths"

(D) West African independence movements were generally led by Pan-Africanists and nationalists while Southeast Asian independence movements were often led by Communists

Part B: Short-Answer Questions
Time: 50 minutes

1. Use the excerpts below and your knowledge of world history to answer all parts of the question that follows.

    "[I]t is shameful for a woman to speak in Church … [for] the husband is head of the wife as Christ is head of the Church."

    -- The New Testament, Christian Bible

    "A virtuous wife should constantly serve her husband like a god … In childhood a female must be subject to her father; in youth to her husband; when her lord is dead to her sons; a woman must never be independent."

    -- The Laws of Manu, ancient Hindu text

    (A) Identify and explain one similarity between ancient Christian and Hindu beliefs as presented in the texts above.
    (B) Identify and explain one Hindu or Christian practice that is based on the beliefs illustrated in the passages above.
    (C) Identify and explain one way Hindu or Christian individuals or groups have challenged this practice

2. Use the excerpt below and your knowledge of world history to answer all parts of the question that follows.

    "The surviving evidence from [the Silk Road city of] Kucha, as partial as it is, suggests an alternative to the standard picture of the fabled Silk Road trade: rather than a long-distance trade initiated and staffed by private merchants, these materials indicate that the Chinese military contributed significantly to the Silk Road economy. When Chinese armies were stationed in Central Asia, money—in the form of coins, grain, and cloth—flowed into the region. When the Chinese troops withdrew, small-scale trade resumed, largely maintained by local travelers and peddlers."

    Source: Valerie Hanson summarizing trade patterns in Kucha, a trading city along the Silk Road, prior to 1000 CE. From Valerie Hanson, *The Silk Road: A New History* (Oxford: Oxford University Press, 2015).

    (A) Identify and explain one way in which Hanson's thesis challenges traditional historical understandings of the Silk Roads.
    (B) Identify and explain one type of evidence which might complicate Hanson's thesis.
    (C) Identify and explain one type of evidence which might indicate whether or not Hanson's thesis also applied to Silk Road trade after 1000 CE. [You must choose a different type of evidence than you chose for part b]

3. Answer all parts of the question that follows.

    Many historians regard the Spanish and Portuguese conquest of much of the Americas in the 16th century as a turning point in world history.

    (A) dentify and explain one way in which this event was an economic turning point in world history.
    (B) Identify and explain one additional way in which this event was an environmental turning point in world history.
    (C) Identify and explain one way in which this event was not a turning point in world history.

4. Use the image below and your knowledge of world history to answer all parts of the question that
   follows.

"The Great Leap Forward." This 1960 poster advertised the economic goals of the Chinese state. The caption reads:
"Start the movement to increase production and practice thrift, with foodstuffs and steel at the center with great force!"

The Great Leap Forward
Stefan R. Landsberger Collections/International Institute fo Social History, Amsterdam/www.chineseposters.net
Chapter 21, *Ways of the World: A Brief Global History with Sources,* Third Edition
Copyright © 2016 by Bedford/St. Martin's
Distributed by Bedford/St. Martin's/Macmillan Higher Education strictly for use with its products; Not for redistribution.

(A) Identify and explain one way the Great Leap Forward was representative of Communist state economic strategies in the 20th century.

(B) Identify and explain one difference between Chinese state economic strategies and state economic strategies in either western Europe or Japan.

(C) Identify and explain one similarity or one difference between state economic strategies in China in the 1960s and state economic strategies in a newly independent nation after World War II.

SECTION II

Total Time–1 hour, 30 minutes

Part A: Document-Based Question

Suggested reading and writing time: 55 minutes

It is suggested that you spend 15 minutes reading the documents and 40 minutes writing your response.

Note: You may begin writing your response before the reading period is over.

Directions: Question 1 is based on the accompanying documents. The documents have been edited for the purpose of this exercise.

In your response you should do the following.

- **Thesis:** Present a thesis that makes a historically defensible claim and responds to all parts of the question. The thesis must consist of one or more sentences located in one place, either in the introduction or the conclusion.

- **Argument Development:** Develop and support a cohesive argument that recognizes and accounts for historical complexity by explicitly illustrating relationships among historical evidence such as contradiction, corroboration, and/or qualification.

- **Use of the documents:** Utilize the content of at least six of the documents to support the stated thesis or a relevant argument.

- **Sourcing the documents:** Explain the significance of the author's point of view, author's purpose, historical context, and/or audience for at least four documents.

- **Contextualization:** Situate the argument by explaining the broader historical events, developments, or processes immediately relevant to the question.

- **Outside Evidence:** Provide an example or additional piece of specific evidence beyond those found in the documents to support or qualify the argument.

- **Synthesis:** Extend the arguments by explaining the connections between the argument and ONE of the following

  - A development in a different historical period, situation, era, or geographical area.

  - A course theme and/or approach to history that is not the focus of the essay (such as political, economic, social, cultural, or intellectual history)

  - A different discipline or field of inquiry (such as economics, government and politics, art history or anthropology).

1. Using the documents provided and your knowledge of world history, analyze the evolution of women's movements from 1792-present.

Document 1

Source: Mary Wollstonecraft, female writer and philosopher, *A Vindication of the Rights of Woman*, (Boston: Thomas and Andrews, 1792).

"Contending for the rights of woman, my main argument is built on this simple principle, that if she be not prepared by education to become the companion of man, she will stop the progress of knowledge and virtue . . . but the education and situation of woman at present shuts her out from such investigations . . .

Consider ... whether ... it be not inconsistent and unjust to subjugate women, even though you firmly believe that you are acting in the manner best calculated to promote their happiness? Who made man the exclusive judge, if woman partake with him of the gift of reason?"

Document 2

Source: Elizabeth Cady Stanton, American activist for women's suffrage, "The Solitude of Self," 1892. From *Hearing of the Woman Suffrage Association Before the Committee on Judiciary, Monday, January 18, 1892*, (N.p., n.d.), 1-5, in ECS Papers, DLC.

"The strongest reason for giving woman all the opportunities for higher education, for the full development of her faculties . . . for giving her the most enlarged freedom of thought and action; a complete emancipation from all forms of bondage, of custom, dependence, superstition; from all the crippling influences of fear, is the solitude and personal responsibility of her own individual life. The strongest reason why we ask for woman a voice in the government under which she lives; in the religion she is asked to believe; equality in social life, where she is the chief factor; a place in the trades and professions, where she may earn her bread, is because of her birthright to self-sovereignty; because, as an individual, she must rely on herself. No matter how much women prefer to lean, to be protected and supported, nor how much men desire to have them do so, they must make the voyage of life alone. . . . It matters not whether the solitary voyager is man or woman. . . . Alike amid the greatest triumphs and darkest tragedies of life we walk alone. . . ."

Document 3

Source: Raden Adjeng Kartini, Muslim Indonesian feminist's letter to a friend, 1899. From Zagnes Louise Symmers, Trans., and Hildred Geertz, ed., Letters of a Javanese Princess (Lanham, MD: University Press of America, 1985).

"I do not belong to the Indian world, but to that of my pale sisters who are struggling forward in the distant West.

If the laws of my land permitted it, there is nothing that I had rather do than give myself wholly to the working and striving of the new woman in Europe; but age-long traditions that cannot be broken hold us fast cloistered in their unyielding arms . . .

I do not desire to go out to feasts, and little frivolous amusements. That has never been the cause of my longing for freedom. I long to be free, to be able to stand alone, to study, not to be subject to any one, and, above all, never, never to be obliged to marry....

And marriage among us – Miserable is too feeble an expression for it. How can it be otherwise, when the laws have made everything for the man and nothing for the woman? When law and convention both are for the man; when everything is allowed to him?"

Document 4

Source: Alexandra Kollontai, Marxist-feminist and member of the Central Committee of the Communist Party of the Soviet Union. From "Communism and the Family," in *The Worker,* 1920.

"Will the family continue to exist under communism? . . . [One] fact that invites attention is that divorce has been made easier in Soviet Russia. . . . A working woman will not have to petition for months or even for years to secure the right to live separately from a husband who beats her and makes her life a misery with his drunkenness and uncouth behaviour. Divorce by mutual agreement now takes no more than a week or two to obtain. . . .

In place of the old relationship between men and women, a new one is developing: a union of affection and comradeship, a union of two equal members of communist society, both of them free, both of them independent, and both of them workers. No more domestic bondage for women. No more inequality within the family. No need for women to fear being left without support and with children to bring up. The woman in communist society no longer depends upon her husband but on her work. . . . She need have no anxiety about her children. The workers' state will assume responsibility for them. Marriage will lose all the elements of material calculation which cripple family life. Marriage will be a union of two persons who love and trust each other. . . ."

Document 5

Source: Combahee River Collective, a women's organization centered in Boston, Massachusetts. From "A Black Feminist Statement," 1977. The Combahee River Collective, *The Combahee River Collective Statement: Black Feminist Organizing in the Seventies and Eighties* (Albany, New York: Kitchen Table: Women of Color Press, 1986).

"[W]e find our origins in the historical reality of Afro-American women's continuous life-and-death struggle for survival and liberation. . . . Black women have always embodied an adversary stance to white male rule. . . . Black feminist politics also have an obvious connection to movements for Black liberation, particularly those of the 1960s and 1970s. . . . It was our experience and disillusionment within these liberation movements, as well as experience on the periphery of the white male left, that led to the need to develop a politics that was anti-racist, unlike those of white women, and anti-sexist, unlike those of Black and white men. . . . [A]s we developed politically we [also] addressed ourselves to heterosexism and economic oppression under capitalism. . . ."

Document 6

Source: Zapatista Army of National Liberation, Chiapas, Mexico, *The Women's Revolutionary Law*, 1994.

"[T]aking into account the situation of the woman worker in Mexico, the revolution supports their just demands for equality and justice in the following Women's Revolutionary Law.

First: Women, regardless of their race, creed, color or political affiliation, have the right to participate in the revolutionary struggle in a way determined by their desire and capacity.

Second: Women have the right to work and receive a just salary.

Third: Women have the right to decide the number of children they will have and care for.

Fourth: Women have the right to participate in the affairs of the community and hold positions of authority if they are freely and democratically elected.

Fifth: Women and their children have the right to primary attention in matters of health and nutrition.

Sixth: Women have the right to an education.

Seventh: Women have the right to choose their partner, and are not to be forced into marriage.

Eighth: Women shall not be beaten or physically mistreated by their family members or by strangers. Rape and attempted rape will be severely punished.

Ninth: Women will be able to occupy positions of leadership in the organization and hold military ranks in the revolutionary armed forces."

Document 7

Brazilian women's demonstration, early 21st century. Carrying a banner calling for "feminist resistance" these women wore sexually provocative clothing to challenge social norms of appropriate female behavior. The sign on the left calls for a "revolution without men."

An Aspect of Brazilian Feminism
© Aaron Cadena Ovalle/epa/Corbis
Chapter 23, *Ways of the World: A Brief Global History with Sources,* Third Edition
Copyright © 2016 by Bedford/St. Martin's

Part B: Long-Essay Question

Time: 35 minutes

Directions: Choose EITHER Question 2 or 3.

In your response you should do the following:

- ■ **Thesis:** Present a thesis that makes a historically defensible claim and responds to all parts of the question. The thesis must consist of one or more sentences located in one place, either in the introduction or the conclusion.

- ■ **Application of historical thinking skills:** Develop and support an argument that applies historical thinking skills as directed by the question.

- ■ **Supporting the argument with evidence:** Utilize specific examples of evidence to fully and effectively substantiate the stated thesis or a relevant argument.

- ■ **Synthesis:** Extend the argument by explaining the connections between the argument and ONE of the following:

  - A development in a different historical period, situation, era, or geographical area.

  - A course theme and/or approach to history that is not the focus of the essay (such as political, economic, social, cultural, or intellectual history).

  - A different discipline or field of inquiry (such as economics, government, and politics, art history, or anthropology).

2. For the period 600 CE–1450 CE analyze the consequences of either the Polynesian or Bantu migrations. *[Historical Thinking Skill: Causation]*

OR

3. For the period 1800 to the present analyze at least one cause and at least one consequence of long-distance labor migration. *[Historical Thinking Skill: Causation]*